# BLACK
# WATCH

# BLACK WATCH

Liberating Europe and Catching Himmler –
My Extraordinary WW2 with
the Highland Division

TOM RENOUF

Little, Brown

LITTLE, BROWN

First published in Great Britain in 2011 by Little, Brown

Copyright © Tom Renouf 2011

A CIP catalogue record for this book
is available from the British Library.

ISBN HB 978 1 4087 0271 0
ISBN CF 978 1 4087 0272 7

Maps copyright © John Gilkes 2011

Typeset in Sabon by M Rules
Printed and bound in Great Britain by
Clays Ltd, St Ives plc

Little, Brown
An imprint of
Little, Brown Book Group
100 Victoria Embankment
London EC4Y 0DY

An Hachette UK Company
www.hachette.co.uk

www.littlebrown.co.uk

In memory of the fallen comrades
of the 51st Highland Division

# Contents

# Maps

# Introduction

I was so proud to join the famous Black Watch as a teenager during the Second World War. The regiment formed part of the 51st Highland Division – almost an army within the British Army – which drew on the Scottish warrior tradition to forge a highly effective fighting force. Scotland's proudest and most ancient regiments, reinforced by tens of thousands of English soldiers, banded together to avenge the destruction of the Scottish forces at St Valéry in 1940. Over the next five years, the Jocks followed the skirl of the bagpipes into some of the most famous battles of the war. Thousands gave their lives in North Africa, Sicily, Normandy, Belgium, Holland and Germany. We were a true band of brothers who were not immune to fear and suffering, but who found courage and fierce loyalty as members of the 'Fighting 51st'.

The Black Watch is Scotland's most senior regiment, and it struck fear into the hearts of the enemy during the trench warfare of 1914–18. German soldiers dubbed the kilted High-landers 'devils in skirts' and rated the regiment the 'most feared'. When my turn came to serve my country, I was hon-oured to follow in that tradition. I quickly learned the awful realities of war in the Battle of Normandy, but my admiration for the officers and men of the Highland Division only grew during that baptism of fire.

*Black Watch* tells the story not only of my regiment but of all the Highlanders who landed on D-Day to retake St Valéry, liberate Holland, fight in the Ardennes and invade Germany. These achievements are now part of Scottish folklore, celebrated in music, song and poetry. In recent years, it has been my privilege to help organise veterans' reunions and pilgrimages to the towns that we liberated in Holland, where we always receive fantastic and emotional welcomes. We have also raised monuments to the men of the Highland Division in both Scotland and Holland.

I am grateful to all those veterans of the division who have allowed me to use their memories in this book, and to the families of those who are no longer with us. I and many others have striven to keep alive the memory of those who made the ultimate sacrifice, and I hope that this book will be part of that process of commemoration.

# 1

# A Place Called St Valéry

I had donned my Sunday suit for the Saturday night dance and the band in the Musselburgh Masonic Hall was in full swing. The girls were glamorous, and couples were gliding across the freshly polished floor to the strains of Hoagy Carmichael's 'The Nearness of You', one of my favourites. I was fifteen and more concerned about girls and rugby than wars in far-off lands. So far, the war had been little more than an exciting diversion in my life. As schoolboys, we learned that the British Empire was supreme and that our country was the world's greatest power. When war had broken out less than a year earlier, we were convinced that our army was invincible and that Britain would administer the Germans a sound thrashing before Christmas.

My boyhood delusions were about to be shattered. Across the hall, through the fug of cigarette smoke, I saw an older friend, a lad I recognised from school. I knew that Sandy had joined the Argyll and Sutherland Highlanders – my father's old regiment – and had already been abroad. He was in uniform, and looked different from how I remembered him – pale, gaunt and seemingly much older than his years. He kept himself away from the dancing crowds who were enjoying the music and the freedom. I caught up with him in the hall-way, coming back from the toilets. A few mutual pals shook his hand and we asked what he had been up to. Without blinking, he launched into his story, a terrible tale of how the famous 51st Highland Division had been forced to retreat, overwhelmed by the lightning blitzkrieg tactics of well-organised and powerful German forces.

We gathered around him, jaws grimly clenched, and in stunned silence hung on to every word. With a creased brow, he told us, 'My unit was overrun. We were completely sur-rounded. We had to travel through the German lines for three nights – no food, hardly any ammunition. We were trying to catch up with the main withdrawal. It was unbelievable.'

Sandy was a survivor of the doomed British Expeditionary Force (BEF). He had escaped from France just a few weeks earlier. We all knew of the amazing rescue at Dunkirk in that summer of 1940. Churchill had made one of his finest speeches praising the 'miracle of deliverance' achieved by an unlikely armada of naval and civilian craft that had evacu-ated 338,000 British and French soldiers from the carnage of the beaches. The Prime Minister had famously vowed that we would fight the Nazis 'on the beaches, in the fields and in the hills'.

Yet, while the nation rejoiced, a dark shadow lay across thousands of homes in Scotland's Highlands and Central Belt, where families still waited anxiously for news of their men-folk. Two entire brigades of the 51st Highland Division had not returned from France. Under wartime censorship, news of their fate was scarce and rumours multiplied faster than rabbits in springtime. Now we listened intently to the awful truth.

But Sandy was not telling us about Dunkirk. He was talking about a place that we had never heard about. A place that neither the newspapers nor the newsreels had mentioned. A place called St Valéry-en-Caux. He told us that a few units had managed to escape, but the bulk of the division had been left behind to fight a losing rearguard battle. Rumour had it that they had surrendered before the navy could pick them up. Thousands killed, thousands taken prisoner.

We could tell that Sandy, close to tears, was telling the truth. As soon as he had finished, he made his excuses and went home, leaving us standing there, mouths agape, unable to comprehend what we had just heard. The thought of the Germans defeating and capturing the Highland Division filled my heart with an anguish that was to haunt me for some time.

It was shocking, almost unbelievable news and led to some bitter recriminations about Churchill sacrificing the Highlanders in a last-ditch gamble to keep tottering France in the war. For me, it really brought the 'phoney war' to a close and raised the very real prospect that, although I was just a boy, I might eventually follow in my father's footsteps and end up fighting against the Germans.

When the war had broken out in September 1939 it had been a source of huge excitement to us schoolboys. We had done our bit at school – filling sandbags down at the beach and addressing ration books. And we were certain that we would win. It never occurred to us that the British would lose even a single battle. Not least because of the spectacular scenes we had witnessed just six weeks into the war.

On 16 October, a group of us were playing on our bikes

down by the harbour when we heard the noise of aeroplanes. We looked up and saw a formation of nine German bombers heading for the giant British naval base at Rosyth, twelve miles across the river on the northern bank of the mighty Firth of Forth. Unknown to us, we were watching history in the making. The surprise raid was the first air attack of the war on Britain, and the planes were initially unchallenged. The Junkers 88s terrified a group of passengers on a Fife-bound train on the Forth Bridge who imagined that they were the target until bombs started falling on HMS *Southampton* in the water below. We could hear the bombing and anti-aircraft fire but could not see the action. Then, as the Germans headed back out over the Forth estuary, we witnessed a stunning spectacle. Out of nowhere, a squadron of Spitfires appeared and pounced like cats on mice. A thrilling dogfight ensued, leaving us kids transfixed, staring skywards and cheering on the dashing young pilots who had been university students, lawyers and farmers until a few months earlier.

Vapour trails streaked the clear blue sky as the Spitfires swooped and dived on the Junkers and their Heinkel escorts. These daring pilots of the 602 City of Glasgow and 603 City of Edinburgh squadrons were such heroes to us. When two of the raiders were shot down and plunged into the grey water of the Forth we were literally jumping for joy, shouting and punching the air in jubilation. Censorship meant that we never learned that three of our ships had been hit, killing sixteen Royal Navy crewmen and wounding forty-four others. The incredible sight simply reinforced what I already thought: The Germans are no match for the RAF. We'll win this war easily; it will soon be over. What fools the Germans are even to try to attack Britain.

We youngsters were not alone. Many people truly believed that it would all be over by Christmas and that our army would, in the words of the popular song, soon be 'hanging out the washing on the Siegfried Line'. But others, who had lived through the First World War, knew it would be no pushover; and many were well aware of just how powerful Germany had become.

At this stage, the war was still not real to us. When two of the German pilots killed in the Rosyth raid were buried just along the coast in Portobello, ten thousand people lined the route and their coffins were draped with Nazi flags. Scottish mothers even sent sympathy letters to the mothers of the dead airmen. St Valéry changed all of that. The news of the disaster was dreadful and it spread like wildfire. All of a sudden, the war seemed a much more serious business.

Until then, I had no thoughts of becoming a soldier. I came into the world on 28 March 1925 in my grandfather's house in Fisherrow. Being the first grandchild, the whole family was in attendance, waiting to pass around the new arrival. Although technically part of the ancient town of Musselburgh, a few miles east of Edinburgh, Fisherrow was a community in its own right. The River Esk, which empties into the Forth estuary, separated it from Musselburgh. The two communities were quite distinct and very different. The 'fisher folk' were fiercely protective of their identity, extremely proud of their heritage and reluctant to share their culture with others. They disparagingly described those who lived on the other side of the river as 'trades folk'. The traditional trades of brewing, net-making, milling and pottery had given a living to town families in centuries past. Then, with the advent of the industrial revolution, cotton, paper and wire mills were developed and Musselburgh became a prosperous town.

My grandfather, Thomas Handyside Williamson, was a
fisherman who was all but excommunicated from his community because he married a 'foreigner' – a lass from
Musselburgh. But his sin was eventually forgiven and he was
allowed to return to Fisherrow to harvest the haddock-rich
waters of the yawning Forth estuary and chase the huge
shoals of herring when the 'silver darlings' arrived off the east
coast each summer. In those days, Fisherrow boasted a fleet
of forty trawlers. Dozens of fishwives, traditionally attired in
shawls and striped aprons, carried their creels up to
Edinburgh and for miles around to sell the fresh catch. Each
September, to mark the end of the fishing season, the whole
community turned out for the Fisherman's Walk, with the
fishermen wearing their traditional blue 'gansey' jumpers following a pipe band and preceded by a box symbolising the
community funds that had been raised to support unfortunate families.

They were a proud, frugal bunch, but the fisher folk
endured their share of hard times and tragedies. In his search
for a better life, Granddad turned to coalmining, where the
money was good and steady. Soon, he sensed even greater
opportunities in the booming coalfields of America and emi-
grated to make his fortune, with plans for his family to join
him in Illinois once he was established. Unfortunately, a long
and bitter miners' strike dashed his hopes, and the family
organ had to be sold to pay his passage back home.

Granddad was to become a powerful influence on my life,
partly due to the unfailing support he gave to our family
when my father died young, but also because he was able to
do any handy-work that was required and encouraged me to
help and learn from him. Although he was never a com-
munist, he was a staunch advocate of workers' rights and,

like so many others in the Scottish coalfields, was very left wing.

My grandmother had died suddenly in 1914 at the age of forty-two, leaving Granddad with a young family to raise. My mother Meg was aged twelve, the middle of five children. She received special dispensation to leave school and look after the family home while Granddad continued to work as a contractor in the mines. It was an enormous challenge for a child to learn all the intricacies of housekeeping, cooking on an open fire and caring for all the family's needs. To add to her difficulties, the First World War had just started and my mother had to queue for butter, sugar and meat. She worked tirelessly to master the basic chores and, in time, was running the house as well as any housewife. With the war over and most of the family bringing home a wage, Mum, working closely with Granddad, was able to add to the loving home that they had provided. They had kept the family together and attained a better standard of living, but at a heavy cost.

Mum had sacrificed all her precious teenage years for the family. While her siblings enjoyed the pleasures of a job and all the outside interests that went with it, she felt deprived and tied to the house. She knew she could not desert the family during the day, but she decided to take an evening job. Luckily, an amazing new form of entertainment had just arrived. Cinema was a sensation. When Mum heard a picture palace was opening in nearby Portobello, she promptly applied for a position and was overjoyed when she became one of the usherettes. The cinema brought a new dimension to her life, and to society as a whole. For a few pennies, people were suddenly transported from the mundane routine and monotony of daily life to a wonderland of make-believe.

Audiences were amazed to see places and activities that they had never known existed. They were captivated by the plots, told in intertitles, and dazzled by the glamour of the stars. The Portobello Central was a phenomenal success and people queued to see whatever was showing.

Mum loved her job and could hardly believe her luck to be getting a wage while watching the wonders of the silver screen. For the first time in her life she was making friends, too – other members of staff as well as some patrons who chose her as their favourite usherette. She would take the tram to work but to save the tram fare always walked back to Musselburgh with her new friends. Walking home one stormy, winter's night, they heard a pitiful cry for help as they passed the open space of Murdoch Green. On investigating, they found Mrs Parry, the petite pianist who played the musical accompaniment to the films. She had been blown twenty yards towards the sea and would probably have landed on the rocks were it not for the safety fence. She was badly shaken, but the girls rescued her and took her home.

Mum was taller than most of her friends, and she carried herself with a certain dignified composure. She was always in her working clothes of skirt and jersey, but when she went out for a special occasion she would dress up in a fine silk blouse. Unusually for the times, she wore glasses from child-hood. Her hair was cut short, and was arrow straight. She tried all manner of things, always unsuccessfully, to put a wave in it. She was a cheerful character with many friends and was friendly to everyone. She would speak to anyone, wherever she was, and could cope with all of the tragic situations that occurred during her life.

By the time she was twenty, she had been promoted to

cashier – quite a step up for someone with little schooling. Every night she had to balance the cash taken against the number of tickets sold. The manager then checked and recorded her sums before depositing the cash in the office safe. The manager, George Bramwell Renouf – an Englishman who was named after the great Salvation Army leader Bramwell Booth – had moved to Scotland from southern England shortly before the First World War. He was employed by John McGuire, the impresario who was busily opening a chain of cinemas in and around Edinburgh. (McGuire later opened the magnificent Playhouse cinema in 1929, which still stands as a showpiece venue for major entertainment in the capital.) The Portobello Central was so successful that McGuire decided to build a larger cinema in Musselburgh. The Musselburgh Central was also to be managed by George, and he chose Mum as his cashier, primarily because of her friendly personality.

The opening night, in 1922, was an eagerly anticipated event in Musselburgh and lengthy queues formed. The film was *Daddy-Long-Legs*, a highly rated and widely publicised romantic drama starring Mary Pickford. A massive crowd assembled on the street and surged forward when the doors were opened, struggling with one another, fighting to get a ticket. The next night, the crowds were even bigger, but a doorman had already been appointed to keep them in order.

It was a good year for George Renouf. He was managing two cinemas and was rewarded with a directorship within the McGuire cinema group. In addition, with his third appearance in the final, he realised his life's ambition by winning the amateur lightweight boxing championship of Great Britain. And now, after a somewhat slow start, romance was blossoming between him and his cashier. George's previous interests were only boxing and work, and he had taken his time getting around to the matter of romance. Courting started as a kind of extension to balancing the night's takings. But it soon flourished and with the prospect of a house in upmarket Parsonage Cottages, Mother married her boss in 1924, much to the envy and excitement of her friends and the rest of the staff. I was born a year later, and my sister Betty came along the following year.

Dad was the middle child of a family of seven. His father had been a missionary and dragged the family around many far-flung outposts of empire. When he retired from evangelising, Granddad Joseph started a lemonade factory in Bournemouth. He was credited with inventing the ball-stopper, which sealed the lemonade and its fizz in the bottle. Rather than entering the family firm, Dad began his working life with Willie Renouf – a family friend who travelled the country exhibiting his 'magic fountain'. This was a spectacular display of dancing water jets, shifting colours and choreographed music – an early version of *son et lumière*. When they put on their show in Edinburgh, they were so impressed with the city that they decided to settle there. Willie was offered the post of manager at the Leith Gaiety theatre, the city's music hall, with Dad as his assistant.

It was around this time, in 1912, that Dad developed his passion for boxing. However, knowing that his devout father frowned upon the sport, Dad felt that he had to keep his new hobby secret, so he changed his surname from Joseph to Renouf, although the family continued to call him 'Bram'. His boxing career was already showing considerable promise when it was interrupted by the 1914 war. Dad joined the Argyll and Sutherland Highlanders and spent almost four years in the trenches with the 51st Highland Division. Although an Englishman, he was proud to don the Argyll kilt, was promoted to sergeant, mentioned in despatches, and fought at Ypres and the Somme. He ended the war at Army Headquarters in charge of Field Marshal Haig's personal transport. Like all men who joined up in 1914 and made it through to November 1918, he was lucky to survive. His most serious injury was a wound to the head, and he always kept the jagged piece of shrapnel that the surgeons removed from his skull as a souvenir.

After the war, Dad returned to the Gaiety theatre and resumed his boxing career at the Leith Victoria Amateur Athletic Club. It was Scotland's oldest boxing club and produced champions in abundance. His close friend James 'Tancy' Lee – a former world champion flyweight who is now in the Scottish Boxing Hall of Fame – gave Dad the benefit of his great experience and acted as his ringside second and manager. They travelled all over Britain and Europe to compete in boxing competitions and international tournaments, enjoying the generous camaraderie of the amateur boxing fraternity. Unlike the murky world of professional boxing today, in my father's day the amateur sport was known as 'the gentlemen's art'. Opponents could knock lumps out of each other inside the ring, then happily share a pot of tea afterwards.

Meanwhile, Dad's business career was also progressing well. The music hall gave the audience live entertainment and allowed them to feel part of it. The Gaiety flourished during the war years but shortly after that, moving pictures were entering the scene. Dad was convinced that movies were going to be the next big thing, so he was determined to get into the cinema business. With big fights put on every weekend in Edinburgh, the boxers were admired and respected local celebrities, and Dad made the most of his fame to secure a position with John McGuire. Soon he became equally well known in the Musselburgh community for his innovation and enterprise, traits he had inherited from his own father. He employed a small orchestra to provide music for the silent films, a step up from the normal solitary piano. Later, he developed his own film projection equipment, which resolved some of the early problems with 'talkies'. Having been under-manager at the Gaiety, he knew many of the local entertainers and put on weekly concerts in the town hall that the towns-folk greatly appreciated. Eventually, he opened his own cinema at nearby Ormiston.

In his spare time, he taught the noble art of boxing to the seniors at the prestigious Loretto private school in Mussel-burgh and organised boxing competitions at boys' clubs in the district. In a pioneering move, he teamed up with radio innovator Alex Low and relayed live ringside broadcasts of the big boxing contests in America to a large number of enthusiasts gathered in the Central cinema in the early hours of the morning. On one occasion, Lord Elphinstone asked Dad to put on a demonstration of films at his nearby Carberry Towers residence for the benefit of his guests, the Duke and Duchess of York, who would later become King George VI and Queen Elizabeth.

When I was four, Dad bought me a toy gramophone with six records. He was puzzled to know how I was always able to select my favourites even when he jumbled them up and were only identifiable by their written titles. He also got me an elastic-band-powered model aeroplane that flew far over the River Esk on its maiden flight, never to be seen again. Summer holidays were a terrific adventure and sometimes meant a long journey south to Bournemouth, where we spent glorious days at my grandparents' beach hut.

Dad worked evenings, so he had some time during the day
to spend with us kids. He would take Betty and me swimming
at Portobello baths, where he was a member of the swimming
club. Its other members included such notables as Ned
Barnie, an early cross-Channel swimmer. On Sunday morn-
ings, Dad would take us to the Leith Victoria, where we met
some of his contemporaries, including Tancy Lee and the
British champions and Olympic medallists Alex Ireland and
George McKenzie. The famous club, set up by workers from
a local shipyard after the First World War, was housed in an
ex-army hut on land rented from the railway company adjacent to the old Caledonian Station. There was no other place
like it, with the smell of liniment, leather and musty sweat,
and we watched future champions like George Bell sparring
and pounding the heavy punchbag. They and the sport fascinated me, and before I long took it up myself. However, I
eventually lost interest and gave it up.

Unusually for those days, Dad was a vegetarian, and totally
committed to constant fitness. He instilled in us that we should
live an active outdoor life supplemented by a healthy, balanced
diet. A bowl of fruit and nuts was always available on the
kitchen table for nibbles, and Mum always cooked nutritional
meals. Dad was slightly built – as a lightweight, he had to weigh
in at under ten stones – but well proportioned. He inherited the
family characteristic of being thin on top from an early age. He
was always very well dressed for work, smart in a collar and
tie, but he also loved to get into his overalls and tinker with his
pride and joy – a sparkling Morris Cowley saloon car.

We spent most of our summer Sundays at Gullane, a little
town near Musselburgh that has a magnificent sandy beach.
It could be reached only by those fortunate enough to own a
car, and therefore indicated quite a class divide. The poorer

folk, without transport, went to the local Fisherrow beach. We spent the days playing games, building sandcastles, swimming in the clear blue sea and enjoying a sun-drenched picnic. It never seemed to rain.

When Dad bought a second-hand caravan, a 1930 vintage, we thought ourselves even more privileged. But on one holiday to the Highlands, we found that the caravan required pushing to overcome the steeper gradients. Near Aberfeldy, in Perthshire, the Cowley gave out and we were stuck on a hill. While Mum made lunch, Dad rooted around under the bonnet and soon discovered that a new part was required. Nonchalantly, he wandered off down the wooded slope, looking, as usual, for somewhere to swim. To our amazement, he returned soon after, pleased as punch, holding the spare part that was needed for our car. Incredibly, he had found a wrecked Cowley in the riverbed, presumably the result of an accident in which the car had plunged into the ravine. This was typical of Dad. He was a carefree optimist, smiled on by fortune, always happy and full of fun, whistling and singing. He was often got caught up in a project, which made him late for another appointment. Mum soon gave up trying to cure his bad timekeeping and decided just to live with it.

Sadly, though, his good fortune was soon to desert him. In 1934, Dad, fit and seemingly in perfect health, still pursuing his highly successful career, suddenly developed a brain tumour. He died within two weeks of diagnosis. He was just forty-two years of age. Mum asked the doctors whether his boxing career or his war injury could have caused the tumour. They were unable to say for sure, but suggested it could have been there from birth.

This cruel blow of fate ended a life that had achieved much

but was still full of promise. Dad had served King and country with distinction, achieved fame and contributed much to the fraternity of amateur boxing. He had enhanced British cinema-going with his innovations, and had contributed generously to community life in Musselburgh.

At the tender age of nine, I walked in my father's funeral cortège. Holding Granddad's hand, we walked for two miles to Inveresk churchyard, where a massive crowd had gathered to pay their last respects. I failed to realise at the time what the loss of a father, and a father's guidance, implied.

Mum, now aged thirty-two and married for barely ten years, once again found herself robbed of the security and comfort of a normal family life. She suddenly faced the responsibility of bringing up two children and running the business on her own, in addition to the heartbreak of losing a dearly loved husband.

In 1930, I had gained a place at Musselburgh Grammar School. It was a venerable institution, founded in 1626, and it was here that I met the boys and girls who were to remain my close friends for the rest of my life. In my second year, the school moved to a magnificent new building on Inveresk Road. At that time, it was a showpiece school with spacious corridors and classrooms well equipped with the latest teaching aids. An old school photograph reminds me that for the first two years there were forty pupils in my class. Our excellent headmaster, Robert Barr, was a strict disciplinarian who encouraged sport as well as serious study. The journey through the primary school was made under the tender care of the lady teachers whom I still remember well, all of them intent on giving us a solid grounding in the essentials. The highlights of those years were the Christmas parties in the holly-bedecked gymnasium. The teachers gave us affinity cards, tied around the wrist, bearing phrases like 'You are Robin Hood. Find your Maid Marion.' Then we would go and search out our partners for the evening. Sometimes it pleased you, and other times it didn't. There was always some unfortunate in the class that nobody wished to be paired with. There was also the annual summer sports day, with races for all and parents shouting support from the sidelines. And our end-of-term play always impressed those parents with its large cast performing in tinselly, homemade costumes. The lasting legacy of this early education was the sense of respect, good manners and integrity that was cultivated within all of us.

Of course, life changed dramatically when Dad died. We all missed him greatly. But my sister and I especially missed the good times that we shared with him. There were no more family outings in the car, no visits to the baths or explorations of the River Esk. We missed his cheerful welcome when we returned home. The cinema at Ormiston was paying off a bank loan, and family finances were at a low. Mum had the situation under control, but we had to go without the extras we had previously enjoyed. Nevertheless, we were better off than most of our neighbours.

The thirties were difficult for Scotland. Most of Musselburgh's workforce was employed in four factories that produced paper, cotton, fishing nets and wire ropes, but a shortage of orders led to large-scale redundancies. Some were fortunate enough to find part-time employment, but most entered the growing ranks of the unemployed. Men searched desperately for work of any kind while women struggled to feed and clothe their families on the pittance dispensed by the state and the parish councils to the needy. Those lucky enough to remain in work saw their wages cut as the firms adopted all sorts of cost-saving measures. But a spirit of togetherness united the community in which neighbour helped neighbour. Troubles were shared. Clothes were patched and exchanged. Children were farmed out to relatives and friends who were in a better position to support them.

The best pupils from the five local primary schools in and around Musselburgh joined us in the upper school. These boys and girls generally went straight into the commercial stream, while the grammar pupils entered the classical stream. Although this might seem unfair, it actually made quite good sense at the time because those in the commercial stream usually wanted to leave school and bring home a wage as soon as possible.

To begin with, I neglected my studies in favour of sport and music. But one teacher stimulated my appetite for learning in the third form, when Pythagoras' theorem and other elements of mathematics started to captivate me. I then gradually developed a serious interest in other subjects, too. This change of heart gave me a new attitude that has remained with me throughout life – I was determined to do everything well.

From early days, I played the mouth organ. I played it going to and from school, while sitting on the toilet, in bed, anywhere. By the age of thirteen, I was saving up to buy a top-of-the-range model with a push slide that gave half notes and would allow me to play practically any tune. My hero was Larry Adler, and I listened to a record of him playing Gershwin continuously. So when I discovered he was coming to the Edinburgh Empire, I was determined to hear him playing live. When Mum denied me permission to see his concert, I was devastated. But defying all threats, I took my worldly savings and at the age of thirteen, set off on my own by tram into the big city. The harmonica maestro entranced me with his wonderful playing, and I was quite oblivious to the punishment that awaited me on my return home.

As my tastes matured, I took up the guitar and Mum paid for lessons. I gained a basic knowledge of chords and harmony that I later transferred to the piano, where I felt much more comfortable.

By the mid-1930s, some of the boys at school were already talking about Hitler's rise to power and the rearming of Germany. Their opinions were formed by their fathers, who had suffered the horrors of the Great War and were now concerned that the government was ignoring the menace. Rumours went around that Hitler was secretly building a powerful air force in contravention of the Versailles peace settlement. Then, one day at assembly, the headmaster told us that two German girls would be coming to the school. They were Jewish refugees who had fled their homeland, leaving their parents behind. The headmaster said that we were all to be very kind to them. The girls duly arrived and one of the languages mistresses looked after them. They stayed with a local family and seemed to fit in well. I remember thinking it was strange that someone or something must have forced these two young girls to leave their own country. But I never imagined that their parents could be hounded by the Gestapo, or that they might end up in a concentration camp run by the dreaded SS, the elite force of black-clad racist thugs who sported the skull-and-crossbones as a badge of honour.

Despite the economic hardship and the suggestions of what lay ahead in Europe, Musselburgh remained a happy place – a holiday resort with many diversions and attractions. Vast crowds would descend for the popular race meetings. There were only five each year, and they were always well supported. The town would heave with people, and many flocked to see Prince Monolulu, a charismatic black racing tipster who wore a feathered headdress and set up his stall at the town hall. Massive crowds would gather round to hear his famous catchphrase 'I gotta horse! I gotta horse!' and buy envelopes that contained his prediction of the winner of each race. He was a giant of a man, very handsome and a spellbinding orator, who travelled around Britain with the racing circuit. For many folk, he would have been the first black man they had ever seen. Most of the townsfolk would watch the horseracing from the roadside, unable to afford the entrance fee and while most refrained from gambling, they enjoyed the atmosphere all the same.

When the Company of Royal Archers, the monarch's symbolic bodyguard in Scotland, came to town each year to compete for the Musselburgh Arrow, everyone turned out to watch them. Each archer was trying to claim the world's first sporting trophy, which dates back to 1603. They would march through the town in their heraldic finery to Musselburgh Golf Course, which has the distinction of being the world's oldest course. Crowds revelled in the pageantry and the pinpoint archery displays. With the Riding of the Marches introduced in 1935, there always seemed to be some great event on in the town.

But the spectre of the 1914–18 war still haunted the Musselburgh of my childhood. Scotland and its Highland regiments had suffered horrendously during the First World War – of all the combatants, only the Serbs and the Turks incurred higher death rates than the Scots. The percentage of mobilised Scots who died was 26.4 per cent, compared with a figure of 11.8 per cent for Great Britain and Ireland as a whole. The fighting between the kilted troops of the 51st Highland Division and the Germans was intensely bitter. The Germans called the Highlanders 'ladies from hell' and 'devils in skirts'. The Highland regiments made the most of their warrior traditions and the Germans learned to dread the skirl of the bagpipes that preceded a fierce fixed-bayonet charge. A myth developed that the Scottish troops never took prisoners. Consequently, the Germans were reluctant to surrender to them and close-quarters combat exacted a murderous toll. German propaganda portrayed the kilted troops as blood-thirsty savages. As a result, if captured, they were frequently singled out for ill treatment, especially as the war wore on. Even English troops would shout over to their opponents that they were the Black Watch in a bid to demoralise the German soldiers.

I grew up with constant reminders of this bloody conflict. Limbless survivors lived at Edenhall hospital in Musselburgh, and I would occasionally see them in town in their blue trousers and jackets with red collars and piping. It was always a welcome adventure to visit the hospital as an eight- or nine-year-old. Some of my friends delivered newspapers or cigarettes and would return with stories of the place. Intrigued, I would tag along, and the wounded men would always be very generous – they would give you a thruppence, a fortune to a child in those days. And they would speak about the war. Some were quite hale and hearty, but many were bed-ridden. There were two or three wards, with about a dozen men in each.

The father of one of my good friends was the local post-man, Mr Fraser, who had lost his hand in the war. Another neighbour had been gassed and was still shell-shocked – he shook a lot. Paddy Nicol, who taught English and history at my school, had also suffered a gas attack, but he was happy to tell us stories from the war. The headmaster, Robert Barr, had served in the Black Watch, while science teacher John Knight was in the artillery. All of them were firm favourites at school. Whenever we re-enacted battles in the playground, I was always in the Highland Division, leading my troops against the Hun. We never lost.

Armistice Day was always a major event. All of the youth organisations took part in a huge parade through the town that ended at the church, followed by a wreath-laying service at the war memorial. The townsfolk always turned out in large numbers.

I never heard my dad speak about the Great War. But he and Mum would discuss it quite a bit, and she would fill me in about things. That's how I got to learn about it, along with information from friends. Some of the other dads would talk to their sons about it. Most of them had been in the war. One day at school, a lad brought in a gigantic German flag – it was a magnificent war trophy and one of the biggest flags I had ever seen.

Mum remembered seeing a Zeppelin over Musselburgh in 1916, when she was a teenager. She said it went down the street, following the twists and turns in the road, and loomed large over the startled townsfolk. She swore she could even see the German crew through the airship's windows. It went on to bomb Edinburgh and Leith, killing and injuring many civilians. Yet, I didn't think of the Germans as being scoundrels, or as nasty, wicked people, but as admirable soldiers. We believed that soldiering in Germany had been an honourable profession. We knew nothing of concentration camps or the activities of Himmler's SS and Gestapo at that time. And even if there had been a whisper about them, we never would have believed it. You could never believe some of the evil things the Germans were doing.

But my friends' fathers knew that trouble was looming, and I started to share their concerns in 1938, when Germany annexed Austria. Women in the shops were worried and started talking. One would say, 'There's going to be another war,' and someone would reply more in hope than anything else, 'Oh no, there will never be another war.' By the time Hitler's forces marched into Czechoslovakia the following year, I was convinced there was going to be another full-scale war. But I did not let it stop me having a good time.

By then, the government, after a disastrous delay in acknowledging the rise of fascism, had finally decided to rearm the nation. This brought much-needed work to the local factories. There was a big drive to recruit manpower and many Musselburgh families escaped from dire financial straits. Several older boys joined the expanding Territorial Army, and they looked most impressive in their uniforms. Some of their fathers joined the Civil Defence Volunteers and learned how to deal with casualties, fires and other emergencies caused by air raids. Many of us at school decided to join the Air Training Corps (ATC), and we lined up at the town hall to register. I attended the training nights for six weeks, and all of my friends were very enthusiastic, but I decided that the RAF was not for me and instead became a messenger in the Civil Defence. This involved carrying important messages by bicycle from the control centre in Newbigging to other units in the area. The construction of air-raid shelters was given top priority.

In the meantime, Germany was on the point of invading Poland, whose sovereignty Britain and France had both pledged to defend. Himmler, in an operation he named after himself, staged a 'false flag' stunt that simulated Polish aggression and provided a pretext for war. Part of the scam was to dress murdered concentration camp prisoners in Polish army uniforms and dump them at the border, then claim that they had been trying to invade Germany.

At 11.15 a.m. on 3 September 1939, two days after Hitler had launched his 'defensive' invasion of Poland, Mum gathered us around the wireless to hear Neville Chamberlain tell the nation that Britain and France were at war with Germany. Air-raid sirens sounded and many people scurried for the shelters, thinking that masses of German bombers would soon be overhead. It proved to be a false alarm, but for the first time I experienced the fear that was to be such an unwelcome companion over the next few years. Later that day, the British Commonwealth and Empire declared their allegiance to the motherland and prepared to send troops to Europe. As in the Great War, many colonial sons soon returned home to join the British forces. The Poles fought courageously, but within two weeks their country was overwhelmed and partitioned between Germany and Russia.

Although the outbreak of war caused a lot of distress and worry to our parents, it did not change our daily lives too much – save for the raid on Rosyth the following month. But gradually things did begin to change as wartime restrictions overtook us. Blackouts, rationing, fire watching, shortages, queuing and the issue of gas masks all became routine. Squads of workmen cut down all the railings in Musselburgh for scrap and we collected old pots and pans in the belief that Spitfires would be made from the aluminium. The new reality truly hit home when the blackout claimed the life of Dad's old boxing instructor. A bus hit Tancy Lee and he died on a pitch-dark Edinburgh street. Each area already had an air-raid warden to enforce the blackout and fire service cover, and before long each would also have a detachment of the Home Guard. Ominously, German bombers started to make more frequent appearances overhead. During one night raid, a bomb struck one of the distilleries in Leith. Whisky flowed down the gutters, causing a stampede among the locals.

One of the first war casualties in Musselburgh was Mr Vass, who was lost at sea in 1940. His two sons were friends of mine. The full significance of the tragedy did not register with me, but Mum explained that hardship would surely follow grief and sorrow for the Vass family. Unfortunately, many similar tragedies would affect our friends and neighbours, and mothers and wives with loved ones on active service lived in fear of receiving the dreaded War Office telegram.

Rumours were rife on the home front despite the massive campaign to guard against information leaking to the enemy. Posters were plastered everywhere, reminding us that 'Loose lips sink ships', but still the chatter continued. Leakage of sensitive information could arise from the most innocent event. The platoon officer routinely censored letters from the front line, but if the sender was a casualty writing from hospital, his mail would usually arrive in its original form. Men on leave would also inadvertently leak classified information. On one occasion I was shocked when speaking to a tradesman who worked on the nearby airfields. He innocently told me of the massive casualties suffered by the RAF bombers, not realising that such information was highly classified by the government.

So, despite the censorship, in 1940 we all knew that the

BEF was on the Belgian border as part of the Northern Armies working to strengthen the defences of the Maginot Line extension. Newspapers and letters home both indicated that there was no initial activity by either side. This stalemate became known as the 'phoney war' when leaflets rather than bombs were dropped on the enemy. The 51st Highland Division joined the BEF in January 1940. They had to endure one of the coldest winters for years. In April the division was sent to gain battle experience with the French Army on the Maginot Line proper in the Saar. Once there, though, all they faced was occasional tit-for-tat shelling and ineffectual patrolling into no-man's land. The Germans seemed docile, but that was soon to change. Like a million other schoolboys, I followed the few events of early 1940 in *War Illustrated* and charted any progress on a *Daily Mail* map that was pinned to my bedroom wall.

Then, on 10 May, the German war machine suddenly kicked into action with an offensive that shattered all opposition and dumbfounded observers. The Germans' Panzer tanks attacked through the supposedly impregnable Ardennes forest and simultaneously violated the neutrality of Holland and Belgium to confront the advancing Northern Armies and the BEF head on. The Northern Armies held their front valiantly, but the German thrust through the Ardennes overpowered the defenders and penetrated deep behind the French defences before turning northwards. Within ten days, the Germans had surrounded the BEF and the Northern Armies, including the Belgian force, and had forced them to withdraw to a bridgehead around Dunkirk. With the capitulation of Belgium and the loss of seventeen divisions guarding the eastern flank, the fate of Britain's only army seemed sealed.

This perilous situation was largely kept from the public, and the heavily censored newspapers could barely hint at the extent of the unfolding disaster. Yet a feeling of impending doom still spread. Then, amazingly, Hitler ordered the Panzers to halt their advance, which gave the defenders the precious time they needed to erect a heavily fortified perimeter. With that in place, the supreme efforts of the RAF, the Royal Navy and the 'little boats' armada allowed the miracle of Dunkirk to take place.

News of the last few days of the evacuation of Dunkirk was shared with a relieved and thankful nation. Newsreels showed our boys arriving home by train and receiving heroes' welcomes, sandwiches and cups of tea, but their grim faces and ragged uniforms reminded us that all the arms, vehicles and stores of the BEF were in German hands. Britain, standing alone and stripped of all her weaponry, now had to find a way to defend her shores against a mighty enemy. I was already beginning to question my schoolboy vision of Britain's invincibility.

When the German blitzkrieg struck, the Highland Division, still in the Saar, was completely cut off from the rest of the BEF, and so had no chance of evacuation from Dunkirk. On 4 June, under command of the French Ninth Army, the division fought a courageous rearguard action on the Somme, where it engaged the main Panzer force. After eight days of gallant defence against overwhelming odds, the Highlanders were ultimately driven back and isolated at St Valéry. Out of ammunition and abandoned by the French, they were forced to surrender.

In Germany this news provided a huge propaganda coup. Major General Erwin Rommel – at this point little known, but soon to become the 'Desert Fox' in command of the

Afrika Korps – was pictured triumphantly in the harbour at St Valéry with the Highlanders' commander, a dismayed and sullen Major General Victor Fortune of the Black Watch. A quarter of a century earlier, these two men had faced each other on the Western Front. Back then, the German Army had declared the Black Watch its 'most feared' enemy regiment. In the run-up to the current war, Josef Goebbels, Hitler's propaganda chief, had derided England's 'Scottish mercenaries'. Now our lads were 'in the bag' and German cameramen lingered on the Saltire shoulder flashes of the captured men of the 51st. Cinema audiences cheered as they watched the newsreels in Berlin, and the narrator was able to announce that thousands of Highlanders had been taken prisoner. Rommel wrote to his wife that the capture of General Fortune and the Highland Division was a 'particular joy'. He also noted that the Highlanders' defence had been 'tenacious' in the face of 'devastating' artillery fire.

Their sacrifice had not been entirely in vain. On the Somme, the 51st had fought alongside French forces led by a newly promoted general called Charles de Gaulle. The prickly de Gaulle was frequently scornful of British efforts, but this battle left a very different impression on him: 'For my part, I can say that the comradeship of arms, sealed on the battlefield of Abbeville in May–June 1940, between the French armoured division, which I had the honour to command, and the gallant 51st Scottish Division under General Fortune, played its part in the decision which I made to continue the fight at the side of the Allies, to the end, come what may.'

After St Valéry, German armies penetrated deep into the heart of France, and on 23 June the two nations signed an armistice. In just seven weeks Hitler had overpowered Belgium, the Netherlands and now France. My wall map was now well out of date. When the new version arrived, the newly occupied countries were shaded ominously in grey. It really brought home the stark reality of Britain's desperate situation.

Now every boy in the land, perhaps not realising the true extent of the threat, was thrilled and captivated as the Battle of Britain began. Dogfights were re-enacted endlessly in the playground, and unforgettable photographs of hordes of German bombers ringed by fighters revealed the mighty task facing the RAF. The Battle of Britain raged from 10 August to 15 September 1940, at which point Hitler realised that the air battle had been lost and postponed his invasion. The Few had prevailed, albeit by the slimmest of margins. Their courage, skill and sacrifice saved Britain.

The following year, the Germans scored a pyrrhic victory in the Battle of Crete. It was their first large-scale use of paratroops during the war; it would also be their last, because of the heavy losses they suffered. It was a bloody battle and the men of the Black Watch distinguished themselves, paying the Germans back for St Valéry. Among the high-profile casualties were three German brothers who clashed with the Scottish defenders in the aerodrome at Heraklion. The von Blüchers were descendants of General Von Blucher who had commanded the Prussians at Waterloo. They were real Prussian blue-bloods. When the Highlanders surrounded the platoon of Lieutenant Wolfgang von Blücher, his nineteen-year-old brother Count Leberecht tried to gallop through the British lines on horseback to resupply his brother with ammunition. He almost made it but was shot and died in front of his brother's eyes. The next day, twenty-four-year-old Wolfgang died alongside his entire platoon. A little later, seventeen-year-old Hans-Joachim von Blücher also lost his life.

In a week of fighting, from 21 to 28 May, sixty-nine men of the 2nd Black Watch died. However, the Germans suffered over three hundred dead in the attack on the aerodrome alone. Most of the Black Watch force managed to escape from the island, but some, such as Dave Hutton, a diminutive private from Dundee, were not so lucky. He recalled:

When the German bombers came on the first day we were lucky that their bombs were well off their mark. We repelled the bulk of their advances and took out a number of planes, but worse was yet to come. The next day the sky was black with paratroopers. It was an almost lovely sight except that you knew death was coming. They came down with pistols and grenades. They were everywhere you looked – in front, behind, beside you, everywhere.

I got blown up on my left side by a grenade and was taken to a field hospital. It was full of wounded and dying – boys without arms or legs. A doctor looked at me and said, 'You'll last till tomorrow' and moved on. Shortly after, the Germans stormed the hospital. I certainly didn't expect to see them and it was terrifying. They made us go outside. My wounds were assessed and I was taken to the airport and flown across to Greece.

Along with the thousands of Highlanders captured at St Valéry, Dave then endured four long years of slavery, misery and starvation in captivity.

On the home front, the mothers held their communities together. With husbands and sons in the forces, they had to care for their families on their own. They had the difficulty of feeding and clothing the family on meagre rations and a tight budget. They had to queue for basic foodstuffs and deal with all the problems caused by the blackout. They had to hide their own worries and fears and keep the family happy. Mothers bonded together to give each other moral support, and they readily shared their troubles and heartbreak.

My mother had the added responsibility of running a business, so Betty and I had our own chores to do. But we were a strong, tight family unit and supported each other. I did a lot of the shopping and could feel the mood of the mothers in the shops. Whenever things were bad they would go about their business in a morose silence, save for an occasional whisper being exchanged, and I could see from their worried faces that their burden was weighing heavily on them. On the other hand, they relayed any good news enthusiastically.

It was around this time that something happened, which completely changed my taste in music for ever. I had always been a bad riser in the morning – Mum had to call me many times to wake me from my slumber. One morning, I sat bolt upright in bed, spellbound by the exquisite music coming from the sitting-room radio. In my semi-oblivion I wondered if I had departed to a higher realm. But no, the heavenly music was an arrangement of Jerome Kern's 'All the Things You Are' – arguably the best of the songs written during the Golden Era.

I was already a fan of jazz, and by the age of sixteen I was playing in several local dance bands. While doing so I met the tenor saxophonist Bob Adams, who became a lifelong friend and who after the war played tenor saxophone in the popular Geraldo Orchestra. It was Bob who introduced me to the jazz masters, and I spent all of my earnings on records by Benny Goodman, Coleman Hawkins, Artie Shaw and Django

Reinhardt. As far as anyone knew, that was my music. But I remained haunted by Kern's masterpiece, which lured me towards the richer melodies of the Gershwin era and eventually, in later life, to the classics.

Playing every weekend was a great experience and it taught me a lot about chord sequences and key changes. I was also earning good money and was able to buy a quality clarinet. However, I knew I was neglecting my studies, so I reluctantly decided to give up performing.

In my final year at school I became head boy and fell in love with Margaret, the head girl, a blonde, blue-eyed beauty. The romance flourished with long walks and serious conversations. I was also now working very hard at my studies and equally hard at my sport. I captained the rugby first fifteen and, with the support of the sports master, set about a most rigorous training schedule. We had a strong set of backs that year, and practised passing the ball while running at high speed until our handling was impeccable. The forwards learned that the dark art of scrummaging depended on good binding and timing a concentrated push. They would also run to exhaustion as they foraged as a pack in open play. We even outlined our tactics on a blackboard to ensure that everyone knew exactly what to do.

Come the first game of the season, we wondered whether our plans would work. Soon it became clear that they would. Jim Munro, at scrum-half, controlled the forwards and the ball came back to him methodically. Tommy Edmond, at stand-off, drew the opposition and timed his passes perfectly to create openings for the centres to exploit. The forwards worked hard to produce good ball and the backs racked up a big score. For game after game our tactics produced good results and the team developed a strong desire to keep on winning. The fear of losing brought out the best in everyone and our winning margins grew and grew. We ended the season undefeated, setting a new school record, which made us so proud. Our success was largely due to the special bond that developed within the team. In that season we all made friendships that were to last a lifetime.

This was one of the most enjoyable years of my life, and I managed to squeeze in plenty of other activities alongside the busy schedule of study and rugby. I formed a jazz quartet, featuring scrum-half Jim on piano, stand-off Tommy on drums, second-row Boyd Gordon on violin, and myself on clarinet. Although our musical skill was limited, we could create a respectable sound by emulating the Goodman quartet and playing comfortably within our capabilities. We chose simple numbers like 'Georgia', 'Lady Be Good' and 'Sweet Georgia Brown', which enabled us to get the quartet swinging sufficiently to entertain ourselves and occasionally our schoolmates.

Friday nights were set aside for the Scouts, where I was an enthusiastic participant. I eventually became a King's Scout and learned many outdoor skills, including first aid, something that would stand me in good stead later in the war. On Saturday nights we would take our girlfriends to the cinema, and I often managed to get the whole group in for free. The cinema was simply the greatest pleasure in everyone's life – a wonderful shared experience at odds with today's fractured, technological society. We all thoroughly enjoyed the superb war films that stirred our hearts and bolstered our morale. Pictures like *Mrs Miniver*, starring Greer Garson, *The 49th Parallel*, about the menace of the Nazis, *The Immortal Sergeant*, set in North Africa, and of course *Casablanca* were all terrific entertainment, but they also gave us an insight into what was happening overseas.

In the summer of 1941, Germany invaded and initially over-ran Russia. However, the Red Army recovered to inflict some hammer blows on the Nazis, confirming Granddad in his view that Joe Stalin was absolutely wonderful and could do no wrong.

The war was getting closer, however. Around this time, six of my friends joined the Merchant Navy. One of them was a boy called Harold Garden. He came from a very wealthy family that had maids, several cars and a large house. But he was determined to join the war effort as soon as he could. Aged just fifteen, he signed up and went on three voyages with the Arctic convoys that Britain sent to aid Russia. Tragically, the third trip was his last: he was killed when his ship was torpedoed.

My sister was desperate to make her contribution, too. To my annoyance Betty, who was very sporty and determined but attractive with lots of friends, decided to join the Wrens. I felt very strongly that with my impending army service she should stay at home and help Mum. But she would not hear of it and insisted on joining up. Mum, of course, would never stand in the way of any of her children leading their own lives.

By then, foreign forces were starting to arrive in Scotland. I saw my first Americans on a trip to Edinburgh. I had always been told that the Yanks were brash and arrogant – not to mention a little late coming into the First World War. Yet, whenever I saw them, they were the opposite of that. In Edinburgh, they would stand outside their hotels and simply watch the world go by, chatting with the locals and handing out cigarettes.

Not all of our new allies were quite so popular, though. We certainly did not like the Poles, who were billeted in Musselburgh. Jealousy inspired much of this antipathy. They were fantastically polite and dashing in their uniforms, so the girls loved them. A few even married them – and that's why us males didn't like them. The local lads reckoned they never did anything, but just swanned about smartly turned out, and very aloof. So we made the most of every chance we got to take them down a peg or two. One day, one of my bandmates was sitting next to a Polish soldier on a bus. A young lady got on and the Pole mumbled something about giving up his seat, so my pal quickly taught him a phrase to help him out. The Pole thanked him, stood up and announced, 'Hey, sit your big, fat arse down here.'

Shortly after my final exams, one of my rugby pals, Lachlan Taylor, persuaded me to volunteer with him for the army. If you volunteered before your call-up papers arrived – which, for us, they surely would – you had a much better chance of joining your chosen regiment. So we headed for the enlistment office, where Lachlan talked me into signing up for the infantry. He volunteered for the Cameron Highlanders, while I opted for my father's old regiment, the Argylls. However, Lachlan failed his medical on account of some kidney problems. Later, crouched in a frozen slit trench with German mortars raining down on me, I cursed my old rugby mate for knowing nothing of the dangers faced by British infantrymen.

At the time, going to war seemed like a normal part of life. I was far from scared; in fact, I relished the prospect of adventure, not knowing it was going to be purgatory. Although people told me that it would be hell, I never took heed. Of course, I had heard about soldiers being killed and horrifically maimed, and I had even met and talked with some of the latter. But I never entertained the thought that something similar might happen to me.

If my father had been alive, he never would have allowed me to join the infantry. As for my dear mother, she always encouraged both me and Betty to live our own lives. She never stood in the way of our plans or aspirations. And, like us, she accepted war as part of life.

2

# The Highlanders Reborn

As my eighteenth birthday drew closer and military service
loomed, my interest in the war intensified. But there never
seemed to be any good news. After the Battle of Britain,
British cities had been bombed and the Germans had seized
Greece and Yugoslavia. The Japanese overran Hong Kong
and then our mighty fortress at Singapore fell, with sixty
thousand troops captured and HMS *Prince of Wales* and
HMS *Repulse* both lost. Rationing at home tightened as
German U-boats wreaked havoc on Atlantic convoys. It was
a grim period.

In June 1942, a government publication written by the
well-known Scottish journalist Eric Linklater gave a near-
complete account of the St Valéry battle for the first time.
Linklater wrote *The Highland Division* to clear up the con-
troversy about the disaster, and I eagerly bought my copy for
ninepence from the corner shop. On first reading, it was clear
that the fate of the 51st Division had been sealed from the
start. They were mainly territorials, ill-prepared part-timers.

They were also vastly outnumbered by nine German divisions, all of them primed in the art of war. So it was remarkable that the soldiers of the 51st were able to stem the German advance for as long as they did. But they paid a terrible price. In eight days of fighting around the St Valéry perimeter alone, over eight hundred men died.

The 51st Highland Division that fought in France in 1940 was like a mini-army, a territorial division of three brigades made up of nine infantry battalions. It consisted of five famous kilted regiments drawn from different parts of Scotland: the Black Watch from Dundee, Perthshire and Angus; the Gordon Highlanders from Aberdeenshire; the Cameron Highlanders from Inverness-shire; the Seaforth Highlanders from the northern Highlands; and the Argyll and Sutherland Highlanders. One anti-tank and three field regiments of the Royal Artillery supported them. The Highlanders also had their own engineers, signals people and medics. The Royal Army Service Corps provided supply and transport.

Many of the officers and NCOs were veterans of the Great War, so they probably had a strong sense of *déjà vu* as they embarked for France. But this time there was a big difference. In January 1940, the War Office informed the Scots that the traditional uniform of the regiments was not considered practical for modern warfare, so the soldiers were forced to hand in their kilts. The Gordons widely resented this order and held a symbolic parade at Bordon in Hampshire before embarkation in which a single kilt was ceremonially burned. A stone memorial proclaiming 'We hope not for long' marked the spot. In fact, it was no time at all before the kilt reappeared: many of the soldiers simply disobeyed the order and donned their traditional uniform at St Valéry. This mild form of rebellion continued throughout the war, with the

Highlanders going to considerable lengths to smuggle their kilts overseas.

On landing in France, the Scots were hastily drilled at Le Havre, where they were greeted by a horrendous winter – one of the worst in living memory. In February, the division joined the rest of the BEF near the Belgian border and took up positions directly behind the main front line near the town of Bethune. Their training continued but was interrupted by the arduous work of building defences, trenches and bunkers for the 'Little' Maginot Line – part of the vast but ultimately useless fortification that straddled the French/German border.

Bolstered by some ancillary units, the division now numbered about 22,000 men. They were attached to the French Army and took over a section of the Maginot Line east of Metz.

At the start of May, a ghostly, ominous silence descended on the region. The villages were deserted. Houses were locked and shuttered, their occupants having already fled. The Highlanders were ensconced in sunken wooden huts and deep trenches, sometimes wood- or straw-lined. This tense waiting game stretched their nerves, but the Scots felt well prepared for the inevitable German push. It was not long in coming. The Germans started to make probing night attacks on selected posts, testing defences and acquiring intelligence. But the Cameron Highlanders outwitted German phone-tappers by speaking in their native Gaelic.

Furthermore, the division refused to sit back and simply wait to be attacked. Instead, they launched their own night patrols, with blackened faces reminiscent of the old raiding days of the First World War, when patrols went over the top into no-man's land in the dead of night. The Argylls excelled in the darkness and made these nerve-racking patrols their speciality. Captain Ian C. Cameron recalled,

> Every night a patrol, with blackened faces, rubber boots, and every type of infantry weapon from a tommy-gun to a hunting knife, would sally forward into 'No-Man's Land'. There were frequent encounters with the enemy, and usually the enemy got the worst of it ... Nevertheless, it was an eerie experience to set out for the first time knowing that any enemy patrol bent on the same purpose might be encountered at any moment. Once this happened there was little time to think – a flurry of flashes, tommy-gun shots, exploding grenades, and then all was over.

Both sides took prisoners during these night-time escapades, but the fighting was no more than sporadic. Then, on 10 May, the Germans conclusively ended the phoney war by launching a massive blitzkrieg. The devastating speed with which the Nazis attacked France and Belgium lived up to the operation's codename – *Sichlschnitt* (Cut of the Sickle).

The Nazis attacked primarily through the thickly wooded Ardennes. The French believed such an assault was impossible, but a million soldiers and fifteen hundred tanks in armoured columns, supported by dive-bombers, showed no regard for French military theory as they blasted through the forest at break-neck speed. They hoped to overrun the French and cut off the Allied forces, driving them to the sea, which necessitated violating the neutrality of Belgium and Holland – but that was of little concern to the attackers. The Maginot Line was neatly side-stepped and its mighty forts isolated as Rommel's Panzers and motorised divisions swept into France, brushing aside the crumbling resistance of a demoralised and disorganised French Army. The Germans secured victory within weeks.

The Highlanders' part in all this began on 13 May, when a heavy early morning artillery barrage near Grossenwald brought them into the war. The Black Watch bore the impact of the early attacks and suffered heavy losses around their outpost at Betting, where men were entrenched in dugouts that were too isolated and strung out over five hundred yards apart. Fierce fighting spread across the front. But the High-landers fought well and defiantly held on to their besieged positions. The Germans cut off several small units, but others rushed to their assistance and managed to repel the attackers. Although dozens were killed and wounded in these exchanges, many of the soldiers felt relieved to be actively involved in the war. They were volunteers and could finally get on with the job they had been sent to do.

But these young Scots were soon disheartened by the speed with which their French allies capitulated. Entire French divi-sions on either side of them were forced back, leaving the 51st in front of the Maginot Line and therefore dangerously exposed and vulnerable. General Fortune consulted with his French counterparts, and issued orders to withdraw. Curses in various Scots dialects rang out from the trenches as the order was given to pull back to match the French withdrawal on either flank.

The French believed that the Germans had set their sights on Paris, and now the 51st were to form part of the defence force to protect the French capital. So, on 20 May, the Highlanders were taken out of the front line and moved to Étain and Varennes. But the antiquated French trains were painfully slow, and the men even had to get out and push them up the hills. The situation was even worse on the roads. Memories of the terrible suffering endured under the previous German occupations in 1914 and 1870, along with Nazi propaganda broadcasts, had sparked a mass exodus and all of the chaos and confusion that went with it. Millions had decided to flee, using any mode of transport that came to hand. There were pitiful sights among the columns of terrified refugees, some of whom pushed along the sick and elderly in prams and makeshift carts. This helpless tide of humanity clogged main trunk roads, country lanes and urban thoroughfares. Adding to the congestion, the British and French troops abandoned their military vehicles when they ran out of petrol. Meanwhile, the Luftwaffe's dive-bombers constantly strafed and bombed the streams of terrified civilians.

Andre Heintz, a French Boy Scout who helped the seething mass of refugees, saw scenes he would never forget:

The German occupation of the north of France between 1914 and 1918 had been so bad that people fled in blind panic motivated solely by one desire – to escape the Boches. Within days, ten million people, one third of the French population, took to the roads. We Boy Scouts jumped onto the running boards of the fleeing cars to offer water and help to those inside. You never knew what you would find in those cars. Wounded people lay moaning, some in bloodstained bandages, others untreated. In one car I was horrified to find a woman holding the dead body of a ten-month-old baby in her lap. I said to her, 'We must bury the baby. Stop the car.' But she would have nothing of it. The people were traumatised. It was sheer panic.

Because of this chaos, it took the Highlanders six days to regroup. By then, the relentless German progress had cut them off from the rest of the British Army, which was being squeezed towards the beach at Dunkirk. Five miles south of there, at the medieval fortress of Bergues, the remarkable Colonel Charles Usher of the Gordon Highlanders led a desperate rearguard resistance that delayed the advancing Germans for five vital days.

During this period, the British Army faced the fanatical Nazis of Himmler's SS regiments for the first time. Within weeks, reports started to filter through of their sadism. At Le Paradis on 26 May, a unit of the SS *Totenkopf* (Death's Head) Division under the command of twenty-eight-year-old Obersturmführer Fritz Knoechlein captured a company of Royal Norfolks. The Germans marched the Norfolks to a group of farm buildings and lined them up along the barn wall. As soon as the ninety-nine defenceless prisoners were in position, two machine-guns opened fire. Then SS men moved among the dead and dying, stabbing and shooting any survivors. Remarkably, Privates Albert Pooley and William O'Callaghan survived by feigning death and then crawling away to be cared for by friendly French farmers.

The very next day, the death squads of the SS *Leibstandarte Adolf Hitler* went into action at Wormhoudt, twelve miles from Dunkirk. A group of prisoners, several of them wounded, from the Royal Warwickshire Regiment, the Cheshire Regiment and the Royal Artillery was marched across fields and crammed into a barn. The massacre began when the SS men hurled stick grenades among their captives. The Germans then ordered any survivors to come outside in groups of five and shot them. Miraculously, fifteen wounded men survived the bloodbath, but eighty died.

On 28 May, the 51st Highland Division finally reassembled along the bank of the River Somme, near Érondelle. They were ordered to fight with the French Army to hold a line running north-west from the town to the coast, a distance of some twenty-three miles. Critically, they were thinly stretched and lacked a mobile reserve. On 2 June, the Scots moved north-west towards Abbeville in a bid to stem the German advance across the river. The Germans had already established two bridgeheads – a large one at Abbeville itself and a smaller one at St Valéry-sur-Somme (a different town from the St Valéry that would become so famous a week or so later). The French had twice tried to eliminate the Abbeville bridgehead, on 20 and 30 May, but had failed on both occasions. Now, it was decided that the Highlanders should tackle St Valéry.

On 4 June, the Scots, with supporting French infantry and armour, attempted to regain control of the high ground overlooking Abbeville and the Somme. They made good headway but were spread too thinly to consolidate their early gains. Tragically, due to inadequate intelligence about the strength of the enemy, they suffered heavy casualties. The Seaforths were 'mown like grass', with the badly wounded Sergeant Donald MacLeod the only man left alive from his platoon of thirty men. The 4th Camerons were wiped out within hours. General Derek Lang remarked later that his troops had been 'cut like ribbons' by machine-gun fire. In total, the Highlanders lost 20 officers and 543 men.

But the Black Watch and the Gordons had at least managed to push back the enemy and send them running. The Gordons took a heavily defended wood, although they lost forty men to machine-gun fire from two concealed German posts while doing so. Later, this action was commemorated in a regimental poem entitled 'The Day the Gordons Took the Woods'. Written during the author's captivity in Stalag XXA in Poland, it ends,

> Though grim, it was a noble fight,
> No cowardice was shown.
> The Hun and Scot in mortal fight,
> For death did claim its own.
> And death indeed was rife that day.
> The corpses were outstrewed,
> In bloodbaths I saw they lay,
> Brave Gordons who took that wood.

But without any help from their flanks, the Scots were again in danger of being cut off. To further dismay, the scattered units were ordered to retreat to defensive positions on the River Bresle.

The next day, the Germans launched a withering assault across the Somme. Now the entire division was slowly forced backwards to the Bresle – but this time they retreated through German-held territory. Two companies of the Argylls, led by Major Lorne Campbell, were isolated. This was my friend Sandy's group, and it took them three days to rejoin the rest of the division. Moving in daylight, they ran the gauntlet of shells, mortars and, most terrifyingly, screeching Stukas, the gull-winged Junkers 87s that seemed to appear out of nowhere to machine-gun and blast exposed troops. There was no respite from the constant need for vigilance, and no food either. Starving, the young Highlanders were exhausted and in desperate need of rest from the repeated digging-in during the withdrawal back to the Bresle. Once the last stragglers had crossed the Bresle, all of the

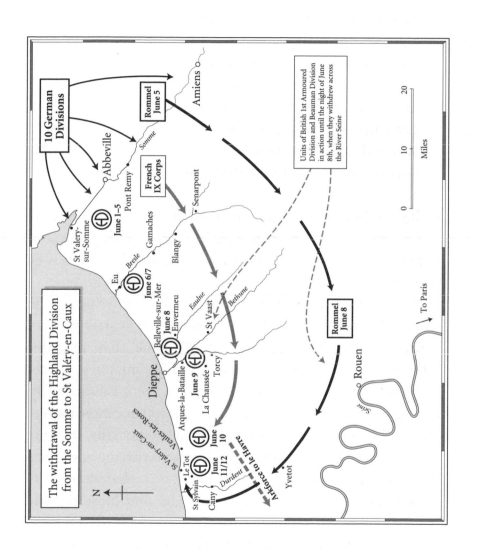

The withdrawal of the Highland Division from the Somme to St Valéry-en-Caux

N

**10 German Divisions**

**Rommel June 5**

**French IX Corps**

Amiens

Abbeville

*Somme*

Pont Remy

June 1–5

St Valéry-sur-Somme

Gamaches

*Bresle*

Eu

June 6/7

Belleville-sur-Mer

Dieppe

Blangy

Senarpont

*Eaulne*

St Vaast

Envermeu

June 8

*Béthune*

Arques-la-Bataille

La Chaussée

Torcy

June 9

Veules-les-Roses

St Valéry-en-Caux

Le Tot

June 10

St Sylvain

Cany

*Durdent*

June 11/12

**A force to Le Havre**

Yvetot

*Seine*

Rouen

To Paris

**Rommel June 8**

Units of British 1st Armoured Division and Beauman Division in action until the night of June 8th, when they withdrew across the River Seine

Miles

0        10        20

bridges were blown up. Another twenty officers and five hundred men had been killed, wounded or captured during this phase of the retreat.

These heavy losses meant the 51st had to fall back yet again, this time to the River Bethune, south of Dieppe. With the situation now more desperate than ever, London sent orders that they were to retreat towards Rouen, so they could be evacuated from Le Havre. General Fortune ordered Brigadier Stanley-Clarke, the commander of 154 Brigade, to organise a safe passage of retreat and a last line of defence outside the port. He took command of the remnants of the 7th and 8th Argylls, the 4th Black Watch, the 6th Royal Scots Fusiliers and supporting units of sappers and artillery. The group mustered in the village of Arques-la-Bataille and adopted the name 'Ark Force' after that village. Its main task was to form a defensive position about twenty miles east of Le Havre, between the two towns of Fécamp and Bolbec, through which the French IX Corps and the other two brigades of the 51st Highland Division would withdraw. It would also establish an inner line of defence closer to Le Havre to cover the evacuation.

The force set off almost immediately, but because of the congestion on the roads – and the fact that the French Army still used horse-drawn transport – the last units did not reach Fécamp until midday on 10 June. At about the same time, news reached the division that German tanks of the 7th Panzer Division were cutting through the line between Ark Force and the rest of the 51st. The Panzers were also closing in on some elements of Ark Force, and fighting had erupted with German infantry advancing behind crowds of refugees.

Stanley-Clarke had been given clear orders by Fortune that, should the Germans cut the line between Ark Force and the rest of the corps, he should act on his own initiative to save his troops. With this clearly now the case, he ordered his men to withdraw to a line between Octeville and Contreville, two miles east of Le Havre, leaving only a small rearguard force on the original line. Stanley-Clarke still hoped that the division might fight its way through, and on 11 June he ordered that the new line should be held to the last man. However, when the navy reported that the rest of the division was completely cut off and plans were being made for its evacuation, he began to plan the rescue of his own force. His troops had been fighting and marching continuously since 30 May and they were thoroughly exhausted. Nevertheless, they found the energy to destroy any usable vehicles, *matériel* and equipment they could not take with them.

Over the two nights of 12 and 13 June, some four thousand men of Ark Force were evacuated from Le Havre and eventually returned to England via Cherbourg. However, two brigades – the rest of the division – remained cut off. An alternative evacuation from Dieppe was ruled out after reports were received that the approaches to the port had been mined and its harbour facilities damaged. In any case, the Germans would probably have beaten them there from the east. That left just one option: the small fishing port of St Valéry-en-Caux – a name that was destined to be seared into the annals of Scottish history and folklore. But it was far from ideal for this type of operation as its harbour was tidal and it sat below towering chalk cliffs. Under normal circumstances, it would never even have been considered.

Attempts were made to set up a box-like perimeter around the town. The division was in position early on 11 June, but the perimeter was never fully established. The Germans had moved at great speed and appeared in strength at Cany, to the south-west. They then advanced from there and along the coast. To the east, the Gordons and the Black Watch were fighting for their lives. Alongside them, the Seaforths, lacking any anti-tank guns, were utterly defenceless in their positions. Rommel's Panzers brutally overran them, crushing the young soldiers to death in their fox-holes.

The gravity of the situation is obvious in the tenor of Fortune's directive to his commanding officers, sent at 10 a.m. on 11 June:

> The Navy will probably make an effort to take us off by boat, perhaps to-night, perhaps in two nights. I wish all ranks to realise that this can only be achieved by the full co-operation of everyone. Men may have to walk five or six miles. The utmost discipline must prevail. Men will board the boats with equipment and carrying arms. Vehicles will be rendered useless without giving away what is being done. Carriers should be retained as the final rearguard. Routes back to the nearest highway should be reconnoitred and officers detailed as guides. Finally, if the enemy should attack before the whole force is evacuated, all ranks must realise that it is up to them to defeat them. He may attack with tanks, and we have quite a number of anti-tank guns behind. If the infantry can stop the enemy's infantry, that is all that is required, while anti-tank guns and rifles inflict casualties on armoured fighting vehicles.

During the afternoon, the Black Watch at St Pierre-le-Vieux came under terrific assault, and by 6 p.m. the defenders had lost some fifty men, wounded or dead. They were reinforced by French cavalry, military remnants from a bygone age who dismounted to fight as infantry, but the position was still overrun at dawn.

To the west, the perimeter was also penetrated, and the Seaforths were cut off in Le Tot. Without their anti-tank platoon, which was on the other side of St Valéry, the enemy tanks were able simply to bypass them.

By now, St Valéry itself was ablaze, having come under heavy bombardment from cliff-top artillery and the air. In the town centre, the divisional HQ, the 51st's anti-tank regiment, some Norfolks and a company of Kensingtons managed to secure the perimeter. They repulsed an assault on the town in the late afternoon, but it remained completely surrounded. Final plans were made for the evacuation. Beaches were assigned and orders given, but these never reached those Highlanders who were still cut off in Le Tot.

A large naval force had arrived off the coast for another Dunkirk-type evacuation on 10 June, but fog had prevented the ships from entering the harbour or approaching the beaches. The following day, Rommel's tanks on the cliff tops forced the fleet to withdraw even further out to sea. So when the order finally came to start the evacuation, it was too late. Banks of dense fog had again rolled in to obscure the coast, several boats had already been lost, and the navy could not risk any more with the Germans in full control of the cliffs. A sloop picked up some troops from the beach, but the German guns sank it and killed the captain. The beach was strewn with the bodies of men who had attempted to climb down the sheer cliffs. One tug managed to pick up a handful of men near St Valéry, but they were the only ones to escape.

Various demands for surrender, made specifically to the Seaforths and one battalion of the Gordons, were robustly rebuffed, and both regiments fought practically to the end. The Black Watch, the Camerons and the other Gordon battalion held out, too. With the evacuation plans abandoned, preparations were made for a last-ditch resistance. Then, at 8 a.m. on 12 June, the French capitulated.

Fortune considered all his options: counter-attack, further resistance or surrender. He weighed all these against the fact that there was no possibility of evacuation or reinforcement. His men were exhausted and virtually out of ammunition, and there were no artillery shells at all. His valiant troops had done all they could. Shortly before 10 a.m., Fortune decided to surrender.

Jack Kidd, a corporal with the Highland Division's military police, described the scene:

> Every building was in flames and there were dead and wounded and dying people everywhere. It was horrific and terrifying. Early next morning the French General, Ihler, raised the white flag but General Fortune demanded, 'Take that down or I'll shoot it down.' After an hour, however, the bugle sounded the ceasefire and we were prisoners surrendering our weapons. I was so depressed that I felt like shooting myself.

As a teenager back in Musselburgh, I imagined the Highlanders gallantly fighting to exhaustion as they were repeatedly forced back to new defences. They had fought in the best tradition of their forebears, conscious that the good name and reputation of the Highland Division rested with them. As the bugle call to surrender sounded, men wept openly and hung their heads before being marched off to prison camps.

At the time, we were unaware of the appalling treatment meted out to these prisoners by their guards. Henry Owens, a gunner with the 51st, recalled:

We were force-marched through France; in fact it would be fairer to say they made us run through France, as it was obvious that they feared that another landing of British troops might take place to rescue us. We were beaten with rifle butts, kicked and abused to keep us moving, anyone falling out of the column ran the risk of being shot – as many were. In some instances men were picked up by motorcyclists and taken away – as happened to my fitter sergeant Ian Macmillan. Much later, we found out he had died.

The march got worse, there was very little food. A mouldy loaf of black bread between six men, and a meagre ration of ersatz coffee for those who had a tin or a dixie, was supplied at Arras, after we had queued for about five hours. The coffee was soon lost, as we had to run, being helped on our way by kicks and oaths.

The weather was extremely hot. We marched on without any water, which was worse than the lack of food, and out of desperation, we drank anything from pools made by rain, or out of cattle troughs. Consequently we suffered from stomach ailments and dysentery. The French women were marvellous. They would leave buckets of water and containers of boiled potatoes at the roadside, which invariably were kicked over by our guards. These ladies took considerable risks, and were often roughed up. Their efforts helped us to survive and we owe them our grateful thanks.

As dysentery took hold, we had to stop more and more to relieve ourselves. We used to dash into the fields and take our trousers down, until the Germans started to use us as target practice. A soldier next to me was shot and we all raced out of the field trying to pull our trousers up. After that, we soiled our trousers rather than go into the fields.

Four long years later, these same men would suffer an even worse ordeal when they were force-marched in freezing winter conditions from Poland and across Germany as the Russians advanced.

General Fortune, who suffered a stroke in captivity but refused to be repatriated, opting instead to stay with his men, was knighted after the war.

Some of the Highlanders who had missed the evacuation still managed to avoid capture. Andre Heintz was near Cherbourg, trying to help his grandparents escape the German advance, when his mother spotted two strange-looking men:

It was a crowded street and the Germans were passing through. My mother told me to ask the men if they needed help. They were both survivors of the famous 51st Highland Division. They stuck out like sore thumbs – it was a miracle they had not been spotted. They were pleased to meet an English speaker and immediately apologised to my mother for being unshaven! The men asked if it was true that France had signed an armistice, if the Americans had entered the war and if the Russians were still at peace with Germany. We had no good news for them but took them to an anti-Nazi priest. He sheltered them until it became too dangerous. Then we gave them a map, food and money and sent them on their way south. They both got back to Britain, one of them thanks to the escape operation run in Marseille by the Church of Scotland minister Reverend Donald Caskie, who became famous as the Tartan Pimpernel for helping Allied servicemen to escape occupied France – until his capture and torture by the Gestapo.

Several officers eventually made it back home and later played key roles in defeating the Germans. They included Major Tom Rennie of the Black Watch, who cycled all the way to Marseille, where the American consul arranged his safe passage to Portugal. He was followed by Captain Bill Bradford, another Black Watch officer, whose amazing escape involved climbing the Pyrenees and then sailing seven hundred miles in a seventeen-foot boat. Captain Derek Lang of the Cameron Highlanders managed to escape twice from the Germans, despite his wounds. He also evaded the Vichy French police before returning home via Lebanon. Colonel Charles Usher, the commanding officer of the unit that had gallantly held up the German Panzers at Bergues, had spent four years as a prisoner in the First World War and he was not prepared to let the same thing happen again. Although he was in his fifties, the former Scottish rugby captain swam out to six ships off the Dunkirk beaches before finally being rescued.

In Scotland, I remained determined to join the 51st, which had been rebuilt under General Douglas Wimberley in the two years since St Valéry. The Ark Force survivors and the 9th Scottish Division, which was also recruited in the Highlands, had been moulded into the reborn 51st and was then supplemented by new Scottish recruits. The Jocks knew Wimberley as 'Tartan Tam' because he insisted on accepting only Scotsmen as reinforcements. (This policy would not last. Horrendous losses in 1944–5 meant that many of the 'Highlanders' at the end of the war were English. In fact, they formed the majority in many Highland regiments.)

During training, Tartan Tam drove the division hard to attain the highest levels of fitness, and the men responded to his infectious enthusiasm and commitment. He insisted that each Jock should display great personal pride and total dedication to his regiment. He certainly set a good example. As a young lieutenant in the Cameron Highlanders, he had won a Military Cross at the Battle of Cambrai in the First World War. Wimberley understood that the 51st had to achieve total preparedness and discipline not only to succeed in combat but to regain the pride it had lost at St Valéry.

Everyone in Britain was facing a similar struggle in the early summer of 1942, when it was especially difficult to remain positive. By then, Rommel had relocated to North Africa, where he was leading the triumphant Afrika Korps. The Desert Fox was besieging the British at Tobruk and making plans to invade Egypt, with the ultimate goal of driving through Iran to link up with the German armies in Russia. Then, on 21 June, came another terrible blow. Tobruk fell with the loss of over thirty thousand men and masses of supplies, including precious petrol. We heard the news with alarm and foreboding. Tobruk and its year-long siege had been regarded as a symbol of British resilience. Now, with the remnants of the Eighth Army scurrying back into Egypt, a cloud of gloom descended on the nation.

It endured for months. Then, in early November, there was finally a glimmer of light. I heard it in the rugby dressing room, when our full-back Walter Lang rushed in and announced that he had just heard on the radio that the army had won a great victory in Egypt. After twelve days of ferocious fighting, troops of the Commonwealth had penetrated the German defences. Our forces were pouring through the gap, smashing Rommel's tanks and forcing him to retreat. We abandoned our pre-match pep talk in favour of a free-for-all babble in which we speculated on precisely who had won the victory and how. We ran onto the pitch in high spirits, inspired by this glorious feat of arms.

It was amazing news. Since the start of the war, church bells had been silent, with instructions that they should be rung only in the event of invasion. Now they were pealing in jubilation. At last we had something to celebrate: General Bernard Montgomery's army had triumphed at El Alamein and the 51st Highland Division had been in the thick of the fighting. St Valery had been avenged.

For days following the BBC's announcement, the newspapers devoted hundreds of column inches to the victory, although the censor ensured that many of the precise details remained secret. We had longed for this triumph ever since the fall of France, and it remained the main topic on everyone's lips for weeks. Churchill called it 'the end of the beginning' and was well aware that it provided a much-needed morale boost. Years of seemingly endless defeat and retreat had left families depressed and fearful. El Alamein gave us hope.

I was desperate to find out as much as possible about the part played by the Highland Division, but such sensitive information was sparse and fragmentary in the popular press. However, a few months after the battle, the government published an excellent account of the Eighth Army's operations between September 1941 and January 1943. This included a lot of information and a detailed map of the battle. Evidently, the Highland Division had fought alongside the Australians on the right, with the New Zealanders on the left as the main attacking force. This was fascinating, but much of the detail was still missing, so it would be many years and a good deal more research before I learned the full story.

The Jocks had sailed to the Middle East via South Africa in June 1942, tasked with slogging it out with the Germans and their Italian allies in the unfamiliar arena of desert warfare. The immense, empty Western Desert is a huge expanse of golden sand dunes, save for a sixty-mile rocky coastal strip that is covered with a crust of fine grit. The two sides' desert campaigns ebbed and flowed on this unforgiving pitch.

For the fair-skinned Scots, many of whom would develop skin cancer in old age, the miseries of the desert included searing, unbearable heat during the day, freezing-cold nights, constant thirst, dehydration and swarms of disease-carrying insects. Every activity depended upon the regular supply of water, transported with difficulty over great distances. The troops had to survive on just half a water-bottle each day for washing, shaving and drinking. It was chlorinated, invariably hot and tasted foul, so it was used to make strong, murky tea.

The soldiers were given a two-course evening meal of tinned M&V (meat and vegetables), corned beef or occasionally a stew, followed by a tinned pudding or fruit. Porridge was the staple breakfast, along with tea and a day's supply of hard tack biscuits. The quartermaster's nightmare was working out the logistics for supplying the forward troops – often at a distance, often under fire.

Sand and grit got everywhere, penetrating deep into equipment and engines. It embedded itself in clothing, causing skin irritations that frequently developed into sores. Whenever possible, officers gave the men the opportunity to bathe in the sea. Sand storms wreaked havoc; the only protection was to wrap yourself in a ground sheet and go to ground.

Flies were another curse of the desert. They thrived on the scores of rotting corpses decomposing on the sand dunes, and hordes would settle on any moist skin especially around the mouth, nose and eyes. They made eating a trial, landing by the dozens on the rims of tea mugs and mess tins and following every spoonful of food regardless of death threats.

Twenty-four-year-old George Sands, a private in the Cameron Highlanders and one of the increasing number of Englishmen in the Highland Division, summed up conditions in the desert:

We learned to do our laundry by washing it in petrol, as petrol was more in abundance than water. Our clothing being bleached almost white, and dry in a matter of seconds. There were occasions when we drank water out of the radiator of a lorry, as that was the only water available. We had tried drinking the water out of the Mediterranean, which caused our lips to swell up, split and bleed, and made us sick. That was what you might call being desperate for a drink.

We discovered that the best way to cook was by

means of a 'Benghazi Fire' comprised of a cut-down petrol can, filled with sand, and then petrol poured into the sand; once lit, it would burn for quite some considerable time.

When we collected our food from the cookhouse truck, we soon learned to cover our plates of food with our steel helmets. Unsuspecting, usually fresh personnel would be carrying their food back to their dugout or tent, when they would be dive bombed by a large bird that would take everything off the plate. Magpies had nothing on these birds.

Apart from the dust storms and the sand getting into everything the most annoying things were the incessant attacks by plagues of flies. Not just the buzzing around you, but it felt at times as though you were being eaten alive.

Standing-to in the line at dawn, waiting for an expected counter-attack with senses and reactions numbed from the cold, brought a sick feeling of fear and helplessness. Soldiers were confined all day to a slit trench with little to do and too much to think about. A shave, water permitting, helped fill the time. Then there would be mail, which was endlessly read and reread, and replies to write. Trench-mates would exchange stories, before silent thoughts of home engulfed soldiers who longed to escape the desert. Night brought fear, with noises amplified and imaginations playing tricks, but it also provided a chance to leave the trench, stretch limbs and grab a hot meal.

Behind the lines there was freedom of movement, but the danger of shelling remained. A shallow trench and a bivouac provided comfortable sleeping for two. A gun crew or an engineer section could share their daily water to advantage. And it was a mystery how, whenever soldiers settled into a new position, no matter how remote, an Arab with eggs would suddenly appear out of the blue, offering to barter for tea and cigarettes. Tank crews enjoyed the protection and amenities of their vehicles, but the infantry did not envy them. The Germans' 88mm anti-tank guns were amazingly accurate and lethal, so there was a high mortality rate among crews, many of whom met a terrible end trapped in their flaming vehicles.

One of the few mercies of the gruelling North African campaign was that there were no substantial SS forces attached to the Afrika Korps. They were busily engaged in genocidal activities in Poland and the Soviet Union, so the desert campaign was spared the routine prisoner massacres carried out by Himmler's henchmen.

By the end of October, the Highlanders were fully acclimatised to their new surroundings. Apprehensive but well dug in, some ten thousand of them waited with bated breath. They had already received a personal message from Montgomery, who did not mince his words. The message reminded troops that it was their duty 'to fight and to kill'. Finally, in bold type for emphasis, it read: '**Let no man surrender so long as he is unwounded and can fight**'.

Some grim preparations had already been made, revealing the expected level of carnage. Private Peter Bruce, from Buckie in Aberdeenshire, was a first-aid man with the Highland Field Ambulance of 153 Brigade. He recalled:

For weeks we had been going up to the front at night at El Alamein and digging out an underground Advanced Dressing Station (ADS). The work had to be very carefully carried out and all the spoil had to be carefully scattered well away from the excavations so that the Germans wouldn't know that such work was being carried out.

Back at our current ADS, which consisted of deep dugout chambers connected by deep tunnels, we carried on as usual. Then one day the Royal Engineers came with bulldozers and started digging out long swatches of sand about four feet deep and six feet wide, row upon parallel row. We asked the engineers what they were doing. They replied that these rows were to be the graves of those killed in a battle to be coming off soon. It made us think.

I will never forget the evening of 23 October. Before we moved up to the front we were briefed that the casualties were expected to be very heavy and we were told not to spend more than four minutes giving first aid. If the casualty couldn't be treated within that time we had to slip two morphine tablets under his tongue and sedate him.

Like their fathers before them, the Jocks were going to fix bayonets and go over the top to advance across open territory, protected only by a creeping artillery barrage in front of them. A piper led every company and each man had a St Andrew's cross marked on his pack. This was the first action of the reformed division since St Valéry, and all ranks were determined to succeed.

Montgomery's strategy was to stage a huge deception operation involving dummy tanks, other vehicles, artillery and even petrol and water-storage facilities to convince Rommel that XIII Corps would launch the attack in the south. Meanwhile, the British commander was covertly increasing his XXX Corps forces in the north. At 9.40 p.m. on 23 October the massed guns of the Eighth Army shattered the silence of the desert with a barrage so mighty that the ears of the gunners were said to have bled. The Battle of El Alamein, Operation Lightfoot, had begun.

The five Commonwealth divisions of XXX Corps – Australians, Indians, South Africans, Scots and New Zealanders – lined up on a 12,000-yard front and prepared to advance. These infantrymen had to break the Axis forces' defences to pave the way for the armoured divisions. Flanked by the Aussies on the right and the Kiwis on the left, the Highlanders had orders to take objectives named after towns in each battalion's recruiting area. So, for example, the 5th Black Watch and 1st Gordons first targeted enemy positions named after the Angus towns of Montrose, Forfar and Arbroath. Then they would move on to Kintore, Braemar, Dufftown and ultimately Aberdeen.

The barrage suddenly stopped as dramatically as it had begun. Huge clouds of dust swirled in the air and were illuminated by two gigantic searchlights that swung their beams to cut across each other and form a giant St Andrew's cross, pointing the way for the Scots. A few excited Highlanders charged too quickly and ran straight into the creeping barrage that was designed to protect them, but most advanced in a rapid yet orderly fashion.

Having sustained heavy casualties, the attack faltered on Miteiriya Ridge due to an extended network of heavily defended enemy strongpoints. The objective of the New Zealanders was beyond the ridge, but the British artillery barrage had failed to take out many of the German bunkers. Consequently, on the crest, intense fire from all directions scythed through the Kiwis, cutting them down like stalks of wheat. Nevertheless, fired by rage, the survivors charged over the ridge to engage in hand-to-hand fighting with the defenders.

During the night attacks of 23–24 October, troops also endured the dreadful fear of advancing through minefields. As they marched into the unknown, they passed the bodies of dead and wounded engineers who had sacrificed themselves to clear dozens of twenty-four-foot wide lanes through the hundreds of thousands of buried death traps that earned this no-man's land the nickname of the Devil's Garden. Each lane was just wide enough for a single tank, so if the lead vehicle was hit there were terrible jams. Mines were also booby-trooped and often wired to each other in sequence, making the advance even more perilous.

George Sands assisted in the mine-clearing operation:

That was the first time that the majority of us had experienced the sight and sound of a huge barrage. It was amazing that there was anyone left to shoot back at us, given the amount of shells that our artillery had fired. I can remember the noise and dust and screams, and our ever-faithful Pipers playing on. The group that I was with acted as a cover for the engineers making vehicle gaps through the enemy minefield. The engineers had to dispense with using their metal detectors. They started probing with bayonets, because the detectors kept registering all the shell fragments and pieces of shrapnel. But I think they were glad to get down nearer the ground, making a smaller target.

The thick smoke and dust blinded and choked the Jocks, who were fearful of losing contact with their comrades.

Private William Black, a company signaller with the Seaforths, remembered the chaos of the battle:

> We lined up behind the guns when they opened up and we waited to get the order to move forward. My mate, big Jock Rennie from Craigmillar, had the wireless set on his back and I was operating it behind him. I can't remember how far we went forward when big Jock stopped a bullet. I had to get the wireless set off his back. Luckily a Bren carrier stopped and I put the wireless set on the carrier. I saw Jock was comfortable and left him for the stretcher bearers. We moved forward again and we had not gone far when the carrier ran over a mine and blew a track. Luckily it was on the opposite side of where I was walking. I got the wireless set on my back and pushed forward on my own. By this time the front line was out of sight and I wasn't sure if I was going in the right direction. There were flares going up all the time and I just seemed to be on the battlefield on my own. There were bursts of small arms fire but the worst thing was the anti-tank shells, which seemed to be swishing all over the place. They must have been expecting tanks to be following the troops. I just kept going and eventually found myself with the Australians. It took a day to get back to my own unit.

At times like these, the company piper played much more than a merely symbolic role. Regimental tunes filled the advancing Jocks with pride, and their foes with fear. Moreover, the brave pipers were vital in rallying disorientated troops. They paid a heavy price, however. Piper Duncan

McIntyre of the Black Watch struck up the regiment's 'Black Bear' march as the Jocks advanced on Montrose. He was hit but kept playing defiantly. Hit again, he continued to play until he died. The next morning, he was found with his pipes still under his arm and his fingers on the chanter. At least three other pipers died that night, too.

Lieutenant William McFarlan, of the Gordon Highlanders, was one of many veterans to pay tribute to the pipers:

Colonel Nap Murray halted us at the start of an enemy minefield to wait for D Company with Valentine tanks. Meanwhile, while digging in, a sniper was giving us a lot of trouble from the direction of Kintore. With a few men we set out to get him. Unfortunately, I forgot to take a compass bearing and, having dealt with him, I had no bearing with which to return. Then I heard 'Monymusk' on the pipes, our company call, played by that great man, Piper Williams. We returned safely to be welcomed by Williams, 'Thank Christ, sir. Everyone else is dug in and here is me left standing up.'

As the infantry moved ahead, the medics followed to pick up the pieces, sometimes literally. Among them was Peter Bruce, who witnessed some awful sights:

We were held back until the troops had got through the first two minefields and then we started mopping up. We came upon our first casualty only about fifty yards from the white starting tape. He had suffered a shell wound to his armpit and another up in his groin and he was flopping about, semi-conscious, on the sand like a broken scarab beetle. From the amount of blood which stained the sand all around him and the mincemeat flesh when we explored his wounds we knew he was beyond all aid, so we had to slip two tablets under his tongue and let him slip away.

The Commonwealth attackers were now locked in a grim stalemate. It was the task of the armoured divisions to advance through areas cleared by the Highlanders and the Kiwis and penetrate the well-defended and entrenched Axis lines. But this failed, partly because the infantry had not reached their objectives on account of the effectiveness of the Devil's Garden defences. After two more days of minor advances, the attack had ground to a halt.

Black Watch private Roy Green, a recruit from the Isle of Wight, recalled the terror of going on patrol during this period:

Having to go forward as a sniper or on patrol was no big problem so far as going in no-man's land on our side. The real problems were on the enemy side. The vast German minefields were between three and five miles deep, strewn with hundreds of thousands of anti-personnel 'S' mines, which exploded about five feet above the ground and were absolutely lethal. It was almost impossible to approach really close unless you were fed up with life! Their minefields were constructed so as to lure attackers into channelled areas to be dealt with by machine-gun fire from bunkers and defensive strong points. No one liked going on patrol. It was stressful and tantamount to suicide on many occasions.

It was decided to step up the momentum and break the deadlock. On 26 October, the 1st Armoured Division launched an audacious night attack to secure Kidney Ridge, the high ground ahead of the Highlanders' positions. Two objectives, code-named Snipe and Woodcock, were taken by a lightning infantry strike and quickly reinforced by six pounder anti-tank guns that could take out a Panzer from fifteen hundred yards. Unfortunately, by now, Rommel had returned from sick leave in Austria to take command, and he promptly ordered a counter-attack. When dawn broke the next day, the enemy launched a powerful offensive with vastly superior forces. But the defenders were well dug in and their guns had been expertly positioned. Their small patch of barren desert was bombarded by mortars and raked by machine-gun fire. However, although they were cut off, they held fast against a furious assault. Ninety tanks of the 21st Panzer Division attacked Snipe in wave after wave. Incredibly, the defenders knocked out thirty-five of them and immobilised a further twenty. This small, gallant band had achieved a triumph of courage and tactics against overwhelming odds.

Success would have been complete if the advancing reinforcements had been able to locate the defenders. But eventually the survivors were forced to withdraw under cover of darkness, leaving the desert ground strewn with men who had given their lives to make possible the victory that followed. Nevertheless, their heroism had seriously frustrated Rommel's last, desperate counter-attack. Lieutenant Colonel Victor Buller Turner, of the Rifle Brigade, won a Victoria Cross for the part he played in the defence.

Incredibly, during lulls in the fighting, the Highlanders took the opportunity to indulge in some dark humour. Roy Green recalled: 'One night at Snipe after the Germans had withdrawn we were gathered around the fire when some nut threw in a handful of .303 bullets unseen and slipped away. Of course it was mad as the bullets were lethal and flew everywhere. But we just laughed and thought it was great fun.' On another occasion, the troops expressed their gallows humour in an even more bizarre way, as Green explained:

We were in the front line at El Alamein when an Italian was seen at fairly short range dropping his trousers to relieve himself – with his white buttocks facing in our direction. Instead of shooting him out of hand we kept up a fire of rifle shots just above his head – our intention was to get his bum sunburned. We never shot him and he duly made his hurried exit. Can anyone imagine doing such a thing in the middle of a major battle? Yet we did precisely that. I called it 'Highland humour' and we all had a great laugh for many a long day.

It was obvious to everyone that a massive and decisive thrust was required, so General Freyberg, of the 2nd New Zealand Division, took command of Operation Supercharge. The units chosen to lead the attack were two fresh brigades that had not yet been involved in the fighting: the Durhams of 50th Division and 152 Brigade of the Highland Division. In support, 133 Brigade of 44th Division would protect the left flank of the thrust and the 28th (Maori) Battalion would protect the right. The attack would be made through the Highland Division's lines to a depth of four thousand yards on a four-thousand-yard front.

The main concentration of enemy artillery was further beyond the infantry's objectives. Of course, it had to be destroyed to win the battle and secure domination. This essential task, which was recognised as the most dangerous of the whole battle and would surely incur a mammoth casualty rate, was handed to the 9th Armoured Brigade.

An impressive diversionary attack was made in the extreme north, where the Australians, drawing strong opposition, continued to engage the enemy infantry along the coast. This gave the launch of Operation Supercharge the crucial element of surprise.

On the night of 1 November, a mighty artillery barrage signalled the start of the attack. As soon as it ceased, 152 Brigade proudly led the assault, advancing in extended order, rifles at the port, bayonets glinting in the pale moonlight. They met little resistance and casualties were relatively light in reaching their objective, although the 5th Seaforths came under fire from dug-in tanks, which they stormed and captured.

By contrast, the area further south through which the Durhams had to advance was an important Afrika Korps defensive line, well designed and garrisoned by veteran Panzer grenadiers who resisted with skill and determination. Fortunately, the barrage had wrought a heavy toll on the defenders, but the Durhams still required immense courage to reach their objective. Many leading platoons were all but wiped out. The support groups protecting the flanks of the salient had hard battles to fight, too, but they managed to take all their objectives. The sappers then quickly cleared the mines from the centre pathway, allowing the 9th Armoured Brigade to make its crucial assault on the Axis lines. The tank commanders knew their only hope was to crash through the fire zone at the greatest possible speed, pierce the enemy lines and, from the relatively safe haven beyond, turn around and fire back on the German guns. It was a case of do or die.

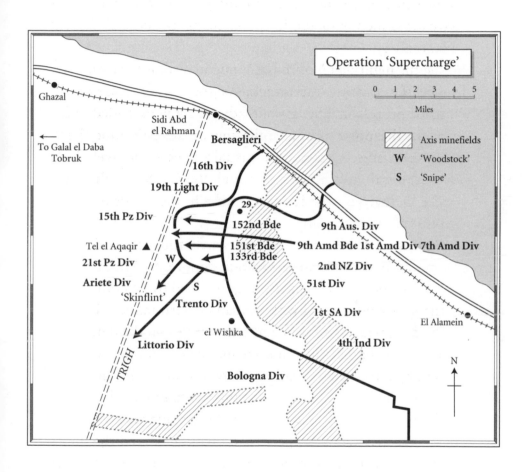

At 6.15 a.m. on 2 November, the British artillery barrage roared once again, and the tanks of the 9th Armoured Brigade thundered through the infantry lines and into enemy territory. In the darkness and dust, neither attacking tank nor defending gun could be distinguished. However, the enemy artillery, which was firing on fixed lines, started to score hits. When the dreaded dawn broke, the tanks became easy targets, and many of the leading vehicles were knocked out, obstructing the way forward. Row upon row of tanks entered the log jam and the German guns had a field day.

Roy Green, watching the battle with his fellow Highlanders from the recently captured Snipe, saw the tragic fate of many tank crews at first hand:

> The German guns had hit our ammunition dump situated in a small hollow. The result was a series of huge explosions of mortar bombs, grenades and boxes of rifle ammunition. An hour later a Sherman tank about forty yards from us took a direct hit and burst into flames. A pair of hands and a face appeared above the turret. But by this time the tank ammunition had started to explode and he slid back inside. It was agonising to watch but there was nothing we could do to help in that situation.

The guns claimed scores of tanks and their burning hulls littered the desert. Yet the courageous crews charged on through the inferno. Ignoring cannons to the left and cannons to the right, they charged into a valley of death. A staggering seventy-six out of ninety-four British tanks were destroyed. The tumult of gunfire and explosions obliterated all cries from the battlefield, banished all thoughts save survival, and numbed all senses. Fear gave way to resignation, and the crews calmly concentrated on the role they had to play – and prayed.

The fortunate few who survived the killing ground now had to hold their objective on the Rahman Track and keep open the pathway they had cleared. This would allow the 1st Armoured Division to charge through to Tell el Aqqaqir, where they would fight the final tank battle.

Rommel reacted to the penetration of his defences by rapidly moving his crack 21st Panzer Division to confront the 1st Armoured Division and defend the Tell el Aqqaqir Ridge, which halted further progress. The Panzers attacked the salient on each flank while all available artillery pounded the area mercilessly, but the defenders held their ground.

Montgomery could have hoped for no more. He now called on the Highland Division, with the 5th Indian Brigade under its command, to punch a second pathway to outflank the Panzers of the 21st Division. On 4 November, the Argylls, Gordons and Indians hacked their way through the minefields and overcame fierce resistance to puncture the Axis defences once again. British tanks then poured through the gap. The game was up for Rommel. The Desert Fox, who had gloated over his capture of the Highlanders at St Valéry, was not laughing now.

El Alamein had cost the Allied forces 13,500 casualties, with 2500 of them from the Highland Division. However, from this point onwards, it was a pleasure to follow the progress of the war on my *Daily Mail* wall map. It was the beginning of the end for the Germans in North Africa. The Highlanders had been reborn and would ultimately fight their way from Normandy across the Rhine and into the German heartland.

But first Rommel had to be chased out of Africa. A few days after El Alamein, on 13 November, Tobruk was retaken. The Desert Fox then made a fighting withdrawal along the North African coast. He still had many troops and plenty of *matériel* at his disposal as he beat a hasty retreat some four hundred miles to Mersa el Brega, where he made his first defensive stand. His strategy was to disengage from the enemy, retreat to a secure defensive position, lay sprawling minefields, and then launch an intense artillery bombardment to inflict heavy casualties. Through these tactics, he still hoped to reclaim the initiative in North Africa.

Mersa el Brega was a village in a bottleneck surrounded by high ground. Patrols reported that the position was strongly held and protected by extensive minefields. However, as the British massed, Rommel withdrew to avoid a Black Watch pincer movement. The village therefore became little more than a footnote in the history of the North African campaign. However, it was much more significant for George Sands:

On 2 December we moved forward to Mersa el Brega, taking over from the 7th Armoured Division. It was here that I knew for sure for the first time that I killed another human being. I had obviously been firing at the enemy but how successful I had been was open to question. Up until now they had been distant targets, impersonal, not even human, just targets.

When we came into contact with the Germans, this guy just leapt up in front of me, aiming straight at me. I can still picture him to this day, a short stocky guy with glasses. It was a case of him or me and I will never forget that look of sheer terror and astonishment on his face as he fell, when my bullet hit him. I dropped down and wept, not sure if I was feeling more sorry for him or for myself. It was not a very pleasant time, but that was to be the last time that I felt those particular emotions. It was far more difficult having to deal with seeing your mates maimed and killed, especially if they happened to be beside you when they copped it. It would get a lot easier to kill. I would get to the point where I wanted to kill. I was to change from a one-time church-going choirboy to being a total animal.

The next destination was Tripoli. Supplies, especially petrol, were running low and Montgomery knew that the advance of the Eighth Army might be halted unless the port's facilities were opened soon. The Highlanders in particular viewed Tripoli as a highly significant target – it might not have signalled the end of the whole desert campaign, but it was at least the halfway marker.

Following a hard-fought and skilful advance culminating in the bloody Battle of the Hills, Tripoli fell on 23 January when the Gordons and Seaforths entered the city. In three months they had fought their way fourteen hundred miles across the desert from El Alamein. Yet there was little jubilation. The troops were simply too exhausted to celebrate. Everywhere, in shell craters and bombed-out buildings, men lay down and slept – some for forty-eight hours.

Just over a week later, on 3 February, Churchill flew to an airstrip outside of Tripoli, where he told an audience of soldiers and airmen, 'After the war, when a man is asked what he did, it will be quite sufficient for him to say, "I marched and fought with the Desert Army."' It was a typically inspiring soundbite from a great orator.

But the next day, the Prime Minister's legendary eloquence deserted him when he witnessed a hastily organised victory parade. Dozens of banned kilts suddenly appeared and the massed pipes of the Highland Division led the troops in impeccable order. Churchill later recalled that they looked as if they had just 'walked out of Wellington barracks'. The tunes that had led the Highlanders into countless desert battles now reverberated through the streets of the ancient Moorish citadel and across the main square, where the Chief of the Imperial General Staff, Sir Alan Brooke, took the salute alongside the Prime Minister.

For General Wimberley, it was a moment to be savoured:

I have never felt prouder in all my life. As the pipes and drums played our famous Highland regiments past in turn to the strains of 'Highland Laddie', 'Pibroch O'Dhomnuill Dubh', the 'Cock of the North' and 'The Campbells are Coming' my heart was very full and there were tears in my eyes. However, I was certainly in good company that day. I noticed the same in Alan Brooke's and, as for Winston, the tears were running down his cheeks.

Brooke admitted:

As I stood alongside Winston watching the division march past, with the wild music of the pipes in my ears, I felt a lump rise in my throat and a tear run down my face. I looked round at Winston and saw several tears on his face ... For the first time I was beginning to live through the thrill of those first successes that were now rendering ultimate victory possible. The depth of those feelings can only be gauged in relation to the utter darkness of those early days of calamities when no single ray of hope could pierce the depth of gloom.

The troops themselves were similarly moved. George Sands remembered: 'The highlight of our time in Tripoli was undoubtedly the march past by the 51st Highland Division, with the inspection and salute taken by Winston Churchill. The sound of the pipes and drums stirring the blood of all who were there was enough to bring a tear to any man's eye.'

But there was still plenty of fighting to do and battle honours to collect in the drive to smash the Afrika Korps. As the chase proceeded across North Africa, the Highlanders started to paint their striking 'HD' insignia on liberated buildings. At first, this was a necessary aid to navigation, but soon it became an expression of pride that earned the division the tongue-in-cheek nickname of 'Highway Decorators'.

The Germans eventually fell back to the Mareth Line, at a narrow point between the Matmata Hills and the coast. Roy Green witnessed the bloody consequences of an unsuccessful counter-attack that they launched at Medenine:

When the Germans attacked we saw a group of them coming forward like a football crowd. What they didn't know was that our mortar platoon were in carriers forward of us in a slight hollow. It was the finest mortar attack I ever saw. The Germans were split asunder with bodies lying everywhere and troops running in all directions. The subsequent German attack was destroyed along with 52 of their tanks.

Even in retreat and facing obvious defeat, the Nazis remained defiant. One group of Highlanders found a novel way of dealing with one particularly arrogant prisoner. Signaller Sandy Dall witnessed the spectacle:

Their officer was a quintessential Nazi: blond, blue-eyed and extremely offensive – in Oxford English. His non-cooperative behaviour was brought to an abrupt halt by two tank crew who took his trousers down and spanked his bottom with a plank of wood, in full view of his own men. To his blond hair and blue eyes were now added red cheeks – four in all – and he gave no further trouble. As he slunk off we dared him, 'Now put that in your bloody memoirs.'

Yet Rommel remained a formidable foe, as the Highlanders discovered at the Battle of Wadi Akarit – a one-day epic described by many as the most ferocious battle fought by the division in North Africa. Partly because of a lack of cover, casualties were higher than at any time since El Alamein: 1289 men killed or wounded. But thirty thousand (mainly Italian) prisoners were taken, and the Seaforths, Camerons and Argylls were able to add the name 'Akarit' to their battle honours. Colonel Lorne Campbell, who led his men to safety through the German lines, was awarded the Victoria Cross for ignoring his serious wounds to carve out a bridgehead for the attacking Highlanders.

George Sands was in the thick of the fierce fighting:

On 6 April, in the early hours of the morning, we crossed our start line and our artillery opened up about a half-hour later. Our rate of advance was too slow, because the following companies started to catch us up, so we moved as close as we could to our creeping barrage. We reached Roumana Ridge just after first light with showers of sparks from shell splinters striking the rocky hillside. The Germans had left the Italians on the forward slopes and we soon sorted them out and consolidated our position on the left-hand bump of Roumana as ordered. Things then began to get decidedly unhealthy. 50th Division had not arrived on our left so the occupants there were throwing everything at us and we came under long-range heavy-machine-gun fire, to which we had no means to reply. Then the German 90th Light Division began a counter-attack from the right, which made the Italians get brave and hold out against us. We were getting a bit thin on the ground. Then we saw 50th Division advancing across the plain under heavy shell-fire which heartened us no end, especially as they rapidly captured their objectives and secured our left flank.

Throughout the entire day we fought the Germans in the wadis and I lost count of the bayonet charges we made. I always used the old, First World War-type, 18-inch bayonet that I had been issued with when I first joined up. The more recent issue of what we called a pig sticker [was] too short for my liking and was only used when being inspected or on guard duty. As far as I was concerned, the further away from my body the enemy was, the better. It was purely psychological as we had been taught that only 2 inches of penetration was enough to kill. Most men feared being stabbed to death.

By nightfall we had secured the position but we were shelled constantly and we did not get a hot meal that night, one of the few occasions throughout the war that we failed to get one. The next morning we found that Jerry had packed up and gone. Casualties had been heavy – at one point my company of 100 men was down to about twenty to twenty-five men. Apparently what we had accomplished with brigade strength should have been carried out with divisional strength. A Reuters reporter wrote at the time: 'Their assault is described by military observers as one of the greatest heroic achievements of the war.'

The Eighth Army had become a highly respected household name. Everyone now viewed it as the fighting force that had turned the tide of the war, and at its heart had been the 51st Highland Division. By the end of the North African campaign, the Highlanders had travelled 1850 miles across the desert in 194 days and had suffered 5399 casualties, including 1151 killed. The division had played a major role in nearly every battle and had won great praise for its dogged determination when facing the full fury of the enemy. It had performed to the highest traditions of its forebears. And it had avenged the tragedy of St Valéry.

General Wimberley's achievement in training the troops was recognised and he was ordered back to Britain to oversee officer training at Camberley Staff College. He was replaced by Major General Charles Bullen-Smith, who would still be in command when the division landed in Normandy in 1944. The Highlanders themselves were given no respite, as they were chosen to lead the assault on Sicily, which began on 10 July 1943.

Roy Green described the Sicilian campaign as 'a long, hard and vicious slog'. It involved thirty-nine days of fighting, during which the Germans frequently refused to take prisoners. By the time it had finished, the Highland Division had suffered 1436 casualties, with 224 dead. The battles of Gerbini and Sferro Hills were especially bloody and demanded inspired leadership at all levels. The only known Highland Division monument to be erected during the war was built high in the Sferro Hills to commemorate one of the greatest achievements of the division. It stands in proud, lonely isolation and marks the spot where a great many brave Highlanders fought their last battle.

# 3

# Back to France

On 1 April 1943, four days after my eighteenth birthday, my long-anticipated call-up papers arrived. I was required to report for duty at Queen's Barracks, Perth, on 6 May. Mum was resigned to my joining up, but she dreaded it just as much as every mother did. She took me on an endless round of formal visits to all our friends and family during which fine china was brought out and we devoured tasty home-baked scones and cakes, the best that rationing would allow. She also insisted that I had a portrait photograph taken and arranged a farewell party. When I boarded the train at Edinburgh a group of friends and family bid me farewell. I was slightly irritated by the attention and wondered what all the fuss was about. It was only much later that I understood that this ritual, which must have been played out thousands of times across the country, was inspired by the fear that I might not survive the war.

At Perth, a corporal awaited our arrival on the station platform. He lined us up in pairs and marched us through the town. On our way to the barracks, a loud voice behind me felt it necessary to criticise all aspects of the proceedings, much to the disquiet of the rest of us nervous recruits. When we arrived we were signed in and taken to a hut that accommodated about twenty teenage warriors. We deposited our belongings on our beds and lined up outside to meet our instructors, Sergeant Alexander and Corporal Amos.

The programme for the rest of the day was hectic but well organised. First stop was the quartermaster's stores. Behind the counter were old sweats with vast experience. We were handed standard battledress that always seemed to fit, despite the recruits varying from short and fat to tall and skinny. Shirts, underwear and socks were flung at us as we were rushed along. We were given different sizes only when it came to our boots and tam o'shanters. At the end of the counter we picked up our webbing equipment: kitbag, large pack, small pack, gaiters, waist belt, straps and water bottle. We barely had time to breathe before we were back in our barrack hut for a kit check and inspection. 'If you lose any of these items,' warned Corporal Amos, 'you pay for them.' We were then ordered to change into our army clothing, and finally parcel up and label our civilian clothes, which would be posted back to our families.

What a day it had been. But I was very impressed with the army's organisation. A draft of a hundred men had been transformed from civilians to fully kitted soldiers without a hitch – or so I thought.

After a surprisingly good evening meal in a gigantic dining hall we returned to our huts. From the bunk next to me came a distinctive, loud voice, one that I recognised from our march to the barracks. 'I'm Alex Corris,' it announced. Then he told me of his lengthy and disjointed journey to Perth, made with his compatriot Mac Mackinnon from his home in Douglas, on the Isle of Man. I took to Alex immediately. He was an intelligent, vociferous rebel, always liable to land himself in trouble, but full of fun and very friendly.

The second day of our initiation into the army was just as hectic. We formed up in three ranks for an inspection to ensure that our uniforms fitted. Next we marched to the barber to have our hair cut, army style, before all of our personal details were recorded. We were given our army numbers and our dog tags, which we had to indent ourselves with number, name and religion, and ordered to put them round our necks and never remove them. I don't think we realised that these were issued to identify bodies that had been damaged beyond recognition. When we were given our pay books we were reminded that we would receive three shillings (fifteen pence) per day, one shilling of which would go directly to our families. This qualified each family for a war pension in the event of our death. Finally, we queued up at the armourer's for our rifles, with the numbers of the weapons recorded in our documents.

We had been in training only two days when Alex had his first brush with army authority. Corporal Amos asked Alex to blanco his gaiters, Alex rather rudely refused, and he was charged with disobeying an order. For this grievous offence, he was sent to the dreaded glasshouse, the army jail, for twenty-four hours. When he returned to barracks the previously irrepressible rebel whispered to me: 'I've never experienced such punishment before. Nobody laid a hand on me, but the psychological abuse was unbearable. If Corporal Amos asks me to kiss his backside, I won't hesitate.' Alex had learned his lesson. He remained rebellious, but from now on he made sure it stayed within the confines of army rules.

The next day, we paraded in front of the barracks' commanding officer. Colonel V. C. Holt made clear that our duty was to serve King and country, and that it was his task to turn each one of us into a well-trained and disciplined soldier who was fit to bear arms in battle. Standing near by was the ramrod figure of Regimental Sergeant Major Andy Drummond, who surveyed the entire scene with a piercing eagle eye. Andy was a Black Watch legend, a tall, handsome and athletic figure who strutted about like a peacock. He never seemed to miss anything, and from the window of his flat overlooking the parade ground he would regularly bellow out a bollocking at some unsuspecting greenhorn. Hailing from Perth, he was considered to be the third most senior RSM in the whole British Army. Although a fearsome disciplinarian, he was quite popular and respected for the way he ran the show. Under his guidance, everything in Queen's Barracks worked to perfection.

The training at Perth was exceptional, with Corporal Amos and Sergeant Alexander, both Argylls, highly professional tutors. They seemed to know the black art of warfare inside out, possessing a vast knowledge of guns, ammunition, close combat, communications, stealth and fieldcraft. Whether we were scaling walls, skewering sacks with fixed bayonets or diving for cover under mock-mortar attack, they drove us hard and persevered until we reached the high standards they demanded. Daily physical training in the gym, and route marches of eight, twelve and ultimately sixteen miles brought us to the peak of fitness. We also attended lectures on current affairs given by a young second lieutenant called Bill Chisholm, whom I would meet later in the 5th Black Watch. Meanwhile, a catering officer showed us how to make meals from the fourteen-man food pack used in an emergency on the battlefield.

I kept my nose clean, but on one occasion, when RSM Drummond took us for drill, he picked on me for failing to wheel properly. It was a mortifying moment. He informed me that I had personally 'ruined' his parade. He bawled and screamed in my face, calling me an embarrassment to the King and a disgrace to humanity. I had never been censured and humiliated like this, and I was on the verge of answering back and walking off the square. But that would have landed me in serious trouble, so I resisted the temptation. With hindsight, I realised that the dressing down instilled the self-discipline to suffer abuse stoically and to obey orders without question – two characteristics that are vital in a crisis.

After a few weeks of training, I had a weekend's home leave. On the bus back to barracks, a very attractive young lady sat across the passageway. We got talking and soon were getting on swimmingly, so when I discovered that she lived in Perth I started to hope that this might develop into a very convenient and enjoyable relationship. As time went on and talk became easier, she asked where I was stationed. I told her that I was at Queen's Barracks and she replied by asking what I thought of the RSM there. I was still smarting from my roasting on the parade ground, so replied that Andy Drummond was 'a nasty lot'. The girl was momentarily taken aback before gathering herself to say, 'He's my father.' My jaw hit the floor and I felt like crawling under my seat. But she told me not to worry – she knew exactly what army life was like. So her revelation put an end to any thoughts of midnight liaisons, which was probably for the best, because if the RSM had ever found out I had designs on his daughter, he would have had me in the glasshouse for sure.

We all thought that our platoon was the best in the barracks. We were dedicated to our training, united by a spirit of purpose and all great friends. Our lads came from all over Britain, so there was a mixture of accents to decipher. We were generally drawn from humble backgrounds, but were upstanding and congenial to a man. We worked hard but played hard, too. After an exhausting day, we invariably spent the evening in Perth, where there were four picture houses, numerous canteens and a popular dance hall. Many of the lads would pair up in unlikely duos, such as Evans from Liverpool and Fraser from the Angus county town of Forfar. Every night I went to the Church of Scotland canteen, where there were delicious sandwiches to eat and a lovely old grand piano to play. I met a very good classical pianist there and we played alternately all evening long. Alex would usually turn up after he had been to the pictures and join in our little music circle. Then, as we walked back to the barracks, he would update me on the latest happenings – he was always the man in the know.

Perth, on the banks of the silvery Tay, is well named the 'Fair City'. Its centre was most attractive and the greenery of the parkland gave it a rural feel. There were many places of interest to visit and beauty spots to explore. The expansive playing fields of the North and South Inches – right in the heart of the city and used extensively for training and early morning PT assemblies – gave Perth its unique character. The townsfolk, proud of their garrison-town tradition, were kind to the recruits and generous with invitations to visit their homes.

When the day came for our passing-out parade, we marched through the city centre turned out to perfection, rifles sloped. We had a farewell supper at a local restaurant and Corporal Amos sang our praises. We certainly had reached a high level

of fitness and had good reason to be proud of our achievements. But we would now split up and go in different
directions. The next day, before going on leave, we bade each
other a fond farewell. I, for one, wondered if we would ever
meet again. Years later, I discovered that several members of
that platoon died during the war.

After ten days' leave, I returned to Perth to train as a signaller. Along with hundreds of others, I was accommodated
in Campbell's Dye Works. The course lasted three months,
during which time our squad of ten would become proficient
in Morse code, semaphore, the Aldis lamp and the several
wireless sets used by the infantry. The work was interesting,
we had good instructors and the months passed quickly.
Every evening, I continued to play the piano at the Church of
Scotland canteen. From time to time, Alex, who was doing his
secondary training at Kinfauns Castle, three miles outside
Perth, would put in an appearance. I also played with one of
the bands at a rather nice dance hall just outside the town
centre.

Then, in September 1943, I was posted to London Scottish
in Chichester, Sussex. The 2nd Battalion was part of the 47th
London Division, housed in the same barracks as the 4th
Black Watch, who had recently returned from the Mediterranean. They had been in France in 1940 but escaped back to
Britain as part of Ark Force. Less than a year later, they were
sent to guard Gibraltar, a key base for the Royal Navy.

I was sorry to say goodbye to Perth, but all of my friends
had already been posted to other battalions. Our draft of
twenty, under the supervision of a corporal, was transported
to Perth station and boarded the train for London. We each
had haversack rations – doorstep sandwiches – in lieu of
lunch, but no liquid refreshment. At King's Cross we

*Above left:* After suffering a head wound at the Somme, my father, a sergeant in the Argyll and Sutherland Highlanders, became head of personal transport for Earl Haig, the British commander in the First World War. (Renouf family)

*Above right:* My father as cinema pioneer and British Lightweight Boxing Champion in 1922. (Renouf family)

A family portrait. L–r: mother, me, father, grandmother Joseph and sister Betty. (Renouf family)

A portrait taken in 1945. I was one of the lucky ones and survived. (Renouf family)

A Highlander in the Maginot Line, these extensive fortifications were simply side-stepped by the Germans during their 1940 Blitzkrieg. (Imperial War Museum, IWM)

The Highland Division holding back the Germans at the River Bresle during the fierce rearguard actions of 1940. (IWM)

Disaster strikes at St Valéry. Rommel, pictured with Highland Division commander Victor Fortune, took special pleasure in capturing the Highlanders. (IWM)

In with the bayonets at El Alamein, the victory that so boosted our morale. (IWM)

Pipers played an important role in rallying the troops when visibility was poor in the desert. Many of these brave men paid with their lives. (IWM)

Victorious Highlanders enter Tripoli in 1942. (IWM)

Churchill wept openly when the Highland Division staged an impressive victory parade in Tripoli. (IWM)

Roy Green remembered 'Highland Humour' during the Battle of El Alamein.

A Black Watch soldier on an unusual mode of transport during the bitter fighting in Sicily. (IWM)

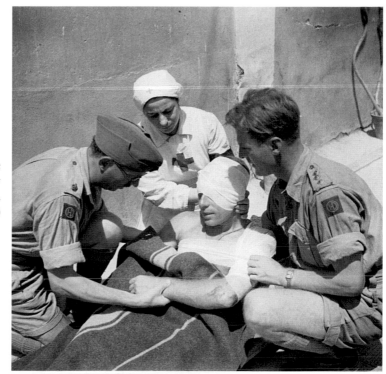

Our medics were
revered and many
were true heroes.
(IWM)

The Black Watch
training for Normandy.
(IWM)

The Highland Division was the only division to fight with Montgomery from Africa right through to crossing the Rhine. Here he inspects the Gordon Highlanders prior to D-Day. (IWM)

transferred to the underground, still carrying our full load. This consisted of waist belt, straps and pouches with large and small packs attached, all worn on top of a greatcoat, plus a bulky kitbag. This was a very heavy load to carry upstairs, downstairs and along endless passageways, with a rifle on one shoulder and the kitbag on the other. I had to stop a couple of times to recover, but the corporal kept pushing us on.

As I shuffled along the King's Cross underground platform, I noticed that one of our group had all but given up the struggle. He had resorted to dragging his possessions along the ground, his bedraggled figure engulfed by his billowing greatcoat, which obscured his five-foot-zero frame. He hauled his rifle and kitbag along without a backward glance, abandoned them in the doorway of the tube train, and collapsed into the corner seat opposite me. Using standard army phraseology, he expressed total disagreement with wartime travel arrangements and, after a brief pause, turned to raise some other controversial point with any potential listener in the carriage. His urchin face was puffed and inflamed to a rosy red. Initially, I took this to be a consequence of his frustration and harassment, but I would later realise that it was his normal complexion and that, more often than not, it was graced with a beaming smile.

'I'm Watson,' he said with a wide grin. I never knew his full name – and I doubt anybody else did, either. He spoke incessantly to everyone and to no one in particular, and always in a critical vein. His shambolic appearance also attracted attention, and he was soon earmarked as a woeful character. Little did we realise at the time that he would become much more than that. He kept on talking for the remainder of the journey, so everyone within earshot learned that he was a farm worker from a large family in Cambridge-shire, that Army travel arrangements were a disaster and that he had volunteered to be a Black Watch soldier, not a London Scot.

In Chichester, I met up with a few fellows from Queen's Barracks who had been posted directly to the 4th Black Watch, including the Liverpudlian Evans and his inseparable friend Fraser. Our training continued, giving us experience of operating as a battalion in the field. We were involved in several large-scale exercises with the 21st Army Group, including Operation Scheme Eagle, which took place on the frozen Yorkshire Moors and was a major rehearsal for the assault on Europe. The generals wanted to try out novel tactics and movements to see if they would work in battle. My company, huddled in slit trenches and paralysed by the cold, played the part of the enemy. Observers identified by their white arm-bands decided who were casualties, or if an attack had succeeded. After two days, one of them walked up to our company and disconcertingly told us, 'You're all dead. You've been wiped out by an artillery barrage.'

Everyone was progressing well, except poor Watson. Our company was often referred to as 'Watson's Company', largely as an expression of sympathy for those of us who had to put up with him. He was usually last on parade, always trailing his shackles behind him, and never prepared for what was to follow. Often improperly dressed – not just a button undone but possibly a gaiter or a cap-badge missing – you might see him with his waist belt wrapped around his chest or his backpack dangling over his backside. Most of all, his steel helmet caused him no end of trouble – it always seemed to obscure his vision.

It is possible to offer an explanation for this endless state of confusion in which Watson functioned. He was active and willing, but always seemed to do things in the wrong order at the wrong time. This was compounded by his compulsion to converse with anyone near him. So even if he happened to be first into the wash-house in the morning, he was inevitably the last out.

Initially, he was charged at regular intervals over some offence or other, which meant that he was almost perpetually on punishment duties. Those with the seemingly impossible task of training Watson to become a well-disciplined and efficient combat soldier would chastise, ridicule and abuse him. Stock army phrases might have been designed specifically for him. He was constantly told that he was 'a horrible little man' and in a 'state worse than China'. Exasperated sergeants would lament, 'Some mothers do have 'em.'

But none of this ever perturbed Watson. He would soon be back on friendly terms with the corporal who had, just a few moments earlier, put him on a fizzer. Eventually, his instructors more or less gave up, and Watson enjoyed a rare immunity from the King's Rules and Regulations.

After Scheme Eagle, we moved to Middlesbrough for a further fortnight of training. Again, we had barely settled before moving on again, this time to Southampton to act as a service battalion in support of the front-line D-Day troops. Then, six weeks before D-Day, 2nd Battalion London Scottish was broken up and we all joined front-line units ourselves. I was sent to the Tyneside Scottish at Thetford, Norfolk, along with the shambling Watson and a few other pals. Our new battalion was part of the Black Watch, recruited originally for the First World War from the large number of Geordies of Scottish descent who lived in and around Newcastle. The Tyneside Scottish had seen action in the Battle of the Somme, where it won numerous battle honours. In 1940 the battalion fought with the BEF and suffered heavy casualties. The survivors escaped from Dunkirk and then took up anti-invasion duties along the south coast. The reformed battalion was then sent to defend Iceland, an essential base for the protection of our Atlantic convoys, for fifteen months. During 1942, it was moved to various training locations to gain first-hand experience of different conditions. In October 1943, it switched from mountain training in Wales to sea-borne assault landing on the beaches of Rothesay. At this point, we trainees in Perth had just completed our basic training. Several of my friends, including Alex Corris, were delighted to be sent to the TS – their first-choice battalion.

When I arrived at camp, it was heartening to see Alex again and to be made so welcome. Despite my vociferous protestations, Watson grabbed the bunk beside mine, while the London duo of Dennis Westcott of Forest Hill and Stan Suskins, who had been with me ever since I'd left Perth, also settled in near by. Next day, on parade, we were each attached to a company. Watson went to A Company, Alex went to C, but most of us, including Westcott and Suskins, were sent to R, the reserve company. The role of all R companies was to act as a reinforcement pool, ready to replace the battle casualties suffered by the battalions. They were to be concentrated in reinforcement camps behind the front line and drawn on as and when required.

We remained with the battalion for about three weeks, during which time we did some intensive training. It was clear that the Tyneside Scottish had reached the highest level of proficiency and was ready to go to war. There was a wonderful spirit and a sense of excitement – a real sparkle in the eye and a spring in the step of the Tynesiders. Everyone was eager to get over there and get to grips with the enemy. The smart turnout of the men, the challenging banter that passed between them, and the familial relationship that was developing between the men and the officers reflected the mood.

We parted from the battalion at Thetford and set off on the first leg of our journey to a transit camp at Micheldever, Hampshire. The travel arrangements – trucks to Thetford station, train to Micheldever and trucks to the tented camp – went smoothly, with no delays or hitches. But we arrived at the camp late at night and as a result everyone overslept the next morning. On parade, I was singled out for not shaving. My three days of extra duties involved peeling an enormous mound of potatoes every evening.

There was a unique sense of anticipation in the south of England, where many of the assault troops were concentrated. The weather was sunny and warm, which created a kind of holiday atmosphere. The troops were at the peak of readiness, their training complete. The entire population was united like one giant family, constantly giving each other encouragement and support.

One morning I walked along the main street in glorious sunshine, rubbing shoulders with every variety of serviceman. Then a commando stopped me. He clearly recognised me, even though for the moment I did not know him. He told me we had done our basic training in the same platoon, and then I remembered him. We talked about our days in Queen's Barracks, I told him what I knew about some of his friends, then we parted. It was an insignificant meeting, but it is etched in my memory because of his appearance. He was turned out to perfection, walked with confidence and assurance, and his eyes sparkled with enthusiasm, proud to proclaim that he was a Green Beret ready to storm the strongest defences of Hitler's Atlantic Wall. To me, he epitomised the aspiration and resolve of the mighty army of liberators who were ready to confront the evil that threatened the whole world. I have often imagined this nineteen-year-old braving the initial assault in Normandy. But I never learned whether he survived.

Not long after that meeting, news began to filter into the camp that the invasion had begun. Word was that things were progressing well and we had caught the Germans on the hop. Sergeant Major Mitchell – a much-disliked Scot from Duns, in the Borders – called us to his tent to issue us with French money. We fingered the odd-looking bills with amusement and wondered if we would be able to buy anything with it. Then Mitchell ordered us to sign a document, almost as an afterthought. Most of my comrades signed the form with scarcely a glance and traipsed out of the tent. When my turn came, however, I took the time to read through it. I hated putting my signature to anything, so I wanted to know what it was all about. When I saw what it was, I refused to sign. The form stated that all those who signed it agreed that they were fit to travel overseas and fight; and if they went absent or refused to fight, they would be treated as a deserter and subjected to the most severe punishment – even death.

A few months earlier, a Bren-gun carrier had knocked me down and damaged my left wrist. I paid a visit to the medical officer (MO), who thought it was no more than a sprain and bandaged it up. For weeks afterwards, though, I kept going back to him to complain about the continuing pain and the fact that I could not fire my rifle. Either he did not realise the true extent of my injury, or he thought I was malingering, but he repeatedly refused to give me further treatment.

When I arrived at Micheldever, I reported to the camp MO, who was more concerned about the injury – especially as I still could not fire my rifle. He sent me to Winchester City Hospital, where the specialist diagnosed a fractured scaphoid – a small bone at the base of the thumb. The doctors then signed me up for a novel course of treatment involving electricity, which was administered three times a week at the hospital and was still ongoing when D-Day arrived. Of course, this meant I certainly could not claim to be fit to fight abroad, yet the British Army wanted me to sign a legal document stating that I was. A stand-off developed between Mitchell and me, as I flatly refused to sign and he demanded that I must. After much deliberation over what to do with me, I was placed under close arrest in the guardroom. I protested to the padre, to the welfare officer, to the MO, to anyone who would listen, but nobody came to my rescue.

The next day, I travelled with the rest of my company to the small East Sussex port of Newhaven. While my comrades were eager and enthusiastic, I was still under arrest and still furious at the injustice. But there was no way anyone could get the better of the army. In fine weather, with the seas much calmer than they were on D-Day itself, we all set sail on a small liner. Once the coast had receded behind us, Mitchell jeeringly said to me, 'Escape now if you like, Renouf.' I replied that I had no intention of escaping – that I wanted to go to France with my company and fight – but I did not want to sign a legally binding document that would deny me my rights. I added, 'And if I wanted to desert, even now, no bleeding sergeant major would stop me.' He ignored my insolence and released me from close arrest. I thought about contacting our family lawyer, to challenge the legality of my situation, but I soon realised it would make no difference whatsoever. And, after all, I was finally going to France, where I wanted to be.

(For years, I hoped to meet Sergeant Major Mitchell again, this time on equal terms, so I could tell him precisely what I thought of him, and let him know how wrong and unjust he had been. Finally, in the 1980s, a Tyneside Scottish reunion was organised which it seemed would give me my chance, but when I contacted his family in Duns beforehand, I learned that he had recently died.)

That night, I sat on the open deck suppressing waves of seasickness, as we crossed the Channel, waiting for dawn and our push ashore. It was my first time on a ship, and the rising and falling set my head spinning. There was no horizon on which to focus, so instead I looked over the side. In the moonlight a deep, green colour shone effervescently on the waves – a beautiful sight that I had never seen before.

Later, unexpectedly, I learned that the ship had quite a nice piano in the lounge. I weaved my way to the stool and spent much of the rest of the crossing playing the classics that were so popular at the time, including 'Over the Rainbow', 'As Time Goes By' and 'Berkeley Square'. It put everyone at ease, and certainly helped my seasickness. I was even able to take advantage of the Royal Navy's generosity. The sailors onboard were very kind to us soldiers, feeding us well and giving us as many goodies as we could carry. I stocked up with Mars bars.

When dawn broke on the morning of D-Day-plus-four, we were about a mile from the shore. The scene ahead of us was unbelievable. The sea was crammed full of boats and ships of all descriptions as far as the eye could see, a vast armada of battleships, cruisers and destroyers alongside a flotilla of merchant ships, steamers and tugs. It was the biggest concentration of ships ever assembled, the like of which would never be seen again. Barrage balloons were tethered to the ships to provide protection from low-flying Luftwaffe raiders, but they were unnecessary as the RAF had undisputed command of the skies. Strangely, the scene was largely peaceful, save for the regular broadsides fired by the battleships, which filled the air all around with a rumbling thunder. Landing craft ferried back and forth to the beach in a non-stop whirlwind of action. From this distance, there seemed to be little activity on the land other than the occasional puff of smoke.

When orders came for R Company to disembark, we lined up loaded with full kit and rifle, ready to descend the scrambling nets. This turned out to be a really terrifying experience. It required every ounce of strength that I could muster to hold on to and climb down the nets. I struggled down to the landing craft, which lurched and dipped with the swell. Near to exhaustion, I feared that I would land in the drink, never to surface, as happened to many men. But a matelot was there to reassure us, and following his command I was safely transferred. I quickly found my allotted place, squatted down and looked around. I could tell that everyone aboard was equally relieved to have made it safely.

With a complement of thirty men, the roar of the engines told us we were heading for the beach in the safe hands of the navy. Our small craft bounced around on the swell, and some of the lads needed to use the sick bags. The shallow water was full of debris and, to my horror, dozens of dead bodies. I tried not to think of them, concentrated on not being sick, and prayed that the navy would avoid the submerged anti-invasion devices.

Not everyone was lucky. Some of the landing craft struck

underwater mines, even though it was thought that most underwater obstacles had been cleared. These unlucky souls had to disembark into chest-deep water and wade three-quarters of a mile to the shore.

Four days later, we were luckier. As we approached Sword Beach, near Ouistreham, at 3 p.m., there was no sign of the Germans. The assault troops, the 3rd British Division, had now penetrated several miles inland. A lot of landing was taking place. The beachmaster was checking unit names on his clipboard and shouting instructions for everybody and everything to move inland to clear the beach for the next group. Some of the large landing craft were delivering tanks and other heavy vehicles. Inevitably there were plenty of breakdowns, but within minutes a squad of engineers would appear with a recovery vehicle and the blockage would be cleared. There were also teams of medics standing by to deal with accidents and any injuries resulting from the occasional shells that landed on the beach.

Once ashore, we were hustled up the beach to the assembly area. We passed rows of German bodies, all carefully laid out, side by side. Later, I would see them stacked like cordwood. But the urgency of the situation meant that I was not as shocked as I might have been. We saw a few prisoners, too. They looked filthy and exhausted, but the initial terror of their moment of capture had gone. Many of the older men looked glad to be out of it; some were even cheerful. The younger ones, however, seemed surly and truculent.

Our company commander, Major Keith, had instructions for us to proceed directly to a reinforcement camp at Cresserons, within sight of the twin spires of La Déliverande, an important German radar station and stronghold. Its determined garrison ultimately held out for twelve days and succumbed only after a massive barrage and an attack by the Royal Marines.

The six-mile march to Cresserons with full kit under a blistering sun along dusty, makeshift roads was tough, but at least there was no shelling – although we could hear the fighting at La Déliverande. A few French farmers who had refused to leave their land emerged to give us a drink of their home-brewed cider as we passed. It was cool, refreshing and thirst-quenching. It was also my first ever taste of alcohol.

When we arrived at the Cresserons camp, we were sent to a large field and told to dig our slit trenches. I shared a trench with an older soldier called MacDowell, who had served as a driver in the London Scottish since the start of the war. Now, aged twenty-five, he was a rifleman. Mac was a good chap and we got on marvellously. He was telling me about his wife and young family when all of a sudden there was a fearsome, high-pitched screaming of sirens – *woo, woo, woooo*. Then the ground all around us erupted. We clawed the earth, willing ourselves to disappear into it as a series of terrific explosions shook the camp and showered the place with red-hot shrapnel that could take off a head or a limb. It was our first experience of coming under attack and it was absolutely terrifying. Slit trenches were surprisingly effective, but they could not withstand a direct hit from one of these shells. We had been caught in the middle of a stonk – our name for a barrage from the giant, multi-barrelled mortar that we nicknamed the Moaning Minnie and the Germans knew as the *Nebelwerfer*. When it was over, Mac and I were badly shaken, but we managed to congratulate ourselves on our luck. Mac's did not last much longer: he was killed a few days later.

The Moaning Minnies would become the bane of our lives,

and being caught in the middle of a stonk was enough to break some men. One attack wrecked the nerves of one senior and highly experienced Highland Division officer, and he had to be sent home. It was the last straw for him. I had never heard of them prior to landing in Normandy, and many of us thought they must be some new secret weapon, little knowing that the Germans had perfected their use in the First World War.

Another unwelcome echo of the Great War came in the form of shell-shock, which could reduce a man to a shambling wreck, no matter who was doing the firing. Ronnie Cameron, a sharpshooter who became a sniper with the Black Watch, landed in Normandy on the same day as me, and he was soon in the thick of the fighting:

> It was after we got dug in that the shelling really started. It was really bad. We had an old soldier in the trench I was in, and he said, 'How are you feeling, lad, after that?' 'Oh,' I said, 'not too good, but thank God it's stopped. At least they didn't do us much harm.' 'Oh, be quiet,' he said. 'That was ours. Wait until the other side starts!' It had been our guns that were firing, and I thought it was the Germans!

After our welcoming stonk, things settled into a dull routine. Bored and frustrated, I was keen to get into action. One day I went for a stroll into Cresserons itself, a village that had once been home to around eight hundred folk but which the Allied guns had shelled ruthlessly on D-Day-plus-one. I had gone for a wander, to try to keep both mind and body active, and to explore the village. As I was going down a deserted street, I could see right into split-open houses, with entire corners blown off to reveal what remained of a living room or kitchen. Then, in the lounge of a badly damaged house, I spotted a piano. I could not resist going inside and playing it. Despite its ramshackle condition, it played quite well, and I was settling into my routine when a sergeant rushed up and shouted, 'Stop that immediately!' I froze, not understanding what I had done wrong. The sergeant soon explained it to me: 'Don't you realise the Germans will detect it and shower shells right down on top of us?'

Ten long days after we arrived at Cresserons, we had a visit from two officers and three other ranks from the Highland Division. I saw them talking to Major Keith, and before long Sergeant Major Mitchell was calling out the names of nearly half of our company. These men were ordered to collect their kits and report back to him immediately. We soon found out why. Shortly after landing, the Highland Division had been sent across the River Orne to support the 6th Airborne Division on the vulnerable left flank of the beachhead. They had suffered massive casualties in a number of attacks. More troops were urgently needed to hold this essential ground, and the recruiting party was visiting every reinforcement camp, looking for Highlanders. The recruits from our company were going to join the 5th Black Watch, which had just lost 110 men killed and some 200 wounded during the Battle of Breville. I longed for my name to be called, but it was not. Ironically, some friends of mine who were reluctant to leave the battalion, such as Tommy Layton and his pal Chugg, both Tynesiders, were on the list.

One member of the recruiting party was Harry Buglass, who had been with me in the London Scottish. Harry had been posted to the Gordon Highlanders when I went to the Tyneside Scottish. I approached him and found that he had changed significantly: the fresh-faced innocent from Hawick now had the grim, stony features and sunken eyes of a seasoned veteran. He was reluctant to talk, fidgeted with his rifle and seemed anxious to be on his way. After a quick look around, he quietly said, 'It's bloody rough up there, Tom. You take care.' Harry always chose his words wisely, so this was an ominous warning. I was already starting to learn that life expectancy among green replacement troops in Normandy was notoriously short.

(Ten years later, I was amazed to see Harry again. I was in the Borders to watch a seven-a-side rugby tournament and he was playing on the wing for a very successful Hawick side.)

While I awaited orders, George Sands was in the heart of the battle with the Camerons. On 12 June, they were ordered to take the village of St Honorine:

We reached our forming-up position without incident and settled down to wait for the field guns to open up, four minutes before zero hour of 0400. We were lying or crouching down when our artillery opened up and, to our horror, the guns had ranged in on us. We suffered twenty or so casualties before we had even moved but as the barrage crept forward we got up and followed our exploding shells toward our objective through the standing corn.

We were to make our way to a large chateau that was surrounded by a wall some twelve to fourteen feet high, which was to be breached by our barrage. Once the wall had been breached, we made our way through the garden and several of my platoon found cover in a ditch. My sergeant, Sandy Sinclair from Stirling, and I made our way forward to the corner of the wall so as to lay down fire on the Germans. We had several new guys with us who were novices at this and we had to keep telling them to keep their heads down. I don't know if it was curiosity, bravery, or stupidity, but they kept on standing up. One by one, they were killed. I was yelling to one boy, he had only just turned twenty, when he was shot through the temple and killed instantly by a sniper. As it turned out, five of the twelve killed in that ditch died of shots to the head. Sandy and I were going frantic, spraying bullets at everything that moved, and we eventually cleared the snipers and things got a bit quieter. By this time it was about 0800 hours. About a half-hour later, the Germans opened up with artillery and mortars and we heard the dreaded Moaning Minnies for the first time.

Sandy and I crept forward to a small orchard for a look-see and to our dismay we counted ten German tanks and self-propelled guns heading our way. We made our way back to our position by the end of the wall and waited for the tanks. Luckily, the tanks sat back and pumped shells over the heads of their advancing infantry. Two or three of the tanks were knocked out by our battalion six-pounder, which persuaded the rest of the Panzers to disappear. However, the infantry kept coming. I was firing the Bren, with Sandy reloading it with fresh clips of ammunition. But we could not halt the Germans' advance. They had set up a Spandau heavy machine-gun and were spraying our positions with heavy fire, inflicting casualties all around us. Sandy was just fitting a fresh clip of ammunition on the Bren when he took a full burst of machine-gun fire through his upper arm, tearing away most, if not all, of his flesh and muscle. I kept the gun firing and Sandy, I don't know how, kept reloading the Bren with his one good arm.

Though eventually ordered to withdraw, George Sands was awarded the Military Medal for his bravery that day, but he modestly felt that others deserved even more credit:

Captain Walter Yellowlees, our medical officer, was awarded the Military Cross for tending the wounded under heavy fire. I think he was probably the bravest man I ever met. At least when you carry a weapon you have the feeling that you can protect yourself, even if it is a somewhat misguided thought. All that Walter Yellowlees had to hide behind was a small Red Cross on his medical satchel. True bravery.

As the reinforcement camp at Cresserons grew ever larger, I became ever more impatient and was desperate to know what was going on. The days slipped by and I repeatedly asked myself, 'How can we win the war if this massive reinforcement force sits around doing nothing?' But the German resistance had been fiercer than anticipated, and our push into Normandy was slowing to a crawl. The vast reinforcements were being amassed to launch a decisive breakout, which meant that the Battle of Normandy would grind on for almost three months.

Word began to get back to us that the fighting was horrendous, and news came through that the Highland Division had come up against fanatical resistance from the 12th SS-Panzer Division – named *Hitlerjugend* in honour of the Hitler Youth organisation. All of the division's privates had been born in the same year – 1926 – and had therefore grown up under the Nazis as members of the Hitler Youth. They were young, agile, fit and absolutely determined. They fought to the last bullet and were devoted to the Führer, as were their officers and NCOs. These die-hard Nazis had committed all kinds of atrocities earlier in the war in Poland and Russia, where they were steeled by their encounters with the Red Army. Their leader was the thirty-three-year-old Kurt Meyer, who had joined the Nazi Party in 1930 and had risen through the ranks of the SS to become one of their youngest divisional commanders. He raced around the battlefield on a motorcycle and was described in glowing terms by his superiors as 'a classic example of an aggressive and ruthless SS officer, he pushed his men and himself to the limit'.

By contrast, the regular Wehrmacht soldiers were appalled by the behaviour of the SS and dubbed Meyer's men the 'Murder Division'. True to form, they had massacred civilians on their way into Normandy, before the fighting even started. On 1 April, at the village of Ascq, the Resistance derailed an SS train. The Nazis responded by seizing eighty-six men who lived near the railway. The youngest to die was fifteen and the oldest seventy-five. Also among the murdered was the village priest.

Meyer had served with the SS *Leibstandarte Adolf Hitler* when it carried out the massacre of British soldiers at Wormhoudt in 1940, and now he behaved in exactly the same way when ordering the execution of Canadian prisoners in cold blood: over 150 were murdered in the week following D-Day. Unsurprisingly, over the coming months, captured SS men could expect little mercy from the Canadians. (The Belgian Resistance captured Meyer after he failed to live up to his boast that he would never be taken alive. He was tried for four massacres, convicted and given a death sentence. This was subsequently commuted to life imprisonment when it was decided that Meyer was, to some extent, 'only obeying orders'. He served less than a decade before being released in 1954.)

The SS forces and Panzers turned the area around Caen – a vital communications junction just ten miles from Sword Beach – into a seething cauldron of death and destruction. The battle for this city, which the Allies had hoped to liberate in the first week of the invasion, became the largest and bloodiest in the whole campaign to oust the Germans from France. It would drag on for over a month, and by 9 July, when the Allies finally liberated Caen, it was little more than a gigantic pile of rubble.

Miraculously, Andre Heintz the Boy Scout who had helped two Highlanders escape after St Valéry, had survived the previous four years despite being an active member of the French Resistance. His group was especially important in sending intelligence about German emplacements to Britain. Two thousand other members of the Resistance in Caen had been arrested, tortured and either executed or sent to concentration camps. Heintz recalled, 'When the SS came we were all frightened of them and their reputation for brutality. Women hid from them. They were a complete law unto themselves. There were signs all over the city, erected by the regular German army, warning against looting, but the SS just ignored them and went on an orgy of thieving.' They murdered, too. On D-Day itself, the SS executed sixty-nine members of the Resistance who were being held in Caen Prison. Among them was the leader of Heintz's group, who had been tortured but had revealed nothing about his comrades.

The Germans turned the medieval market town into a fortified citadel, with tragic consequences for much of the population. More than eight thousand civilians trapped in Caen died in Allied bombing raids and bombardments, joining the long list of victims of 'friendly fire'.

The Battle of Normandy was turning into a long, drawn-out and bloody business. I was soon to discover for myself just how bloody it could be.

# 4

# Into Battle

After the five beach landings, the main task of the Allies was to expand and consolidate the bridgehead. This involved the assault divisions in battles on their immediate front to push back the Germans. Many of these were extremely ferocious, and the area around Caen turned into a vicious epic of blood-letting.

Montgomery planned to break out of Normandy, liberate Paris and drive north to expel the Germans from Belgium and Holland, where the people were starving. From Holland, we would invade Germany and cross the Rhine while the Red Army closed in from the east. As the front-line battles raged, we built up our fighting reserves, ammunition, tanks and supplies of every description. This went very well until terrible storms between 17 and 20 June halted all landings and seriously damaged the Mulberry harbours. Montgomery had planned to launch a major offensive on 22 June, employ-ing fresh units from the reserves, but this had to be postponed.

The Germans were likewise engaged in amassing a force to attack and destroy the bridgehead. These reinforcements approached from all directions, but the RAF targeted and delayed them. The storms then grounded the RAF for four days, which allowed a substantial build-up of German reserves, but the US forces' capture of Cherbourg on 22 June reduced the potential of the planned counter-offensive. Hitler, dissatisfied with the lack of progress, ordered four SS-Panzer divisions to launch an attack from Caumont across the American–British boundary to the coast at Arromanches. If successful, this would be a masterstroke that would split the Allied armies.

Montgomery knew that he must strike first with his break-out forces. So, the day before the Panzers were due to attack, he launched Operation Epsom, which forced the Germans back on to the defensive. It was in this maelstrom that I and the other raw recruits of R Company were to be blooded in battle.

On 25 June, 49th Division launched 146 Brigade in an attack to capture the sprawling village of Fontenay-le-Pesnel, a key road junction for the movement of troops and supplies. But fog hampered the early morning assault, which was supported by tanks and a massive artillery barrage, resulting in disorientation and utter confusion. When dawn broke, enemy fire from the Spandaus and snipers of the 12th SS-Panzer Division resulted in devastating casualties. On reaching Fontenay, bitter house-to-house fighting raged all day against the fanatical resistance of the *Hitlerjugend*. By 8.30 p.m., 146 Brigade had captured the western side of the village, but dug-in Panzers and further German reinforcements held the rest of the village for many hours before the brigade finally out-flanked them.

The following morning, the front-line troops of the Tyneside Scottish entered the battle. Their task was to protect the right flank of Operation Epsom, part of a force whose goal was to capture the Rauray Ridge. Thereafter, they were to push due south in a diversionary thrust. First, though, they had to capture La Grande Ferme in support of the 11th Durham Light Infantry, who were attacking towards Rauray village. There was good tank support from the 8th Armoured Brigade, but little assistance from the artillery, whose firepower was concentrated on the opening attack of Operation Epsom.

At 6.50 a.m., A Company, to the skirl of bagpipes, led the attack and immediately came under heavy fire from enemy tanks and machine-guns. The Germans were skilfully concealed in the thickets and hedgerows, making it difficult to return fire effectively. To make matters worse, as the infantry advanced, the supporting tanks were knocked out when they failed to penetrate the double hedgerows. Nazi resistance stiffened, and before long most of A Company's officers had become casualties, including Major MacGregor, their inspirational leader. New troops experiencing withering fire for the first time and without a leader to rally them could do no more than keep their heads down and try to hold their ground. At noon, B Company managed to get a platoon across the stream guarding the approach to La Grande Ferme, but the farm was heavily defended by the *Hitlerjugend*, including four of their tanks, dug in to untouchable hull-down positions. These knocked out another six of our Shermans as they tried to approach. With no artillery support and the RAF once again grounded by bad weather, the attack halted at 4 p.m. and the battalion withdrew.

Two days later, the Durhams, with good tank support, courageously captured the village of Rauray, while Operation

Epsom overcame stiff opposition to cross the River Odon. The Tyneside Scottish were now ordered to clear the adjoining villages of Tessel and Brettevillette of Germans and protect the right flank of the Durhams.

At 7 a.m. on 28 June, the Tynesiders moved forward behind a massive artillery barrage that flattened the way ahead. The leading companies picked their way through the debris, making full use of any cover afforded by the hedgerows, fearful that the sudden crack of a machine-gun might herald devastating fire from hidden bunkers. Against all expectations, though, Tessel Brettevillette was not heavily defended, which allowed C and D companies to consolidate in defensive positions around the village.

At noon, orders came for A and B companies to continue the advance towards neighbouring Brettevillette. As the leading companies moved forward behind a much lighter artillery barrage, the resistance suddenly increased. But using the dense bocage to advantage the companies made good progress, despite the heavy Spandau fire. At 2.30 p.m., the four companies reported that they had taken all of their objectives, but they feared that an enemy counter-attack was imminent.

By this time, the Durhams, on the left flank, were attacking along the Rauray Ridge. This was a key feature that they had to take in order to protect the right flank of Epsom and gain observation over the whole battlefield. In addition, the ground won by the Durhams would be crucial when the predicted German counter-offensive began.

In Brettevillette, the battle-hardened 2nd SS-Panzer Division, newly arrived from the Eastern Front, were already launching powerful counter-attacks. They were determined to hold on to the village for at least a few hours, and the fighting was ferocious. With all reserves committed, the battalion was unable to consolidate and orders were given for a withdrawal to Tessel Brettevillette. Overall, the Allies had gained valuable ground during the day; but they had also suffered heavy casualties, numbering around a hundred, including two company commanders.

To the front the enemy were preparing the strongest of defences. These were not to repel invaders, but to mount a mighty attack.

Throughout 29 June, our artillery and the RAF mercilessly bombarded the enemy forces deployed around the salient. Nevertheless, the Germans launched their expected counterattack at 6 p.m. and the battle raged from copse to hedgerow for the rest of the evening. Some penetration was made, but the Epsom force of VIII Corps held their ground and the enemy suffered very heavy losses. The Tyneside Scottish, who had been heavily shelled during the day, were relieved and withdrawn to a reserve position behind Rauray village to reorganise.

After three days, Epsom had gained precious ground. It had penetrated six miles into enemy territory and had crossed the Odon. But its troops remained well short of their final objective and they had to battle hard to keep the ground they had gained. The 49th Division had captured the Rauray Ridge, but the Germans heavily resisted its planned advance southward. Montgomery's breakout had faltered, but at least he had succeeded in drawing most of the German armour on to the Epsom front, where a decisive battle could now be fought.

It was at this point that R Company left the Cresserons camp and joined the rest of the battalion. It was a dull day with rain hanging in the air and a sullen mood hanging over those who had survived the last few days of fighting. Sunken eyes, sallow faces and a lethargic unease had replaced their bright eyes, lively body language and enthusiasm for the task in hand. I looked around and saw none of my friends, but then I heard an unmistakable voice in the distance babbling incessantly to nobody in particular. 'That's Watson,' I told the sergeant major. To my astonishment, he replied reverentially, 'Thank God for Watson. That little man has held this company together ever since we went into action.' Seeing my surprise, he explained, 'The Germans never let up their fire, but it didn't matter what they threw at us, Watson remained calm and indifferent to danger. When others were diving for cover, Watson was moving around searching for the enemy. His running commentary of the action and his encouragement to get at the enemy boosted the morale of everyone.' Finally, he added, 'When his platoon officer was killed by a sniper, Watson went off on his own to stalk the culprit, found him concealed in a tree and took his revenge. And he is quite oblivious to the fact that he is regarded as a hero by all of us.'

I tried to speak to Watson but got little sense out of him. He was obsessed with revenge and blethered on about his great friend and trench-mate Gerry Kingston, who had been wounded in the last attack. As I left him and walked off to dig my slit trench, I reflected on how strange it was that the man we believed to be the worst soldier in the British Army should rise above all others when it came to a real test of bravery. (From hereon, I caught only fleeting glimpses of Watson from time to time. He survived the war, and years later his trench-mate Gerry tried to track him down, but he could find no trace of this unlikely hero.)

As I added the finishing touches to my slit trench, I heard the words 'Am I glad to see you.' My old friend Alex Corris had come to welcome me. But it was not the old jaunty Alex. He tried to be cheerful but he could not contain his despair or exhaustion. 'We've been through hell in these attacks,' he said. 'The enemy are hidden in the undergrowth and as soon as we move forward we are machine-gunned. Their snipers are deadly and their dug-in tanks pick off our Shermans at will. The Hitler Youth fight to the death. Most of my pals are gone.' Alex named a series of mutual friends who had been killed, including one whom he bleakly revealed had been 'cut in half by shrapnel'. With a weak smile, he concluded, 'Tommy, we'll be lucky to survive this,' and then returned to his own company.

It was good to see Alex again. We were still great friends, even though we had met in passing only three or four times since our first six weeks together in Perth. But he painted a disturbing picture of being in action – very different to what I, in my innocence, had imagined it to be like. Could it be as bad as that? I wondered. All too soon I would discover that it was even worse.

The next day, which dawned dull and damp, was 30 June. A Company was busy reorganising. It had suffered the heaviest casualties and desperately claimed most of the reinforcements. Even then, though, its numbers were well below normal. Platoons and sections had to be reformed, and every man had to be briefed and equipped in great haste. However, reports from the front unexpectedly stated that there was practically no enemy activity. In mid-afternoon, we learned that the battalion would relieve the 10th Durham Light Infantry, who three days earlier had courageously taken most of the Rauray Spur.

There was talk among the troops of a massive, five-hundred-bomber raid on enemy forces, where elements of six Panzer divisions had been identified, but no bombing on that scale ever arrived.

Around 8 a.m., A Company moved forward, passing through the 11th Durhams, who were deployed in the defence of Rauray. Most of the buildings of this ancient Norman village were in ruins. We followed a sunken lane bordered by thick hedgerows for half a mile before moving into a large field on the right. The sunken lane was the boundary between VIII Corps, who had launched Epsom, and our XXX Corps. Behind the hedgerows on the other side of the sunken lane were men from the King's Own Scottish Borderers, dug in to defend the base of the Epsom attack.

We took over the positions from the Durhams on the southern edge of the field, with slit trenches dug behind an earth banking topped with tall trees. A voice called out, 'Hey, Jock, here's a good trench for you.' I accepted the invitation and found that it was partially roofed with logs. The generous Durham man assured me that everything was quiet and peaceful. But it would not stay that way for long, and I'm sure that the trench's makeshift roof helped me survive the forthcoming battle.

The positions chosen by the Durhams and now occupied by the Tyneside Scottish were to prove crucial in the Battle of Rauray. The four rifle companies of 320 men were situated to give combined cover across the whole front and fire support to one another. Little did we realise that the Germans had selected Rauray as the primary target for their major counter-offensive. It would develop into an exhausting, ferocious battle for both sides, but the Tyneside Scottish would ultimately disable the SS-Panzers to such an extent that Rauray would become a battle honour of the battalion.

To the right of A Company's field was a gap in the bocage

of some two hundred yards, providing an ideal pathway for enemy tanks. On the other side of the gap was the southern hedgerow of rectangular field stretching back towards Rauray. B Company's three platoons, under the command of Captain Calderwood, were positioned in the open, next to this hedgerow. This gave them an unobstructed view of enemy territory, but very little cover and no decent protection. The right flank was defended by C Company, three hundred yards to the west, in a position that was protected by hedgerows but had a limited field of view. D Company was in reserve, dug in some four hundred yards behind B.

Our anti-tank platoon took over the six guns left behind by the Durhams. These were skilfully positioned with overlapping fields of fire covering the approach to the battalion and any areas that were likely to be infiltrated – in particular the gap in the bocage between ourselves and B Company. The deployment was such that they also gave cover to the rifle companies.

We were in a relatively secure defensive position. Looking over the top gave an excellent field of fire towards the woods that lay three hundred yards ahead – the enemy's front line. It gave good protection against enemy fire and was also an effective anti-tank obstacle. But if we were to suffer a direct mortar attack, the bombs were liable to explode in the tree-tops, causing a deadly shower of shrapnel and branches to hail down on us. Open slit trenches gave little protection against this hazard, something the previous tenants of my trench had obviously realised.

I shared the trench with an old regular soldier called Johnston. He was a funny sort, quite different from my conscript comrades, and never spoke much. During the night, he and I took turns on guard duty, peering into the dark space ahead.

I struggled to stay awake, but was kept vigilant by the flares that both sides routinely fired to light up the field of view and ensure that there was no enemy movement. We heard noises in the distance that resembled the rumbling of tanks, but didn't think too much of it.

Just before daylight on 1 July, the platoon sergeant roused me from my trench and said, 'Go and help get breakfast rations for the platoon.' I joined three others and trekked sleepily through the lifting mist and the churned-up mud to our company HQ, two hundred yards behind our trenches. The quartermaster gave us large vacuum flasks and we lugged them back to the front. I left the sergeant to dish out the food and returned to my trench. As I climbed in, the first shell arrived with a whistle and a terrific explosion. But still none of us suspected that this was the start of a major battle in which the Tyneside Scottish would play a decisive role and we rookies would learn the art of war.

The Germans were about to launch a concentrated attack along the Rauray Spur into what they had decided was the weakest point on the front – the boundary we were defending between VIII and XXX corps. It was a desperate gamble to cut off Epsom at its base, split the British forces, and drive for the coast. German losses over the past few weeks had been so enormous that such a drive to the coast was doomed before it even began. Rommel knew this and fully understood that an Allied breakout that would threaten his entire Army Group B was inevitable. He therefore advocated a retreat to the defensive line of the River Seine. But Hitler overruled his most esteemed general and ordered that his forces must stand firm and fight to the last man.

For the next hour or so, mortar bombs landed intermittently all around us, but none came too near my slit trench.

Then, at around 8 a.m., the shelling suddenly increased in concentration and accuracy. This was the first time I had come under a major barrage. The whole earth shook and trembled. The whirring and whizzing of killer shrapnel filled the air above me. I wriggled further into the trench, finally understanding just how essential these simple defensive excavations are, and vowed to pay more attention when digging them in the future. Johnston remained grimly silent beside me, as frightened as I was. The shells seemed to be landing ever closer. Soon, they were exploding directly above us, bursting in the trees. The white-hot shrapnel showered down, travelling at tremendous speed, screeching, tearing through the air and anything in its path. As we cowered, we could hear jagged metal fragments slamming into the log roof, just inches above our heads.

The barrage rained down for half an hour – almost long enough to break our spirits. It was easily the longest thirty minutes of my life and absolutely terrifying. This was a true baptism of fire, but I knew worse was to come. Even as a rookie, I was well aware that the Germans were simply softening us up before they made a tank-led charge across the field.

Every now and then, I rushed to the top of the earth bank to try to gauge the situation, but I couldn't see a single German. The barrage was too intense to remain exposed in the open for long, so after a few minutes I would scramble back down to the trench. By now, our casualties were mounting, with a continuous stream of groaning, wounded comrades crawling past my trench. They had to get back to the regimental aid post (RAP) urgently, while they still had the strength. But to do so meant running the deadly gauntlet of shellfire and mortars.

The RAP was in the sunken roadway, behind our field, but it was being targeted by German machine-gunners. So the only safe route to it was right through the centre of an enormous hedge, thick with thorns and thistles. As the wounded men crawled past, Johnston and I shouted encouragement: 'Don't stop lads. Keep going! Keep going!' Near to collapse, with many close to giving up, they needed all the encouragement they could get. If they took cover in a shell hole or a trench, they might die through loss of blood, so they had to brave the fire and keep going.

When the shelling subsided, those of us who still could clambered to the top of the embankment. Across the field, we could see Germans mustering at the edge of the wood, but our artillery was keeping them at bay. We held our fire for fear of giving away our positions. Our defensive position remained strong and despite the casualties suffered we could still raise a reasonable fire power. Any enemy infantry who tried to attack would surely pay a heavy price. Suddenly a heavy barrage descended on our positions once again and we all scarpered back into our trenches. The mortaring was deadly accurate and we suffered further casualties.

Ten minutes later, the barrage stopped again and we scrambled back up the embankment. This time, I saw four tanks supported by infantry advancing on the far side of the field, heading straight for us. I was terror struck, but when I looked around there was no sign of panic, everyone around me was standing fast. Men versus tanks was a lost battle before it started, with few survivors, an infantryman's nightmare, but I suppose we felt safe behind the embankment, which the tanks would be unable to breach. I was swallowing hard, my stomach churning as we held our fire until the enemy was within range. When they were close enough, we opened up with rapid fire. My training came back to me: 'Steady, steady, steady, mark your target, fire!' Several SS men fell, but their fanatical NCOs drove the others forward, firing their Schmeisser machine-guns from the hip. As they continued to advance, they took cover behind the tanks, which were now using their machine-guns to keep our heads down. We knew that the footsoldiers would re-emerge and assault our positions as soon as the tanks got within fifty yards. And I had serious doubts that we would be able to stop them, given the casualties we had suffered in the barrage. Then, suddenly, like the answer to a prayer, the leading tank burst into flames. Unknown to me, two anti-tank guns had taken up positions just along the embankment, about fifty yards to my right. The guns fired again and a second tank was disabled. It was fantastic. The two remaining tanks returned fire, knocked out one of our guns, but then withdrew. The warriors of the *Hitlerjugend*, robbed of their cover, were now easy targets as they scampered for the woods. We opened up a devastating fusillade of rifle fire on them. It was like a turkey shoot.

I was still firing when orders reached our platoon that the whole of A Company was to withdraw. This came as a surprise, since we had just repelled a very strong attack. Although we had suffered a lot of casualties, our morale was high and we all felt that we could continue to hold these excellent defensive positions. If we withdrew, we would certainly lose one of our precious anti-tank guns and the whole left flank of the battalion would be wide open. This would have serious consequences for the now-exposed B Company and would give the enemy an ideal spot from which to attack the inter-corps boundary.

I would later question the decision to withdraw from the

bund. At the time there seemed to be a lot of confusion, mainly because we had lost most of our officers and NCOs. Perhaps the decision was made to reduce further casualties from mortar fire or through fear of being overrun. But I still believe that it was premature, or at least unlucky in its timing. If the situation had been assessed just ten minutes later, it might have been viewed differently.

Either way, there was never any question of us disobeying a direct order, so I was soon crawling out of there, past the shattered remains of breakfast flasks and untouched rations, with five other survivors. Still under fire from the German gunners, we made for the hedge running alongside the sunken roadway with bullets flying all around us. Trying to make myself as small as possible, I crawled into the hedge and was soon scratched to pieces by the thorns. Blood was seeping from my hands and arms before I had ventured a yard. But adrenalin and the whistling bullets drove me on. I realised that my small backpack was catching on the thick branches so I tossed it behind me, abandoning my daily essentials. We crawled on for a hundred yards through the hedge, fighting the urge to cry out from the pain of a thousand pricks and cuts, until we finally popped out, exhausted, the other side.

Now, with five other stragglers, we withdrew at pace, crouching along the edge of a field. We passed some of the 15th Scottish Division, who were frantically digging in under accurate Spandau fire from the eastern flank. A Tyneside Scottish officer suffering from a bad groin wound was courageously trying to rally his troops and pinpoint the Spandaus. As we ran past, I saw one chap – about my age – hit in the chest with a single bullet. Blood fountained from him as his mates tried in vain to stem the relentless flow. It was horrific – the first time I had seen someone killed. The memory still lingers with me, but at the time I was more concerned to reach cover.

We marched on, looking for a stragglers' post where we could assemble and keeping our eyes peeled. We stumbled upon a British artillery officer concealed in a hedge with a view overlooking the field we had just abandoned. He acknowledged us as he chattered into his wireless, giving our guns some new enemy coordinates. A few hundred yards beyond the field, two large trailers sat in a sheltered hollow. A single private soldier was busily operating some of the signals equipment that they contained. He was too occupied to notice us as we passed.

As we wandered along the track, the battle noise behind us started to diminish. After a mile or so, we saw a sign pointing the way to the stragglers' post. Ominously, it also warned, 'Beware of Snipers', but it was still a reassuring marker because there were no other British troops around. Before long, we arrived at the camp. A mechanised unit gave us a hot meal and listened to our story. Merely being with them was a real morale boost. Later, they encouraged us to get a good night's sleep.

I found an unoccupied slit trench lined with straw and came across a German blanket, which I wrapped around me. I fell asleep swiftly, but the tanks moved around camp all night and I kept waking up with a jolt, terrified that I was about to be run over. Lice had also infested either the straw or the blanket, so I scratched and itched throughout the night – and for the next few days. At one point I realised that a creature had invaded the trench, so I tramped around in the darkness in an attempt to destroy my adversary. I heard a pathetic little squeak and satisfied, I returned to sleep. It was not until morning that I found the terrorist had been a shrew.

The poor little creature had been prepared to share its domain with me, but I had demanded and taken all of it. I felt an overwhelming sense of remorse at the wanton destruction of its life, and Burns' poem 'To a Mouse' sprang to mind. But I had no time to reflect on 'the best laid schemes o' Mice an' Men'.

After breakfast, a sergeant major gave a morale-boosting speech and told us to rejoin our unit. We were at a complete loss as to where our unit might be, but he pointed down the road and said, 'Over there.' Refreshed and reassured, our group made its way back through the thickets, hedges and fields for two miles in the indicated direction. By sheer good fortune, we came across Major Mirrielees, who was sitting on a large boulder in shirtsleeves with a clipboard, ticking off the names of stragglers. He also listed any equipment we had salvaged.

'So, you've managed to hold on to your rifle, Renouf,' he said. 'Well done.'

A few more stragglers showed up, all with a similar story to tell. Our reinforced company of eighty men now numbered about a dozen. No one knew for sure what had happened to the battalion, but we all presumed it had been overrun. All I knew was that there had been massive casualties, and what was left of A Company had withdrawn in disorder. I saw that the enemy force was large, well supported by tanks and seemed to be well organised. We had no doubt that it was now in control of the embankment we had defended, a good position from which to attack the base of Epsom and penetrate towards Rauray village. I felt that my first battle had ended in defeat.

Considering that the assault was being made by SS Panzer Divisions it seemed certain that our dug-in infantry would be unable to halt this mighty force led by tanks. The battalion was facing impossible odds. We were facing eradication it seemed to me that there was no other option but to withdraw. I believed that the battle of Rauray had been a disaster, an ignoble defeat for the Tyneside Scottish. I could not have been more wrong, but it would be some time before I discovered the full details of what happened at Rauray on 1 July 1944.

The battle started with a barrage of such intensity that it indicated the presence of a powerful force. Several Panzer divisions were in the area, with the 2nd and 9th SS-Panzers concentrating around Bretvillette, to the right of the battalion front. To achieve their objectives, the enemy first had to capture the Rauray Spur, defended by the Tyneside Scottish.

In the grey mist of dawn, B Company, with their wide field of view, were the first to spot a column of some twenty Panzer tanks and infantry support moving eastwards. As they crossed the battalion positions a detachment of infantry peeled from the column and veered left to advance on C Company, on the right flank. But C Company held fast during the ensuing bloody and chaotic infantry battle, barring the way to Rauray village.

Next, a group of five Panzers advanced across the open ground between B and C companies. Then another five tanks, this time preceded by grenadiers, advanced on the exposed B Company. Terrified and on the verge of panic, the defenders faced annihilation and were ready to run for their lives. But Captain Calderwood, with courage and calm assurance, inspired his men to stand fast and repel the enemy. The troops responded magnificently and halted the grenadiers. The tanks soon came into the sights of Sergeant Dave Watson's nearby anti-tank gun. With great skill, he managed to knock out four of the five invaders. Meanwhile, a troop of the divisional anti-tank regiment that was defending Rauray engaged and destroyed the five tanks that were infiltrating between B and C companies. Finally, the remaining tanks in the column that attacked A Company and the King's Own Scottish Borderers on the far left flank were also destroyed or forced to retreat.

The enemy regrouped and made another attempt to penetrate the defences, but this time a massive artillery barrage forced them to retreat.

B Company had performed particularly heroically by holding the key position on the front and repulsing the might of the Panzers. With support from the anti-tank crews and the pinpoint barrage launched by several artillery units, a total of fifteen German tanks had been knocked out.

A platoon from D Company was detailed to reinforce the much-depleted B Company. However, because of infiltration by SS machine-gunners, the latter was virtually cut off, so the platoon led by Lieutenant Murray faced a long, hard fight to reach it. The undergrowth afforded ideal cover for the Germans to infiltrate their Spandau teams and snipers, allowing them to penetrate deep into the battalion area and approach Rauray village. The men of C Company faced such a serious threat from their open right flank that they had to withdraw. This removed the right-flank protection that was essential to B Company.

Any thought that the enemy was finished was soon dispelled when a second attack was mounted later in the morning. First the German artillery launched a brutal barrage, and then the Panzers concentrated their attacks on the flanks. They swept on to A Company's now-deserted embankment and seriously threatened the remaining King's Own Scottish Borderers defenders. On the open right flank, enemy tanks penetrated all the way to Rauray village. By now, all eight of our Tyneside Scottish anti-tank crews had been knocked out, but the divisional anti-tank regiment, supported by strategically positioned Shermans, destroyed most of the enemy Panzers that came within range. The beleaguered B Company, at this point still without reinforcements, was mortared mercilessly and then attacked by a troop of tanks. However, Captain Calderwood saved the day by calling down a concentrated artillery barrage.

Next, our vigilant forward observation officers spotted the 9th SS-Panzers mustering at Queudeville and the 2nd SS-Panzers doing the same at nearby Bretvillette. Massive artillery barrages poured on to both positions, causing great disruption and many casualties. This effectively scuttled the next German attack, due to be launched at midday.

However, the most ferocious barrage yet soon shattered the short lull in enemy activity. Shells and mortars rained down on the remaining Tyneside companies with ever-greater intensity and accuracy. Casualties mounted alarmingly and the need for reinforcements became urgent. By now, though, at least Lieutenant Murray's platoon had finally reached B Company, while C and D had linked up with the Durhams to defend Rauray.

Enemy tanks formed up again and attacked right along the front. B Company reported Panzers approaching from right and left, seemingly determined to get the better of the heroic outpost. Others reached the defences of Rauray village, where they threatened to overrun C and D companies. The advance was halted by our anti-tank gunners, the Sherman tank support and another ear-splitting artillery barrage, but more

German troops were arriving and the situation was declared critical. In a desperate search for reinforcements, drivers, storemen, clerks and cooks were all transported to the front and added to the ranks of C and D companies.

Now the battle raged at its fiercest. The Germans launched a concentrated attack on Rauray, forcing the forward platoons of C and D companies to give ground. However, the defences manned by the 11th Durhams, the divisional machine-gunners, with tank support, were sound and held off the attackers. Reinforcements in the form of flame-throwing tanks then arrived and attacked the Spandau-infested hedgerows around the village. The grenadiers panicked and retreated, leaving their tanks vulnerable. It was a rare sign of enemy weakness.

Meanwhile, German tank reinforcements were closing in on B Company and threatening the survival of the gallant defenders. In desperation, Captain Calderwood, forgetting wireless procedure, shouted into his microphone, 'For mercy's sake, give us more firepower,' whereupon the most intense barrage of the day decimated the attackers. The depleted Panzer force dispersed and was soon engaged by Shermans. Next the flame-throwers came to the aid of B Company, torching the hedgerows on both flanks and causing many Germans to flee.

The German infiltrators in the centre were well entrenched and continued to hold fast, but all around them the enemy assault was starting to falter. After twelve hours of resistance against continuous shelling and mortaring, Spandaus, snipers and wave upon wave of Panzer attack, despair finally lifted from the defenders when they saw the enemy retreating and heard the order to attack. C and D companies, each supplemented by a company of Durhams, moved forward under a smoke screen with tank support on call. D Company bypassed several enemy pockets to reach B Company as fast as they could, just in time to witness the hasty departure of the German grenadiers. They found only twelve survivors in the company of heroes. The Durhams engaged in a brisk encounter with some demoralised grenadiers before recapturing A Company's embankment. Meanwhile, C Company and its Durhams flushed the enemy out of their original positions. Fourteen hours after the first enemy attack, all the Tyneside Scottish positions had been reclaimed.

The Battle of Rauray was a notable achievement for the Tyneside Scottish. The battalion withstood the full force of a German counter-offensive that was planned to drive a wedge between the Allied armies and destroy the Normandy beachhead. The Tynesiders' defences repulsed the might of the 9th and 2nd SS-Panzer divisions. The enemy lost over thirty tanks and suffered an estimated eighteen hundred casualties (although some of these were inflicted on the Epsom front). The Tynesiders lost 132 men, the majority of them from B Company, and five tanks. The battalion's anti-tank crews accounted for ten Panzers, while the mortar platoon delivered a total of three thousand bombs. There were many heroes that day, but Captain Calderwood stands out: he displayed a courage rarely seen in battle and instilled a fighting spirit in his men that brought honour and pride to the battalion.

The successful defence of Rauray relied upon the support given by the tanks of 24th Lancers, the 217th Battery of the 55th Anti-tank Regiment and several Royal Artillery units. But nobody could deny that this was the Tyneside Scottish's day. Our commanding officer, Lieutenant Colonel de Winton, received a message from Major General E.H. Barker, commander of the 49th Division, which read: 'Will you please pass on to your troops my congratulations on the magnificent stand made by you today. You have made a great name for yourselves. I deplore the casualties you have sustained, but it is most gratifying to know that the gallant band who remained were successfully relieved.' At the end of the war, Miles Dempsey, General Officer Commanding the British Second Army, told Montgomery that he looked on Rauray as the turning point in the Normandy campaign.

Afterwards, the remaining Tyneside Scottish troops were reorganised into just two companies. Two hundred South Wales Borderers, a hundred troops from the Hertfordshire Regiment and fifty Gloucesters all joined us to form a full battalion once again.

Our next task was to hold the line near Tilly, specifically at a little village called Pont de Juvigny. The Germans had been using the local chateau, a mile to our front, as their base, and my platoon was ordered to go forward on patrol and determine their strength. An hour before dawn, as our patrol prepared to move out, the artillery shelled the chateau heavily. We moved off with no equipment save for our rifles, wearing plimsolls and with our faces blackened. Under the command of Lieutenant Murray, we crept forward in the darkness and then paused to ensure we remained in contact with the man in front, all the time striving not to make a sound. As we approached the chateau, we found the bodies of eight Tommies, killed during a previous failed assault, so it was with some trepidation that the leading section made their assault on the entrance. However, they found the chateau empty.

The rest of the battalion was now able to move forward and take up positions around the building. Meanwhile, our platoon secured some high ground further forward, where we came under heavy Spandau fire. A bullet hit our corporal, Sam Clarke from Elphinstone, near Ormiston, in the leg, severing an artery. He died shortly afterwards despite the best efforts of Private Neaves, from Dundee, who tried to stem the flow of blood with his own emergency dressing. This was my first experience of direct Spandau fire. All you heard was a short burst and then people were falling. One round struck a concrete telegraph pole in front of me; another the pick-shaft I carried; another my small pack, only to be stopped by a wad of writing paper that I had recently received from home. Three extremely near misses. I later wrote to my mother – on some of the paper that had saved my life – to tell her that Sam's death had been an unfortunate accident, hoping to quell any fears she may have had that I was in danger.

On 21 July, we were withdrawn to a rest area. A few days later, we joined the 49th Division at the eastern end of the Normandy beachhead as part of the build-up for Operation Totalise. Our task was to follow the breakout force and mop up any remaining strongpoints. The Tyneside Scottish were ordered to capture the heavily defended town of Mézidon and the high ground beyond it. Fighting forward from house to house, we had cleared the northern outskirts of the town by 1 a.m. on 16 August. We then battled against stubborn opposition and heavy shellfire to reach the centre. Come daybreak, the battle for the high ground was still raging when civilians suddenly started to appear in the forward area, a sure sign that the enemy was withdrawing. The townspeople welcomed their liberators with wild enthusiasm. Men and women, young and old laughed and danced, sang and cried as they waved improvised flags. We were fêted with a genuine gratitude, which provided a great morale boost after a night of hard fighting.

By this time, A Company, led by Major Mirrielees, had captured the important crossroads south-east of the town. Four-thousand-pound bombs had peppered the area, obliterated the roads and left massive craters half full of stagnant water – an ideal breeding ground for insects. Mosquitoes attacked us mercilessly as we dug our slit trenches, even though we covered ourselves with repellent cream.

The capture of the high ground meant that the 49th Division could now pass through and head for the Seine along a route that ran parallel to and several miles north of that of the Highland Division. Within a month, the two divisions would fight side by side in the battle to liberate Le Havre.

After the liberation of Mézidon, our battalion was again withdrawn to a rest area, where the other two battalions of 70th Brigade joined us. While awaiting orders for our next action, we were stunned to learn that the entire brigade was to be broken up to serve as reinforcements for other units. This was a devastating blow to the Tyneside Scottish, who had gained a fine reputation over the previous few weeks. Our corporal – one of the few remaining Geordie originals – gave vent to his feelings by launching a furious condemnation of the army.

But, for me, this cloud had a silver lining. The Highland Division had suffered massive casualties in the breakout drive to Lisieux, with some battalions now below operational level. On 24 August, those Tynesiders who still wore the red hackle, the famous trademark cap plume of the Black Watch, were posted to either the 5th or the 7th Battalion of the Black Watch, with the remainder going to the 7th Argyll and

Sutherland Highlanders. When I learned that I was going to the 5th Black Watch, I was overjoyed. At last I had achieved my ambition to join the Highland Division – the 'Fighting 51st'. Little did I realise that the division had built its legendary reputation on a high level of activity and risk. And I certainly had no inkling that I would soon join its massive casualty list.

# 5

# Wounded

I arrived at Lisieux with Alex Corris, a brusque Londoner called Ken Bidwell and others from the Tyneside Scottish. We joined A Company, in Corporal Chapman's section. I was not altogether happy about this, ironically because Alex was my best friend. You heard plenty of stories about two pals standing alongside each other and one of them being killed. I didn't want to experience that.

Corporal Chapman, an El Alamein veteran, was only twenty-seven, but he had a family back home and he soon became a father figure to us, too. Ginger, a Yorkshireman and the amiable platoon runner, told us that our corporal was a 'friendly' NCO, 'one of the good guys', which put us new recruits at ease. We quickly felt at home and enjoyed a hot meal. My section occupied a house on the high ground above Lisieux. There were no civilians in the vicinity, and I wondered where they had all gone. I wondered *why* they had left, too, since we were a long way back from the front line.

As Ginger showed us around the house, I recognised some old Tyneside Scottish faces who had joined the 5th Black Watch earlier. Propped against a wall was Tommy Layton, whom I knew from even before the war. He was from Houghton-le-Spring, between Newcastle and Durham, in Northumberland. My uncle Pete ran a butcher's shop in the town, next door to Nicholson's fish shop, where Tommy had been a delivery boy. I spent school holidays kicking about with him, chatting with the girls who worked at the nearby sweet factory for free handouts. It was great to see a familiar face, but this was not the same carefree Tommy I had known in those halcyon days. His eyes had shrunk into their sockets, he had lost all colour from his face, and his cheeks were hollow. He moved like a zombie. I found him sitting by his pal, Chugg, also from Northumberland. They both seemed to be in deep despair and had obviously been through hell. Neither was willing to talk about their battles. All they did was shake their heads whenever I asked.

It was extremely humbling to see Tommy. I tried to reminisce with him about our happy childhood days, but again I garnered little response. He had seen so many comrades perish that his own life had been shattered. He was completely numbed to the vicious ferocity and daily death, seemingly under an imminent, unavoidable death sentence himself.

The 5th Black Watch had joined the 6th Airborne Parachute Regiment after D-Day. Together they held the Orne bridgehead under tremendous pressure. In their first attack, on Breville and Chateau St Come, 110 men of the 5th were killed. They also suffered massive casualties during an attack on a factory at Colombelles, north-east of Caen. I had known nothing of these disasters before joining the battalion.

Their sacrifice had been immense, and they had done more than their fair share, which made me feel guilty and helpless. In comparison, my first two months in France had been easy. They had fought alongside the 9th Parachute Battalion on the most critical front, which they had been ordered to hold at any cost. The paratroopers were rightly ranked alongside the commandos as the cream of the British Army. They were men of great quality, but they also suffered greatly, especially in their courageous attack on the Merville battery: they were reduced to just 120 men in that single action. Thereafter, the Black Watch shouldered a good share of the burden alongside their illustrious comrades. Regrettably, though, whenever the veterans of the 6th Airborne reunite to celebrate their achievements, they fail to acknowledge the contribution made by the Highland Division. That is very sad, especially when you consider the casualties suffered by both divisions.

The Highland Division could list some remarkable achievements in those first few weeks in Normandy, but Tommy Layton was far from alone in feeling shattered by the experience. He and his comrades had all been part of one of the finest hours in the division's glittering history, but their morale was now at rock bottom. Fortunately, spirits improved immensely when Montgomery replaced our commander, Charles Bullen-Smith, with Major General Tom Rennie, the dashing and courageous Black Watch officer who escaped by bicycle to Marseille after St Valéry.

We spent two nights in the house overlooking Lisieux before learning that we would no longer participate in front-line battles. The division stood down, and from now on would be involved only in mopping-up operations. This came as a major relief to all of those who had been fighting non-stop since D-Day.

Our first task was to clear one or two pockets of German resistance, left behind to disrupt our advance. We travelled east towards the Seine and prepared to attack a strongpoint. However, shortly before the assault, we learned that the Germans had already departed, so we moved on and prepared for another attack. Then the defenders abandoned that, too. So a third attack was planned. This time the target was Chateau Mauny, adjacent to Mauny village, which sat on a cliff-top overlooking a snaking meander of the Seine.

On 26 August, A Company advanced; 7 Platoon was to make the attack, with my section leading. It was a warm summer's day with clear blue skies. As we hiked across the open farmland, it was so pleasant you could almost forget there was a war on. We munched on the hard tack biscuits that lined our pouches, along with tins of bully beef and sardines, all mixed in with our hand grenades. We came across a pioneer platoon clearing mines from the road to the chateau, carefully picked our way through and carried on, in staggered formation, loose fingers on our triggers, albeit with no sign of enemy activity. Next we met a roadblock of three fallen trees, with another pioneer team trying to clear it.

As we made our way over the logs, there was a sudden burst of machine-gun fire from the woods, just twenty yards in front of us. Without thinking or knowing how I got there, I found myself behind a roadside tree stump, flat on my belly. The stump provided just enough cover, for now. I looked around and saw that everyone else had managed to find some sort of cover, too. The unseen machine-gunner fired intermittently in short bursts at each of us. I wriggled from side to side as bullets hit the stump and kicked up earth as they ricocheted. On my right was Alex, lying in a fold in the ground that was barely sufficient to protect him. Ken Bidwell had been carrying our Bren gun and was pinned down in a ditch. By now, I was sure that the machine-gun was firing from a raised position in the woods, to the left of the road. I reached into my pouch for a grenade but could find only tins. I called out to Ken to throw one, but he was struggling under the weight of the Bren.

None of us could move. Seconds seemed like hours. There was nothing we could do but hold tight.

After a while, Alex called out to me, 'Tom, you all right?'

'Aye, I'm fine,' I said. Then I felt a warm liquid trickling down my back. Strangely, though, there was no pain. Quite calmly, I shouted, 'Alex, I think I've been hit.'

At great risk to his life, Alex crawled over to me. He pulled aside my shoulder pack to see two patches of blood seeping through my tunic, which led him to think that two bullets had hit me in a very vulnerable area. In the gravest of voices, he said, 'Tommy, get back to the RAP as quick as you can.'

Using every piece of cover I could find, I did as he suggested, fully aware that the machine-gunner might still have been in the woods. Once off the road, I slowed to a walk across a field that led to battalion headquarters. Wondering why I still felt no pain, I heard a most suspicious voice calling out, 'Renouf, where do you think you're going?' I turned to see the highly respected Lieutenant Murray, who knew me from the Tyneside Scottish. He was taking cover in a ditch with his own platoon.

'I've been wounded, sir,' I said defensively, annoyed that he thought I was doing a runner. To prove the point, I turned and showed him by back. As soon as he saw it, he told me to get back to the RAP smartly.

I trundled on, still feeling fine, and even picked an apple from a tree and munched on it. I happily contemplated evacuation back to the UK and a reunion with my family, even for a short spell.

When I reached the RAP, the MO examined me. 'You're a very lucky boy,' he said, pointing me in the direction of a waiting ambulance. I still had no idea what had happened. As I headed for the ambulance, mortar bombs started falling all around. I was more alarmed than usual and crawled under a nearby tank. As soon as the mortars subsided, I climbed into the ambulance. Three more walking wounded and two stretcher cases soon joined me.

The ambulance drove slowly along the bomb-pitted roads, and the Military Police delayed it at many checkpoints. Priority was always given to men and stores heading for the front line; as we were travelling against the main flow of traffic, our progress was agonisingly slow.

Our first stop was at the divisional casualty clearing station (CCS), where the medics gave essential medical treatment, but we were soon on the road again. The stretcher cases were both motionless, but they groaned every so often. I found the noise distressing, and looked over to check on them. It was only then that I saw, to my horror, that one of them was Corporal Chapman and the other was Ginger. My corporal had a head wound, while our company runner had been seriously wounded by mortar shrapnel. Both of these veterans who had survived the long journey from El Alamein to Normandy were in a bad state.

The next stop was a Canadian aid post. The doors of the ambulance opened and the medics escorted us into the reception tent with the greatest of care and attention. The doctors then handed each of us a cup of sweet tea and a cigarette – a Sweet Caporal, a favourite of the Canadians. I was a non-smoker but still had a puff.

The MO stood by and waited for us to finish, then he gave the worst cases some treatment. We had a short rest and then went back on the road. By now it was dark and the ambulance had to negotiate the potholed road with restricted headlamps. After another two hours of bouncing along, we finally reached a British aid station. We waited for the doors to open, but they never did. This time, we had to make our own way to the reception tent. Once there, the medics seemed quite indifferent to our plight. I told them two stretcher cases required urgent attention, but this had little effect. Eventually I got angry and started shouting at them, calling them a disgrace and telling them how superior the Canadians had been. It was twenty or thirty minutes before an MO arrived. He conducted a brief examination of each of us and left. One of the other medics then came over for a look at Corporal Chapman and Ginger. In a casual, off-hand manner, he said, 'They've had it,' and started to stroll away.

I jumped to my feet and grabbed him. 'Don't you dare speak in that way about our comrades. They have been doing all the fighting while you big, fat, useless base-wallahs sit and do nothing. You should be on your knees thanking these chaps for doing all the fighting!'

I was shaking and had obviously frightened the medic. As he scurried away I sat down, suddenly feeling faint – I guessed from the loss of blood. Before long, we were back on the move. Another two hours, another stop, this time with the attentive Canadians again. They escorted us inside and allowed us to rest. A distant radio was playing music, and I managed to identify the tune: Tino Rossi singing 'J'attendrais'.

Ginger had previously told me that this was his favourite song, so I rushed over to tell him that it was on the radio.

However, a medic intercepted me to say that he had just passed away.

Soon after, Corporal Chapman died from his injuries, too.

I was filled with sadness and remorse. These two men had fought so hard for their country – had done much more than their fair share – and now they had been killed within sight of victory. It seemed so unfair that I had survived while they had perished. I wanted to trade places with them.

A little later, the rest of us piled back into the ambulance. There was one more stop at a British aid station, where we again received most unsatisfactory treatment. This shocked me, because the consensus was that the medical officers and medics did a uniformly wonderful job throughout the war. Whoever wrote the reports certainly always gave them high praise. So I could not understand why my experience of them was so different. Perhaps I visited the few exceptions to the rule. Maybe the strain of night duties weighed especially heavily on the medics I met. But I doubted it.

The journey to hospital took some eighteen hours in total. We finally arrived at a Canadian facility in Bayeux in the middle of the night. It was one of more than a dozen hospitals concentrated within an area that the Germans recognised as a Red Cross zone.

I was examined by a young Canadian MO, who said, 'You're very lucky.'

'So they keep telling me,' I replied.

He told me that a bullet had gone in, missed my spine by a fraction of an inch, and come out again. A tiny bit lower, and I would have been paralysed. The bullet had travelled inside me for about three inches, but had even missed my ribs.

The MO said, 'We'll operate to disinfect the wound tonight

and you'll make a quick recovery.' He gently tapped my shoulder and added, 'We'll have you back with your unit in no time.'

Of course, this dashed my hopes of returning to the UK for some leave. After the operation, I was given the new wonder drug, penicillin, and told to rest for ten days.

I had, indeed, been lucky. The battalion had suffered another four fatalities during the attack on Mauny, including Major Mirrielees, my commander at Rauray. So a total of six comrades died on the day I was wounded.

After crossing the Seine, the battalion moved through Rouen and headed north, with the joyous, newly liberated French fêting them along the way. They were on this route because Montgomery had decreed that the Highland Division should finally restore its honour by liberating St Valéry. So the division, led by General Rennie, moved into the very positions they had last occupied in June 1940. The honour of being the first troops to enter the town fell to the 4th Camerons and 5th Seaforths, led by a pipe band. The mayor was on hand to pay tribute to the returning heroes, and a massive party was soon under way. It was a truly remarkable return, with our troops cheered all along their route by the local population, which did much for their spirits.

I was hugely disappointed to miss out on this historic and poignant return, but at least in hospital I enjoyed a level of luxury I had long since forgotten – clean cotton sheets, excellent meals served in bed and pretty nurses giving expert medical care. A few days after my operation, the doctors allowed me to get up and walk around. I soon learned that some of the other patients in the ward had very nasty wounds. In particular, one Canadian was receiving a lot of attention from the nurses. Rumour had it that he would not recover, yet when I spoke with him he was always bright, cheerful and in good spirits.

After a week in hospital, I was sent to a nearby British Army convalescence depot to complete my recovery. I was directed to a numbered tent where I found stretcher beds for eight patients. Life in the depot was quite different from the usual army routine. There were no parades and no duties. You could queue up for meals at any time you wished, within certain hours. The excellent food was served on plates that you took into the dining tent, where there was the luxury of tables and benches. The rest of the time, you simply relaxed and recovered your strength.

Once I had settled in, I decided to go for a walk and headed for open ground. Only then, as I passed row upon row of tents, did I realise the full extent of the camp. I was a bit groggy by the time I reached the outer limits. Realising I must be weaker than I thought, I decided to turn back. But just then I bumped into another patient. Not only was he from the 5th Black Watch; he had previously been in the Tyneside Scottish. He told me his name was John King and I learned that he had joined up six months ahead of me. He was in D Company in both the 5th and the Tynesiders, and had been wounded by a piece of shrapnel in the leg at Le Havre on 12 September. His tent was in a different part of the vast camp, but we met up a few more times.

Back at the battalion, John had a reputation for being reliable, steady as a rock and prompt to answer any call to duty. He was quickly promoted to full corporal and much respected as a section leader. In February 1945, during the bitter fighting of the Rhineland offensive, and still at the tender age of nineteen, John was promoted to sergeant. It was in the front line that the battalion really depended on its

sergeants, perhaps above all other ranks. They had responsibility for both their men and the administration of the
platoon. They had to report all casualties to headquarters,
ensure that every man was doing his duty, supervise the
supply of meals, ammunition and other essentials, and attend
quickly and efficiently to any problem that arose. Moreover,
whenever the platoon's officer was injured or killed, his
duties would fall on the sergeant, too. This meant leading the
men into action, directing each section in the attack, and
making critical decisions in the heat of battle upon which
men's lives depended. It required mature men of experience
and strong character to shoulder such immense responsibilities. The teenage John King never flinched from doing his
duty.

(I did not see much of John in the battles that followed, but
we became firm friends when we both received our commis-
sions at the end of the war. We spent the last of our army days
training recruits at Redford Barracks in Edinburgh before
being demobbed in 1946.)

One of my tent-mates was a friendly Londoner called John
Slipper. A gunner in the Royal Artillery, he had suffered a
bad attack of jaundice. Although he was six years older than
me, we chatted easily and soon discovered a common interest – a love of music. John was a trumpeter who had played
professionally with one of the big bands before the war.
Unsurprisingly, his prized possession was his instrument,
which he never let out of sight. When I mentioned that I
played piano, he told me there was a piano in the NAAFI and
suggested we should play some numbers together.

We soon discovered we were very compatible and shared
the same taste in music, so John thought we should try to
form a small group. At that time, the convalescence depot

housed several thousand patients, so we thought it was only a matter of time before we found some other musicians. Our playing in the NAAFI soon attracted the keen interest of one chap in particular – Elwyn Hughes of the Durham Light Infantry. He borrowed an alto sax from the camp's concert party and joined us the next day in the NAAFI. Elwyn generated a beautiful tone that he had honed playing in Blackpool bands as a teenager.

All three of us were familiar with the standard jazz repertoire, but we still needed a drummer. Then, as luck would have it, we met Sid Soar, a Yorkshireman from the 3rd Division. Very soon, under John's direction, we were playing good music, and many fellow patients came to hear us practise in the NAAFI tent. Each convalescence camp had its own resident entertainment group, and ours had a top-notch singer, so it was not long before we invited him to join our quartet.

John arranged for us to give several concerts and the NAAFI was always full. Our fame spread and invitations to play at the nearby hospitals came in readily, as did offers to play in the officers' mess when they hosted parties. We welcomed any excuse to play. During that whole period, I never once noticed my injury or felt hindered by it. But it did leave two large scars on my back that are still visible today.

Playing in the band gave us great pleasure, and there were other bonuses, including special meals during intervals. This life of privilege, so different from what we had experienced in the front line, continued for several weeks because we were kept in the camp long after our nominal discharge dates. In fact, we remained there until the convalescence depot closed down in late September and moved to the protected Brussels area, along with all the other hospitals, to be nearer the fighting.

A column of three-ton trucks lined up in the parking area of the convalescence depot and we were divided into groups before being shepherded to our respective vehicles. John went in one direction as I went in another. We had been fully kitted out so were carrying quite heavy loads. In addition, of course, John was gripping his trumpet case, which I could see was the most important item in his baggage. We shouted goodbye to each other then suddenly he was gone as the momentum of the army juggernaut abruptly closed an important chapter in my life.

(Some twelve years later, Kathleen, my wife to be, and I attended a ball in Melrose. The music evoked some vague memories from the past. 'He's a very good trumpet player,' I said to one of my friends. 'Yes, he's the leader of the band. They're called the Silver Slippers.' It took a while for the name to register, then suddenly I realised it was John Slipper. He must have put on over two stones, which had changed his appearance drastically. I asked Kathleen to go over and request a number that had been one of our staples in the con-valescence depot – 'If You Want It, You Gotta Buy It, 'Cos We Ain't Giving Nothing Away'. John was taken aback and said, 'That's an old one. I used to play it in my army days.' Kathleen replied, 'I know.'

As we danced, John stared at us, his mind furiously search-ing for a connection. At the end of the number I walked towards the stage, but before I could speak his eyes lit up in recognition and he blurted out, 'Tommy, it's great to see you. I've often thought of our days in the depot and wondered if you had survived the war.'

At the end of the evening, John and I spoke for some time before the band left. We exchanged addresses and I subse-quently visited him and his wife several times. Immediately after the war, he had played with several big bands in London and had made a very good living for a time, but then he was overwhelmed by nervous depression and felt he could not go on. One night he picked up his trumpet, headed to the station and chose a train at random. He had no idea where it was heading. That was how he arrived at Galashiels, where he recovered from his depression and built a happy and fulfilling life for himself.)

Each truck set off from the convalescence depot with up to sixteen men standing and holding tightly on to the roof frame. Travelling east from Bayeux, we passed through the British bridgehead where there had been some desperate battles, near places that were unknown to me at the time. Now their names are synonymous with the Normandy campaign. This journey stirred up a paradox in my mind: I had no desire to return to the horrors of the battlefield, yet I missed my battalion and felt guilty that I was not there to support my comrades. I desperately wanted to get back to the Highland Division, currently fighting in Holland, and now I finally seemed to be on my way. I was sure that in a few days I would be sharing the warm comradeship of my pals. Much to my chagrin and frustration, however, things did not work out that way.

Rumour had it that we were going to a transit camp near Amiens – a journey of almost two hundred miles. The roads were still in a poor state of repair, so it was going to take most of the day, allowing for a lunch break. Before long, the truck was lunging back and forth as it smashed into potholes and bounced over bumps. Not a single building was still standing. There was merely a mound of rubble along each side of the excavated road, then individual piles of debris and gigantic craters. A railway locomotive rested on top of one pile, but there was no sign of its carriages. We guessed that they had been smashed to pieces along with everything else. This was Caen – the result of more than twenty five-hundred-bomber raids, each of which dropped two thousand tons of explosives on the city. Amazingly, as soon as each raid was over, the defenders would emerge from cellars and bunkers to fight on. Caen was the central hub of the German defences. It was a primary D-Day objective, but it remained in enemy hands until 9 July. The British and Canadians attacked it continuously for over a month, while diehard units of the 12th and 21st SS-Panzer divisions put up an equally fierce defence.

By the time we passed through the city, Andre Heintz was openly sporting his Free French Resistance armband. He was helping the Allies and ultimately became a translator for the prominent Highland Division officer Colonel Charles Usher. In addition to his other exploits, it was Usher who ordered the ceremonial burning of the kilt at Bordon in 1940. So it was no great surprise that in June 1944 he appeared amid the sniper-infested rubble of Caen in a kilt and eschewed a tin helmet for his beloved Glengarry cap. His role was to get aid and restore vital services to the embattled citizens of the town, who had spent a month living in tunnels and cellars. He became a model civil affairs officer, but also found the time to fight alongside his fellow Gordon Highlanders, even though he was officially too old for active service after his escape from Dunkirk.

The terrible battle was etched in the memory of Heintz:

We didn't have street fighting because there were no streets left. The Allies and Germans fought over piles of rubble. Caen was bombed twenty-six times between

D-Day and its liberation on 9 July. Sometimes, hundreds of Halifaxes and Lancasters would come over to drop bombs. It was a terrifying sight.

The city was practically razed to the ground, except for two places: the abbey and the hospital, thanks to a huge red cross that my sister and I had made from white sheets dipped in buckets of blood. These two buildings were hit by nearly 200 shells, but that's little compared to the 600,000 shells that rained down in the month after D-Day.

People were very scared. Many took refuge in the abbey because William the Conqueror was buried there, and they believed the Allies wouldn't dare bomb the grave of an English king. Of course, the abbey is also a very strong building, and provided a good place to shelter. A legend soon started among the thousands of people sheltering there. They said there was a saying in England that, if William's grave was ever destroyed, it would be the end of the English crown. I think it was just something they repeated to keep up morale.

A traumatised but grateful population greeted the Allies when they finally took Caen. Heintz recalled:

After the liberation, when the city was being cleared up, they came across a cellar where a man had died of suffocation after being trapped. They found a note with him that said, 'I feel that I am dying. It is terrible to know that I'm going to die because I have been expecting the liberation for so long. But I know that, because of my death, other people will be liberated. Long live France, long live the Allies.'

We arrived at the transit camp in time to be allocated a tent and get a hot meal before darkness fell. Next morning, I looked around the camp to find an array of tents stretching in all directions. The camp was only half full, an indication that it would soon be moving nearer the front line. The food was good and the camp well kept, but most of the entertainment and other facilities had already been moved forward.

The others in my tent were also recovering from wounds and injuries and were now en route back to their regiments. It was revealing to hear their experiences and learn what had happened to other divisions in other parts of Normandy. Some of them had been in the camp for two weeks or more, but I felt sure I would not share a similar fate. After all, the Highland Division was desperate for reinforcements. I scrutinised the noticeboard every day to see who had been drafted to other camps, but after a week my name still had not appeared. I enquired at the camp office and learned that they processed each man in strict order. Moreover, getting a soldier back to his unit depended upon complex logistics that might take some time to organise. Each man simply had to wait for his individual case to run through the system. It was frustrating, but clearly there was nothing I could do to speed up the process.

One of my tent-mates was a very friendly Cameronian. He was a bit older and certainly more streetwise than I was, and he offered to show me the sights of Amiens, just a few miles from the camp. After a quick walk round the city centre, where there was little sign of serious damage, he led me into a well-appointed café. He ordered a spirit but I stuck to lemonade. In our alcove, we chatted about the progress of the war, our battle experiences, our homes and families, and I was fascinated by his lively conversation. Two immaculately dressed ladies were sitting in the next alcove, back to back with us, and seemingly engrossed in each other's company. However, after a while, one of them unexpectedly turned round and caught the eye of my new friend. The astonished look on his face rapidly mellowed into a sly grin. He exchanged a smile with the lady and then fell unusually silent when she resumed her conversation. I failed to grasp the obvious connection between the two of them and broke the silence by asking if he was all right. In a coy whisper, he said, 'That was the one I had in the brothel yesterday.' The lady never turned a hair, my Cameronian friend was strangely amused, and I was hugely embarrassed, shocked and speechless. I was also terrified to be sitting within inches of a prostitute. Of course, I had heard all the soldier talk about brothels, but such places were still unreal and vague to me. Now I seemed to be in the middle of a very different world.

However, within two weeks, I was on my way to another transit camp, this time in Belgium. We passed through a series of towns that I recognised as Highland Division battlefields from the First World War – Cambrai, Valenciennes, Mons, and so on. It was now mid-October and the weather had turned wet and damp.

After standing all day in the back of the truck, we were aching by the time we reached our destination, near Louvain. This was another tented camp, erected on both sides of a gully. After a day of continuous rain, the whole area had become a sea of mud. The wet weather confined us to our tents, except at mealtimes, when we had to negotiate the gully to and from the cookhouse with our mess tins. This nasty, muddy, dreary place caused a cloud of gloom to descend on everyone and everything.

My misery was even greater because I found it difficult to

get on with my new tent-mates. Nearly all of them had been medically downgraded for one reason or another. By the time I met them, they seemed incapable of doing anything save for the most menial jobs. These unfortunate, morose misfits had been in the camp for months. They only increased my desperation to return to my own unit. Little did I know that my pals were about to embark on one of the most brutal campaigns of the whole war.

# 6

# Going Dutch

After the failure of Operation Market Garden – the unsuccessful assault on Arnhem – it had been decided that the approaches to Antwerp and the Scheldt estuary had to be cleared of German forces. This liberation of the bleak and exposed countryside of southern Holland would be achieved by two great operations – code-named Colin and Ascot – with Montgomery's ultimate aim to cut off the German Fifteenth Army. A Canadian force would thrust north-eastwards from Woensdrecht on the coast, pass north of Roosendaal towards Moerdijk on the Maas, and join up with the British XII Corps driving west from s'Hertogenbosch. The Highland Division's role would be to clear the enemy from North Brabant, between s'Hertogenbosch and Geertruidenberg.

There was plenty of action before Operation Colin even began, as the Allies maintained the pressure on the Germans. Night patrols were especially nervous affairs, as Stan Whitehouse, a private with the 1st Black Watch, recalled:

One cold, damp night, soon after arriving in Holland, our platoon was sent up front to watch for enemy patrols infiltrating the lines. We were dug in to a field about twenty yards from a metalled road. We had an excellent view of no-man's land, which was lit up by Monty's Moonlight – our boffins had come up with the ingenious idea of bouncing searchlight beams off low-lying clouds to illuminate the enemy's positions and no-man's land. It worked well during those autumn nights, with thick cloud acting as an ideal reflector. On this particular night German flares were also active, keeping us fully alert.

I heard unusually noisy footsteps on the metalled road just behind us and looked around to see Black Watch bonnets and hackles intermingled with German helmets. The Jocks were quite vociferous though not loud enough for us to distinguish the words. I assumed our boys were escorting prisoners to the pen. 'Where are you taking that lot?' I called out. This was the signal for pandemonium to result. Firing began, with bullets zipping past us, followed by shouts and screams. Three Germans rushed off the road and into our field, running between our slit trenches. We opened fire on them – they were easy targets silhouetted against Monty's Moonlight and soon fell. I could see a scuffle under way on the road with much grunting. Several of our lads were killing a German officer with their bare hands.

It turned out a German patrol had penetrated our lines and taken six of our lads prisoner. The Jerries had taken their bootlaces and belts and the noise I heard on the road was our boys shuffling along, holding up their trousers as they went.

By now, many of the Highlanders who had fought their way across North Africa and pushed the Germans out of Normandy were showing signs of strain. The top brass were well aware of this, and granted the men leave as often as they could. But this did not always have the desired effect, as George Sands recalled:

> Along with a dozen others, including Captain Lamb and Major Parker, I was sent to Antwerp for four days' rest and relaxation. There is no doubt in my mind that our commanding officer knew I was close to breaking point. I was feeling particularly low and probably showing the first signs of battle fatigue. Although the leave was given with the best intentions, it turned out that we were subjected to almost non-stop bombardment by V-1 flying bombs and V-2 rockets. Just after we arrived in Antwerp, a military policeman, who was directing traffic at a crossroads, received a direct hit. All they found was one of his white gauntlets.

Operation Colin began in the early hours of 23 October 1944, the second anniversary of El Alamein. Attacking the German front north of St Oedenrode, the Highlanders of 152 and 153 brigades would punch a hole in the Nazi defences, through which 154 Brigade would advance towards the River Dommel, a major obstacle in the advance westward.

The initial objective of 153 Brigade was the town of Schijndel. The Gordons led a silent attack from Eerde to Wijbosch, a village on the outskirts of Schijndel, to find that the enemy had already withdrawn. The 5th Black Watch then formed up in the village, ready to move with tank support on the south-east corner of Schijndel itself. At dawn, under a creeping barrage, two companies, some 240 men, attacked across the fields towards the town. Meanwhile, the engineers cleared the main road into the town of mines, closely followed by the other two companies. The battalion instantly came under mortar and shell bombardment, and, on entering the town, Spandau machine-guns opened fire from several different directions. The engineers almost reached the town centre but suffered many casualties before withdrawing. Then the Allies unleashed a ferocious artillery barrage, which allowed the battalion to push towards its objective. Finally accepting that they were defending a lost cause, the Germans made a fighting retreat from the town.

The beleaguered citizens emerged from their shelters and welcomed the Jocks in amazing scenes of jubilation amid the blazing ruins of Schijndel. With them was a group of shot-down American airmen, hidden from the Germans for several weeks by brave Dutch families who would surely have been shot if caught helping the enemy. Later in the day, the Gordons occupied the west side of the town, which allowed the Highlanders to consolidate and form a solid base.

Private John Tough, of the Gordons, was in the thick of the fighting:

We had moved through the blazing town Schijndel and on to the village of Esch when the Jerries gave us a terrible stonking with their Moaning Minnies. Our section leader, Lance Corporal Fenwick, was killed and we had several wounded. My mate Macmanus, who landed on D-Day, said it was the worst mortaring that he had experienced. As we advanced, I spotted one of my mates, Tony Barton, lying dead by the roadside. It was a bit upsetting but you just got on with it.

Then we went into a farm where the Dutch people gave us a tremendous welcome. It was just great, but when the joy subsided the farmer's family told us that their daughter had just been killed in the shelling. We were stunned. It made such an impression on me that these people could have given us such a welcome at a time when they were grieving for their child. We stayed in their barn that night in a very sad and subdued mood.

Unfortunately, the thrust by 152 Brigade, on the left flank, did not go so smoothly. The Camerons were up against battle-hardened paratroops who fought tenaciously and inflicted many casualties on the Highlanders, including Major Nigel Parker, a popular figure throughout the regiment. The hellish battle raged all night and drove George Sands to the very brink. He vividly recalled his terrible ordeal:

The plan was for A and B companies to seize their initial objectives and that we, in D and C companies, would pass through them and form up ready for a second assault the following morning. We were to have the usual weight of artillery, mortar and heavy machine-gun support. We were to advance under Monty's Moonlight but, as it turned out, the defenders rather than the attackers gained an advantage from the light.

As soon as A and B companies crossed the start line and hit open ground they were met with intense defensive fire, mainly from Spandau machine-guns, and sustained heavy casualties. Only a depleted B Company reached its objective. A Company lost their company commander, wounded, and were nearly wiped out. We, in D Company, were launched round B Company's flank in an attempt to gain A Company's objective.

Again, as soon as we were in the open, the machine-guns opened up on us. The two guys either side of me were both hit. The one on my immediate left was killed instantly as Spandau bullets hit him. He was ripped open diagonally across his body, from shoulder to opposing hip. It was as if his body had been unzipped. I managed to lie flat on the ground in a furrow on the edge of the field we were in, wishing it were a lot deeper. Machine-gun bullets and tracer rounds whistled over my head. I was powerless to do anything. I laid like that for most of the night, listening to the screams and moans of the wounded and dying.

By dawn the following day, the Camerons had cleared the woods and moved west to consolidate and recover.

This assault was typical of the fighting the Camerons faced during both Colin and Ascot, so it should come as no surprise that the regiment earned an unprecedented number of gallantry awards during these campaigns. Moreover, like all front-line troops, they had to cope with the dangers of friendly fire and lethal accidents. Having come through the hell of the attack on Schijndel, the Camerons suffered a tragedy of their own making. Again, the incident was etched on Sands' memory:

I had a bad experience of having to follow an order that I knew to be pointless. It has haunted me ever since. I had been ordered to take my platoon to clear some woods and farm buildings. I tried to argue that it was a pointless exercise as we had already cleared that particular area. But I sent six guys forward up an avenue of trees and was just organising another squad when the tank, which was covering our advance, loosed off an air burst. When covering an advance, the tank always had its gun loaded and ready to fire over our heads. It was a total accident but the tank commander slipped on the firing mechanism and fired a premature round.

The shell was an air-burst and unfortunately it hit the trees and caught the six guys who were about twenty yards away from me. The blast from the explosion singed my hair, and what turned out to be part of a young boy's head hit me in the face. When I got to my boys, three were dead and three had been terribly maimed. One had all his buttocks shot away; another had an arm and his shoulder missing; the third seemed to be bleeding from every part of his body. I can still picture the young lad to this day. He was only eighteen years of age and ginger-haired. I believe he came from Glasgow. The wounded were screaming at me not to leave them: 'Sarge! Sarge! Don't leave me, Sarge.' I was trying to reassure them, to calm them. I told them I would not leave them and administered the morphine that I always carried round my neck. I wanted to cry but knew that I must not let them see that I was scared for them. I knew there was no hope for any of them as I watched their colour turn to grey. I ordered the carrier forward and we took a door off the nearest building to act as a stretcher on top of the carrier. I got them to an aid station but one had died before we got there and the other two died shortly after. It was an utter waste of life. After more than fifty years,

I still hear their screams and see their faces – faces of death. 'Sarge! Don't leave me, Sarge.' When I was on my own, later that night, I shed many tears; I sobbed uncontrollably.

I always tried to look after the boys in my section. They never went short of a smoke or a dram of whisky. Sergeants had a monthly whisky ration. There might be twenty or so sergeants going into an attack but there might be only ten left after the attack, so the remainder would share the whisky and cigarette rations. I always shared it out among the boys in my section. I always thought that if I looked after them, they would look after me. It seemed to work.

The tank commander went bomb happy once he realised what had happened, even though nobody blamed him. It was an unpleasant thing to see – he seemed to go instantly insane. He had to live with that tragedy all his remaining days. Our officer, on the other hand, wasn't to be forgiven. On my return, I reported to the commanding officer that the officer concerned had been drunk. I could not forgive him then and I still can't forgive him to this day. We were all in the same situation, living on our nerve ends, wondering if today was to be our last. Subsequently, he was relieved of his duties and disappeared from the 5th Camerons. I don't know his full punishment, but whatever he received, he had it coming.

Compared with the Camerons, the Seaforths on the extreme left of 152 Brigade had a much easier time of it and faced little resistance during their initial advance towards the town of Boxtel. They reached the Dommel to find the bridge blown, but still managed to get a foothold across this barrier. Early the next morning, the enemy repulsed their first attempts to cross the river in strength with intense fire. However, during the day, the Germans suddenly withdrew. After an unopposed crossing in canvas boats, the 2nd Seaforths reached Boxtel without any further incident. They were greeted not by hostile Germans but by over a hundred Allied aircrew, who were proudly paraded by an ecstatic crowd. Dutch families had sheltered the downed airmen since the previous September.

Captain George Lisle took his company of Seaforths to the nearby village of Den Dungen. He was busy clearing mines from the main road when he received an unusual welcome:

I was amazed to see a priest striding down the road and waving his arms. He introduced himself as a member of the Dutch Resistance and told us that the Germans had pulled out overnight. But our lads nearly had a fit when the clergyman welcomed us as *American* liberators. My wireless operator put him right, pointing at our tartan shoulder flashes and shouting, '*Ecosse! Ecosse!*' Then the priest produced a camera from beneath his cassock and insisted on taking our photograph. Next he insisted that we follow him and arrest a collaborator he described as a 'Quisling'. When we got to the house indicated by the priest, the prosperous-looking occupant denied any Germans had ever been there. But the house had that indefinable smell that always lingered wherever Germans had been for any length of time. (Our medical officer thought it was due to the anti-louse powder that they used.) I was convinced that the priest's accusations were correct and decided to detain the man. By the time we got the collaborator outside a large crowd had gathered, baying for blood.

With Schijndel secured, 154 Brigade prepared to pass through 153 Brigade. The 7th Black Watch – mounted on troop-carrying Kangaroos, with the tanks of the 33rd Armoured Brigade in support – made rapid progress. They entered St Michielsgestel around midday on 23 October, at the cost of two tanks, to find that the Germans had withdrawn and blown up the town's bridge across the Dommel. Nevertheless, the Highlanders crossed the river on boats and rafts, secured a bridgehead and consolidated in strength. By mid-afternoon, the 1st Black Watch had arrived to reinforce the bridgehead. During the night, the divisional engineers displayed amazing teamwork and determination to erect a Bailey bridge over the Dommel, despite suffering regular shelling and increasing casualties.

Overall, it had been a good start to Operation Colin. All of the initial objectives had been achieved, casualties had been relatively light and two hundred prisoners had been taken. However, the German 59th Division had recently been reinforced by freshly trained paratroops and they remained a serious threat.

The next target was the little town of Vught, some five miles north-west of St Michielsgestel. Famed only for its bell-tower, nothing much had happened here for centuries before the Germans arrived. Now, it was the main objective of 154 Brigade. Early on 24 October, the 7th Black Watch set off to secure a crossing of the Halsche Water, a tributary of the Dommel. But the Germans made good use of recently acquired self-propelled (SP) guns to delay the advance. So it was midday before the Highlanders reached Halder, where they found that the bridge had been blown. The advance on Vught had to wait until the hard-pressed engineers could erect yet another bridge across the river. Meanwhile, the 1st Black Watch struck out towards Hal, a crossing point further south, only to find that the Germans had blown the bridge there, too. Two companies managed to clamber across the wreckage to form a bridgehead and await construction of a Bailey bridge. The engineers, labouring all night, eventually completed a bridge three hundred yards upstream, safe from shell and mortar fire.

When the Black Watch tried to cross the new bridge on 25 October, they encountered terrific resistance. A company led by Major Graham Pilcher came under heavy mortar and Spandau fire and was pinned down in flat, open country. Any movement out of the cover of the ditches drew fire, and snipers were picking off the Jocks at regular intervals. Realising that the situation was critical, Pilcher made a dash across the open ground to his forward units. He braved intense fire to organise and then lead a determined assault on the enemy, dug in on the main road two hundred yards away. The assault party wiped out two enemy machine-gun posts and killed or captured several Germans. The sniping continued, but Pilcher crossed and recrossed the bullet-swept ground to consolidate his defensive positions. He was awarded a Military Cross for his bravery under fire and was decorated by Field Marshal Montgomery.

The same day, a concerted attack on Vught was finally launched. The 1st Black Watch, attacking north along the main road and supported by the Northamptonshire Yeomanry, fell victim to the deadly SP guns. Their advance was halted at a roadblock, where five tanks were trapped and systematically destroyed by a single SP gun: the Germans knocked out the rear tank first, which prevented the others from escaping, and then picked off the rest, one by one. The enemy also launched a counter-attack that seriously threatened the whole battalion. Fortunately, the Argylls in the rear were able to pass through the Black Watch and engage the enemy in a fierce battle. The combined force halted the counter-attack, but it was unable to advance further.

The 7th Black Watch, attacking Vught from the east, ran into similar resistance and their advance was also held up short of the town. General Rennie, the divisional commander, ordered the troops to await back-up, which would require yet more bridge building.

The following morning, the advances from both directions were given full artillery and tank support, and by midday both the 7th and the 1st had managed to enter the town. They were received with overwhelming joy and gratitude from the townsfolk. The burgomaster's wife was especially grateful as she was Scottish and had spent years hiding from the Nazis. She hugged her liberators, who could not believe their ears when they heard her accent. The Highland Division ensured that word was quickly sent to her family in Perth that she was safe, in good health and had been liberated.

But for the young Jocks the quiet market town of Vught held one more surprise. It was an altogether grimmer discovery. George Sands and his men chased a group of retreating Germans through some woods and exchanged small-arms fire with them. Richard Massey, an eighteen-year-old from Warrington, was with Sands' platoon. He had lost two elder brothers in the war, so he knew about its horrors, but nothing had prepared him for what they stumbled across in those woods. Massey recalled:

After the Germans made their getaway, we found this huge camp. It had ditches around it and was surrounded with large rolls of barbed wire. When we went in, the SS guards had gone, and so had the prisoners, who had been taken to Belsen. But as we went through the main gates we were horrified to see the bodies of two male inmates hanging from gallows. It was a terrible sight to see. We all saw it and were disgusted. We went to the crematorium and you could see the barrows and you could see it had just been used. It was a haunting place.

This was the first time that Allied troops had liberated a concentration camp in Western Europe. It was not equipped with gas chambers, but when the Camerons explored further they found torture cells, mass graves and execution sites.

Hundreds of Jews, many of them children, had died at Vught and hundreds more political and resistance prisoners had been tortured and murdered. In total, thirty thousand people had passed through the camp since its completion at the end of 1942. It was split into two sections. The first was a transit camp for Jews on their way to the death camps, although hundreds died of disease and starvation in Vught itself. The second was a security camp, guarded by the SS, which held both male and female political prisoners – many of them active in the Dutch Resistance. This was a place of unmitigated terror. The guards starved, shot, beat and tortured their victims. They used clubs wrapped in barbed wire and trained dogs to savage the genitals of tethered prisoners. Over seven hundred inmates were murdered in under two years, with the rate of executions increasing after June 1944, as the Allies approached.

In one particularly horrific incident, the guards terribly tortured a group of women. They had spoken up for another female prisoner, and their punishment was to squeeze into a cell of barely nine square metres. Seventy-four women remained wedged in the cell for over fourteen hours. Ten of them died, their corpses still standing upright amid the survivors until the guards unlocked the door. Several others suffered permanent physical or mental damage.

Elsewhere, the advance progressed and benefited greatly from excellent cooperation between the tanks of the 33rd Armoured Brigade, the Derbyshires' reconnaissance, the artillery and the infantry. It was delayed on several occasions, often by one of the two main rivers of the area, and it was then that everything depended upon the engineers building their Bailey bridges at speed. As expected, the German 59th Division fought hard to hold their ground, and with the support of their SP guns they regularly brought the advance to a halt. Also, the nature of the advance was very different from that in Normandy. Now, the Allies' objectives were mainly buildings of strategic value, which gave the infantry cover from enemy fire and protection against the colder weather.

While 154 Brigade succeeded in taking Vught, the other two brigades made good progress on the left flank. The two Gordon battalions of 153 Brigade crossed the Dommel at St Michielsgestel and swept south, towards a crossing of the Halsche Water at Esch. They arrived just in time to see the bridge blown. The 5/7th Gordons managed to get across the wreckage and establish a bridgehead, but soon they had to fend off a powerful counter-attack. Fortunately, just as the Gordons were on the point of withdrawing, they were reinforced by the 5th Black Watch and the attackers were driven back. Further south, the bridgehead at Boxtel was expanded to the north by the 2nd Seaforths to join up with the Esch bridgehead and south to liberate Liempde.

General Rennie had been informed that the 7th Armoured Division, the Desert Rats, would be passing through his front to launch a parallel southern thrust in a move that was designed to increase the threat to the entire German Fifteenth Army. This meant that the bridges across the Dommel and the Halsche Water had to be strengthened, which further delayed the Highland Division's own advance. During this enforced rest period, some mopping up and a northern thrust by the 5th Seaforths to connect with the 53rd Welsh Division attacking s'Hertogenbosch were undertaken.

At dawn on 26 October, 153 Brigade headed west from Esch towards Haaren with the support of the 4th Royal Tank Regiment. Meanwhile, 152 Brigade moved north-west from Esch to widen the gap in the enemy defences and give free passage to the Desert Rats. A mile from Haaren, a single SP gun knocked out two tanks, halted 153 Brigade's advance and caused an immense traffic jam at the Esch bridgehead, where the Desert Rats had formed up in preparation for their advance. This delayed the latter's thrust, but before long they were making good progress.

The 5th Black Watch, leading 153 Brigade, suffered more casualties as they advanced on Haaren. On entering the village, they initially encountered considerable small-arms resistance, but then the enemy suddenly abandoned all their positions and withdrew. This was part of a general withdrawal of the Fifteenth Army to a line centred on the ancient town of Loon Op Zand. With the enemy in full retreat, General Rennie ordered the Highland Division west to confront the new line of defence. The 7th Armoured Division had already made a surprise attack on this strategic point but had found it heavily defended and had bypassed it. Now that it was reinforced, it would present even greater resistance to the Highland Division. Rennie decided that a two-brigade attack on the strongpoint was required, so he ordered 153 Brigade to make a frontal assault while 152 Brigade made an outflanking advance on the right.

At 3 p.m. on 28 October, after a heavy barrage, the 1st Gordons launched the frontal attack. Initially, there was the predicted stiff resistance, but this unexpectedly decreased as the advance continued. Soon it had crumbled altogether and the enemy made a hasty retreat. It was later learned that the defenders were in the process of being replaced by another unit at the precise moment when the Gordons attacked. Moreover, the German command feared that 152 Brigade's flanking manoeuvre might isolate the town.

Rennie was disappointed that the defending garrison had escaped capture, so he ordered the 5th Black Watch to continue the chase throughout the night. The Black Watch passed through the Gordons' lines and advanced northwards along the main road to Kaatsheuvel under a full moon. Silhouetted against the bright moonlight, the Highlanders were vulnerable to attack from Germans concealed in the undergrowth and casualties mounted. At one point, the two leading companies were cut off by enemy infiltration and very heavy fighting and tank support were required to re-establish contact with them. A final concentrated thrust was made at dawn. Under accurate shell and mortar fire, the battalion drove on to the village of Horst, still south of Kaatsheuvel. Exhausted and vulnerable, they deployed in all-round defence and waited for the rest of the brigade to catch up.

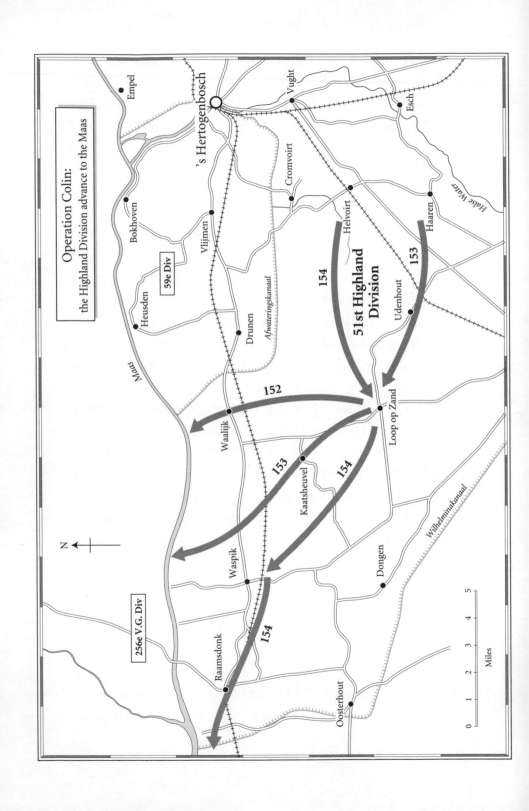

Operation Colin:
the Highland Division advance to the Maas

's Hertogenbosch

Empel

Vught

Esch

Cromvoirt

Bokhoven

Helvoirt

Haaren

*Halse Water*

59e Div

Vlijmen

154

153

Heusden

51st Highland
Division

Udenhout

Drunen

*Afwateringskanaal*

*Maas*

152

Loop op Zand

Waalijk

153

154

Kaatsheuvel

154

*Wilhelminakanaal*

Dongen

256e V.G. Div

Waspik

N

Raamsdonk

154

Oosterhout

0   1   2   3   4   5

Miles

The road to Kaatsheuvel was now open, a heavy barrage paved the way to the town, and at midday the 5/7th Gordons, supported by tanks, advanced. However, the Germans fought a skilful rearguard action and retreated slowly. At 3 p.m. most of Kaatsheuvel was still in enemy hands, so Rennie ordered 154 Brigade into the battle to the west of the town, where they met equally stiff resistance. The fighting continued well into the night, until gradually the resistance started to crumble. Then, suddenly, the enemy was gone.

Next the Highlanders moved quickly to liberate Sprang-Capelle and Capelle. Then, after a short march, they were the first troops to reach the River Maas. It was now impossible for any German stragglers to move west and join their retreating comrades.

While the battle for Kaatsheuvel raged, 152 Brigade plodded unopposed across the sand dunes on the right flank. Their patrols reported that the area had already been abandoned by the enemy. During this advance, the 5th Camerons entered Waalwijk, where they were given another tumultuous welcome by the townsfolk.

The plan that had been laid by Montgomery was now nearing completion. The Canadian force, attacking from the Belgian border, had made good progress past Roosendaal to the Maas and was now pushing eastwards to join up with the British XII Corps, which was driving westwards. But a final concentrated effort was required to close the trap. The German command, recognising their situation was hopeless, requested and received Hitler's permission to withdraw the Fifteenth Army across the Maas. However, they ordered the 59th Division to remain behind and defend the pocket contained within the Afwaterings Canal. This division had battled courageously throughout, and now they were sure to do everything in their power to keep the escape route open and save as many of their comrades as possible.

In their thrust to the Maas, 154 Brigade was driving straight towards this determined and skilled enemy rearguard force. The 1st Black Watch led the brigade towards Waspik, which they took only after a bitter fight in which they suffered heavy casualties. The bridge over the local canal was blown and the battalion consolidated. Next the 7th Argylls came forward and set off with tank support towards Geertruidenberg. Very soon the battalion ran into fierce opposition and two tanks were knocked out. Several hours' heavy fighting halted the advance overnight. The following morning, the Argylls first survived a counter-attack and then withstood heavy mortar and machine-gun fire to advance to the village of Raamsdonk, where it established a base from which the 7th Black Watch could continue the last few miles of the assault.

A platoon of Black Watch set off at top speed in Kangaroos, escorted by tanks, and was making good progress until it was confronted by a battery of anti-tank guns at close quarters. A courageous battle was fought, but the convoy was forced to withdraw. A second convoy, this time aided by a mighty barrage and an immediate follow-up attack, finally broke the strong ring of defenders who were protecting the German evacuation. A brave dash was then made for the bridge at nearby Keizersveer, only to find it destroyed.

The performance of 154 Brigade in this last stage of the advance was acknowledged as outstanding. The enemy resistance had been desperate and determined, the Highlanders had fought to the brink of exhaustion, and over two hundred prisoners had been taken.

Operation Colin had lasted nine days and had liberated southern Holland by driving the enemy across the River Maas. This had greatly aided the Canadian troops battling hard to clear the Scheldt estuary and open the desperately needed port of Antwerp. (In that operation, the achievements of Scotland's 52nd Lowland Division in the desperate battle for Walcheren Island were also critical.)

During those nine days, each unit of the Highland Division, including the Derbyshire Yeomanry Reconnaissance, had fought stiff battles. They sustained total casualties of 700, with 122 killed, but these would have been much greater without the accuracy of the divisional gunners and the excellent support provided by the 133rd Armoured Brigade. Enemy casualties were extremely heavy and 2400 Germans were taken prisoner. As ever, though, they proved to be masters in the art of withdrawal, mounting a successful rescue operation that allowed a substantial body of their Fifteenth Army to escape before the last bridge across the Maas was blown.

With the bridge at Keizersveer blown and the last of the stragglers rounded up, all that remained was to tackle the 59th Division, who had been left behind as a rearguard on the south of the river. They occupied what was effectively a six-mile-wide island between Waalwijk in the west and s'Hertogenbosch in the east. It was known simply as 'the Island'. Bordered to the north by the Maas and to the other three sides by the Afwaterings Canal, it could be reached only by boat. Consequently, an assault crossing of the canal had to be made before the final battle was won.

The canal itself was forty yards wide, but the distance between the protective dykes was nearly eighty yards. Crossing this stretch was fraught with difficulty and danger, so a careful study of the terrain was essential. Once this information had been assessed, Rennie decided that 152 and 153 brigades would cross on the southern stretch of the canal. To give the infantry protection, he arranged for twelve flame-throwing Crocodile tanks to take up positions halfway up the nearside dyke, so that they could project their flaming jets on to and beyond the far dyke and burn up the enemy defences. A massive barrage, delivered by some 232 guns, would also be laid by the artillery regiments of XII Corps.

In addition, tanks would be sited every twenty-five yards along the front, and these would move to the top of the dyke to give covering fire as the infantry advanced. The Middlesex machine-gunners would fire continuously at the enemy as the Highlanders moved over the open ground. With their Vickers guns peeping over the top of the nearside dyke, it was hoped that they would force the Germans to keep their heads down.

All of this took days of intense planning before the launch of Operation Guy Fawkes was fixed for 5 November. However, it was then decided that the assault should be brought forward by twenty-four hours.

The mighty barrage first opened up on the enemy dyke defences before being moved to other strongpoints. The village of Drunen was all but destroyed and twenty-eight civilians were killed. Next the Crocodiles spurted their deadly fire as the infantry started to move forward in fear and trepidation. They faced a dash over the dyke, a run to the sixteen-man canvas boats, jostling to get into their allotted place, then an impatient wait for the boat to fill with their comrades. Next would come a zigzag across the open canal, where they would be sitting ducks, without any cover. If and when the boat hit the far bank, there would be a scramble and a rush to the far dyke to gain some protection.

Meanwhile, the brave ferrymen, supplied by the reserve companies, would have to row the boat back to the near bank to pick up another load. This nightmare would then be repeated over and over again.

At 4.35 p.m., the 5th Camerons and the 5th Seaforths of 152 Brigade crossed the canal and met little opposition. So, in a combination of relief and confusion, they pushed towards their objectives. As the Camerons approached Drunen, they saw the Germans running away in disarray. The Seaforths found the enemy dyke abandoned and then also witnessed the enemy fleeing towards the Maas bridges. The two battalions entered Drunen from different directions to find the town all but deserted and badly damaged.

153 Brigade was not quite so lucky. Crossing the canal east of the 5th Seaforths and forty minutes later, the 1st Gordons suffered several casualties in their advance. The leading boat of the 5th Black Watch was hit by a Panzerfaust bazooka, causing more injuries. Nevertheless, many Germans began to surrender as the advance continued against weak resistance. Both battalions reached their objectives around the ruins of Nieuwkuijk in good time, and at 10.30 p.m. the 5/7th Gordons arrived, followed by light supply vehicles that had been rafted across the canal. During the night, the 4th Royal Tanks, coming from the diversionary attack at s'Hertogenbosch, arrived to give support to the earlier attacks.

After a meal and a brief rest, the advance continued with tank support. The battalions of 152 Brigade fanned out towards the Maas from Drunen while those of 153 did likewise from Nieuwkuijk. The primary objective of the 5/7th Gordons was the large village of Vlijmen, which was taken unopposed, but they suffered ten casualties from shelling and mines in the approach. In the early hours the 5th Black Watch moved on Haarsteeg without trouble and took more than ninety compliant prisoners. Patrols were sent towards the Maas, only to report that the enemy had evacuated in haste and were blowing the bridge.

The 5th Camerons, advancing towards the river town of Heusden, was the only battalion to meet serious resistance. A group of some thirty Germans had set up ringed defences to allow the evacuation across the Maas to continue. Stiff fighting took place, but the enemy could not be dislodged. A flame-throwing carrier was finally used to breach the defences and allow the Camerons to liberate Heusden. By 6 p.m. on 5 November, the Highlanders had reached the Maas, but all of the bridges had been blown and, once again, most of the enemy had escaped.

Those who had not were now in grave danger, as George Sands recalled:

On 6 November we were again on the move, this time to Heusden. The battalion suffered more heavy mortaring. Advancing through Heusden, we heard a tremendous explosion ahead of us and we soon came across the burned and bombed remains of what looked like a church. It turned out to be a municipal building. The SS had herded women and children into that building. Then they blew it up. The next building to be liberated was being held by men in the black uniform of the SS. As we closed in on them, the survivors emerged shouting, *'Nicht scheissen! Nicht scheissen!'* and *'Kamerad, Kamerad!'* I thought: *Nicht scheissen* my arse! I shot them without a second thought.

From that day on, any German wearing the black SS uniform would rarely get the option of surrendering to us. Even the green-clad Wehrmacht would get only one chance to surrender. If they did not accept the first offer, they did not get the chance again.

The Pioneer boys got the job of clearing that building. My mate Ted Murcar, on his return to Heusden in 1994 for the fiftieth anniversary of their liberation, could not face entering that building again. The horror of all those bodies, especially the children, had stayed with him in his nightmares.

Sixty women and seventy-four children died when the Nazis blew up the town hall in which they were sheltering. Before the detonation, the Germans had excavated underneath the bell-tower to ensure that it would fall on top of the terrified civilians. Heusden's small population was decimated by this single atrocity.

Operation Guy Fawkes succeeded in clearing the enemy from south of the Maas within thirty-six hours. Several hundred prisoners were taken and Allied casualties were light. Overall, the assault crossing of the Afwaterings Canal had gone very smoothly. The infantry had been well protected by the combined barrage and the support had arrived in good time. Thereafter, the advance across the Island had been a textbook example of movement and control. It rightly received much praise from the army top brass.

Before the assault began, it was thought that the enemy's 59th Division, which had fought so effectively throughout Operation Colin, was at full strength and had been reinforced by two SS units. In fact, the Highlanders' opponents were shadows of their former selves. As soon as the barrage was launched, the Germans abandoned their arms and equipment and fled. Some looted, some were drunk, most were ready to surrender. The German defences were abandoned and the chain of command was broken; the 59th Division had lost its pride. These were low-grade troops who were generally unable and unwilling to fight, and the Highland Division overcame them almost effortlessly. The four days of precise planning and the mighty barrage from every available artillery regiment contributed to the speed of the victory; with hindsight, however, the elaborate preparation and intense bombardment were probably unnecessary.

Better intelligence would almost certainly have led the generals to downgrade the operation and send the artillery elsewhere. But they were rightly cautious after earlier disasters at Breville and Colombelles. Moreover, the operation provided a valuable model for the planning of future canal crossings. On the downside, it also caused massive, largely unnecessary destruction and loss of life to Drunen and most of the other villages on the Island.

The fighting was far from over. Another enemy bridgehead across the Maas in the province of Limburg still had to be cleared. A strong German force occupied the triangular area roughly defined by Venlo and Roermond on the Maas, where it runs north-east to south-west, and Nederweert, twelve miles to the west. This force had previously been a threat to the Nijmegen corridor during the drive by XXX Corps towards Arnhem. But it had been contained and pushed back to the river. During Operation Colin, although they were guarded by the 7th American Armored Division, these Germans had broken out from their bridgehead and regained much of the area. They were now threatening the important supply centre of Eindhoven. The 53rd Welsh Division, having liberated s'Hertogenbosch, was sent south to help contain the threat, but the Welshmen needed reinforcements to push the enemy back across the Maas. These reinforcements came in the form of the 15th Scottish, on the left, north of the Noorder Canal, and the Highland Division, in the centre. The 53rd Division was to attack on the right, bordered by the Maas.

Most of the enemy were now contained within an area bordered by the Noorder and Wessem canals, which crossed just over a mile south-east of Nederweert. The Noorder then ran north-east some twelve miles to enter the Maas near Venlo, while the Wessem ran south-east to join the Maas upstream from Roermond. The whole area was flat, with no cover save for a few small woods. Rain drizzled continuously on sodden fields, a heavy mist blanketed the ground and all the villages and farms had been heavily damaged. There was also a network of ditches and deep canals that gave the Germans a ready-made defensive system.

Each Allied battalion was issued with a complement of canvas assault boats, and each knew they would have to make at least two of the dreaded canal crossings. The divisional engineers, with the support of several corps bridging units, would have to build numerous Baileys across the canals. B Squadron of the 11th Royal Tank Regiment supplied amphibious Buffaloes, the Fife and Forfar Yeomanry provided Crocodiles, and tank support came from the 144th Royal Armoured Corps and units of the Desert Rats, the 7th Armoured Division. The area was defended mostly by Luftwaffe units that had been integrated into paratroop divisions.

Before the operation began, the Highland Division was sent to a rest area for several days. Trucks ferried the men to and from Eindhoven, which had good facilities and where life was returning to normal. Troops would barter a couple of hundred cigarettes for a prized Philips dynamo torch, which proved to be invaluable in night operations. A favourite destination was the Hot Bath Unit, which provided open-air showers to wash away three weeks of sweat and grime, and exchanged clean, dry kit for mud-caked uniforms.

All too soon the respite ended, and the division moved south to the villages around Nederweert. Some training allowed the men to become familiar with assembling the collapsible canvas boats, loading and unloading them efficiently, rowing and steering. Practice runs were made on the local canals, and anyone who threatened to capsize the boat or lose a paddle overboard received heated words of censure.

Operation Ascot, which came to be known as the 'Battle of the Canals', was launched on 14 November. The plan was for 152 Brigade to attack across the Noorder Canal, less than a mile from the lock gates where the canals intersected, and for 153 Brigade to attack across the Wessem Canal, some two miles from the lock gates. Meanwhile, 154 Brigade would stand by, ready to seize the lock gates, and then advance through 153 Brigade's bridgeheads to Heythuysen, six miles to the east.

In the approaching dusk, at 4 p.m., 153 Brigade set off, supported by Buffaloes carrying jeeps and anti-tank guns, flame-throwing Crocodiles and the ever-present Middlesex machine-gunners. The crossing by the 5/7th Gordons on the left was successful, no serious resistance was met and all objectives were secured, even though the Buffaloes were unable to make the crossing because of the steepness of the banks. The famous BBC broadcaster Chester Wilmot covered the whole event and sent back an impressive report.

The 1st Gordons' simultaneous crossing on the right flank was much more difficult. They suffered some forty casualties in the approach to the canal, a result of two long-range mortar bombs landing on B and C companies. Sergeant Herbert Harding, a Londoner but a proud Gordon Highlander, had a particularly fortunate escape:

> I was squatting on the side of the bank, pulling a boat back to reload it with more men. We were taking mortar fire but carried on getting the men across. All of a sudden there was a whoosh and a crump. A mortar shell had landed right between my legs. It was a dud and as I put my hand into the hole and felt it, I thanked my lucky stars.

The 5th Black Watch, following on the heels of the Gordons at 6 p.m., found the enemy resistance stiffening as the defensive fire concentrated on the crossing point. Crossing the canal in darkness and chaos, with the sound of shells getting nearer and Spandau fire sweeping the water, generated indescribable terror among the Allied troops. Men paddled madly with their rifle butts to escape this watery killing zone. Then, lying in the lee of the far bank, they received the dreaded 'prepare to advance' order. The men scrambled to the top of the bank, where a burst of Spandau fire tore into one of the platoons.

The advance continued across sodden fields and the Black Watch reached its objective – a wooded area that secured the road to Roggel – just before midnight. Company transport and supplies had arrived by 5 a.m., courtesy of the engineers, who had erected a bridge over the Wessem at incredible speed. The 5/7th Gordons occupied Ophoven and Brumholt, and the 1st Gordons, riding in Kangaroos, soon entered Roggel itself.

The 5th Camerons and 5th Seaforths' crossing of the
Noorder was greatly assisted by the support of Buffaloes that
ferried men and equipment swiftly across the canal. The
Camerons' advance was led by a piper playing continuously
in the leading vehicle. The operation was planned down to
the last detail and achieved all of its objectives in good time.

The Seaforths, attacking on a broad front on the right, had
more mixed fortunes. C Company crossed in Buffaloes in
record time, but A had insufficient boats and B found that its
stretch of the canal had been drained, leaving a waist-high
mud barrier. The company overcame this ingeniously, by
laying a walkway of boats from bank to bank. The enemy
offered no resistance, thirty-five prisoners were taken, and by
6 p.m. all three companies had taken their objectives to form
a thousand-yard-deep bridgehead. Next day, the battalion
advanced, again unopposed, towards the Zig Canal. The 2nd
Seaforths, in reserve, met no opposition as they crossed the
Noorder and moved into position to consolidate 152
Brigade's bridgehead.

With bridgeheads established over both canals, the 7th
Argylls now launched 154 Brigade's attack on the lock gates
at Nederweert. The weak resistance was soon overcome, but
a few casualties resulted from explosions of the Germans'
new anti-personnel mine – the Schu-mine. These were made
of wood to avoid detection and could be easily camouflaged.
Whenever one detonated, it tended to result in the loss of a
foot or leg. The corps engineers were standing by with a
ready-made bridge, carried on a Churchill tank, to place
across the canal. Within a few hours, tanks were speeding to
the front, ready to give support to the infantry.

While the Argylls consolidated to protect the lock gates,
the two Black Watch battalions of 154 Brigade crossed the

bridge and entered 153 Brigade's bridgehead. On the morning of 15 November, the 1st Black Watch advanced in Kangaroos to Leveroy, where the blocked road required clearing. Then the 7th Black Watch passed through with a squadron of tanks in support and made for the town of Heythuysen, which the enemy had evacuated, losing two tanks to mines on the way. Next day, the troops entered the town of Neer. Again the enemy had evacuated.

Now at its halfway stage, Operation Ascot was going well. Despite the rain, the wind, the cold and now the Schu-mines, all units had taken their objectives on time. In no small measure this was thanks to the support given in the canal crossings by the artillery barrage, the Crocodile flame-throwers, the Middlesex machine-gunners, the tanks and especially the Buffaloes. The newly trained, young German paratroopers sometimes put up strong resistance from their defensive positions at the crossing points, but they were reluctant to stand and fight when exposed in the open. Most of the Allied casualties were caused by shell and mortar fire and the already loathed Schu-mines.

The next major obstacle was the Uitwaterings, better known as the Zig Canal. This narrow, deep, steep-sided canal lay across the entire front and was assumed to be the enemy's main defensive line. The attack would be led by 152 Brigade on the left, where the Zig joins the Noorder, followed by 153 standing by ready to exploit the situation. The Camerons met little resistance as they advanced four miles from their bridgehead and formed up within a mile of the Zig. Patrols reported that there was enemy movement and small-arms fire coming from the junction of the two canals and that the bridge there was blown.

At first light on 17 November, a short but heavy barrage

pummelled the bridge area. Then C Company, led by Major Melville, went forward. At 7.50 a.m., the leading platoon dashed over the collapsed bridge and took up defensive positions. They were soon joined by the rest of the company.

The enemy quickly realised the threat that this bridgehead posed to their defences, and soon intense bazooka, shell and mortar fire rained down on C Company. The battalion committed its entire firepower in support of the bridgehead, and Major Mainwaring led over A Company to reinforce the defenders. The enemy bombardment persisted for two hours until, under cover of a thick smokescreen, a counter-attack was launched. The German infantry charged across open ground and closed on the bridgehead with great determination. The full weight of the Allies' field and medium artillery was brought to bear on the attackers by the forward observation officer, Major Douglas Tilly, and halted their advance. Under devastating fire the Germans displayed great courage and continued to attack. The two defending Cameron companies held their ground and the battle raged in full fury until 1 p.m., when the enemy finally withdrew.

During the night, the engineers constructed a temporary bridge to facilitate tank support so that the advance might continue. The new structure was named Cameron Bridge in honour of the battalion's achievement, and their gallantry was immediately recognised by the corps commander, General Sir Neil Ritchie. Other observers have described the action as the most courageous battle fought by the Camerons during the entire European campaign.

The second crossing of the Zig was to be made by 153 Brigade, which had been making steady forward progress since crossing the Wessem. The 1st Gordons had entered Roggel without any trouble on 16 November, riding on

Kangaroos, and the 5th Black Watch had then passed through to take up positions in a wooded area close to the Zig, where they were heavily shelled.

When it was realised that the Camerons were under serious threat, orders were given for 153 Brigade to make an immediate crossing of the Zig. It was hoped that this would serve as a diversion and relieve some of the pressure on the Camerons. At 2 p.m. on 17 November, Brigadier Sinclair ordered the 1st Gordons and the 5th Black Watch to prepare for a crossing as soon as possible after 5 p.m. Three hours' notice was totally inadequate to make the arrangements for a major attack. Much more time was needed to organise even a brief recce of the crossing point, devise a plan and liaise with the supporting arms. Moreover, men had to be fed and supplies replenished. The 1st Gordons' commanding officer, Lieutenant Colonel Cumming-Bruce, made his views known and then raised a further concern over officer casualties. He explained that the battalion had already lost all but two of its twelve platoon officers and that it was barely battle worthy. Sinclair replied that there was no alternative: the Camerons were pinned down, the situation was urgent. Nevertheless, Cumming-Bruce succeeded in postponing the Gordons' crossing time to 9 p.m., which at least allowed for a brief recce of the ground to be made and for the men to have a hot meal.

The Gordons crossed the Zig at two points on a six-hundred-yard front. Buffaloes could not be used as they were unable to negotiate the steep-sided banks, and the sodden ground prevented some of the supporting arms reaching their battle positions. Fortunately, though, there was little enemy resistance and the whole battalion got over without delay. By 11 p.m., they had occupied positions that brought relief to the Camerons' right flank. Very few casualties were suffered, which was taken to be a consequence of attacking on a broad front. By morning, the sappers had completed a second bridge over the canal.

On the right of the Gordons, crossing at the same time, the men of the 5th Black Watch were not so fortunate. They had suffered such heavy shelling in their marshalling area that they were reluctant to leave their slit trenches, even for a hot meal. They were also becoming far too familiar with the new hazard of the Schu-mine. Flail tanks were supposed to clear these mines and open a passage to the canal, but they got bogged down in the mud so the track had to be cleared much less efficiently by pioneers and engineers. The supporting arms vehicles also got bogged down, including the carriers transporting the assault boats, which then had to be man-handled over half a mile to the canal.

The prospect of yet another canal crossing worried the men. By now, they knew they would be helplessly exposed, unable to take cover and bunched closely together to make an inviting target. Their nerves were stretched to breaking point as they waited in silence before making their weary way to the boats in a state of deep despair. However, spirits started to rise as every stroke of the oars took them closer to the far bank. The voyage lasted just a couple of minutes before the men could jump ashore and hug the steep bank for protection against the shelling and gunfire. Once there, they answered a roll-call, rested and waited for the next order. They could barely see one another in the darkness, and were guided forward by a whisper from their corporal. The fence at the top of the bank barred the way into a field. The enemy had identified this as a likely target, and their Spandau teams fired on fixed lines along the top of the bank. Consequently, the Black Watch lost several men here.

Private Davie Reid experienced the terror of crossing the Zig:

The assault plan for crossing the Zig Canal included massive artillery, tank and heavy-machine-gun support. Unfortunately, the return of severe wet weather prevented all of this and we went ahead without most of the extra cover. As a result, the assault company was attacked before it even reached the canal and suffered several casualties. My company, A Company, followed but the enemy were well positioned on the far bank and directed deadly fire towards the crossing points, even though they were firing blind in the darkness. We reached the near bank and tried to take cover. As we lay there in the darkness, we could only hope that the sporadic bursts of Spandau fire would not land too close to us. Suddenly we felt the rip of a short burst of bullets around us and we hugged tighter to the ground. Immediately on my left, I heard a strange noise coming from my mate, Max Natskin. I stretched a hand towards him and felt him covered in blood. I could tell that he was mortally wounded.

As we moved down to the boats and crossed to the far bank, the enemy fire continued. A Spandau burst could come at any time and we were completely exposed and defenceless. We were filled with fear but something kept driving us on. All we could do was pray that we would be spared. Crossing that canal was one of our worst experiences.

Incredibly, our platoon reached the far bank without further casualties. We took cover below the rise and awaited further orders. Soon we were told to move up the bank and prepare to advance. At the top of the bank

there was a wire fence that had to be crossed. I crawled
under the fence but Bob Stoker, who was next to me,
climbed over it. At that moment there was a burst of
machine-gun fire and Bob was killed outright. It was a
tragedy. He was such a cheerful bloke and kept our spirits up. The same night we also lost our platoon sergeant
Reubens Cooper. He was always very friendly and kind.
He got his stripes the day before he was killed and came
round us all to show us them.

The two attacking companies pushed forward to their
objective some thousand yards ahead, while the two follow-
up companies positioned themselves on the flanks to give
all-round protection against counter-attacks.

Next, the 5/7th Gordons, having crossed the engineers'
bridge, pushed forward towards Helden to establish an
extended bridgehead. In the meantime, the Camerons had
advanced a thousand yards beyond the Zig Canal. They had
broken the hard core of the German force, albeit at considerable cost, and it was now thought that the enemy would
fight a rearguard action back to Venlo. The Highland
Division was finally well positioned to make a strong final
thrust.

Meanwhile, the two Seaforth battalions of 152 Brigade had
made remarkable progress. Starting with a trek of a mile
along a track that was knee deep in mud, the 2nd Battalion
led the way over Cameron Bridge in the early hours of 18
November. Then, in total darkness, the two battalions
advanced in single file, guided by compass bearings. The 2nd
headed due north, through the Cameron lines and along the
side of the Noorder Canal to Beringe. The 5th went north-
east across country to Zelen. Realising the dangers of men

losing contact in the dark, which would result in a battalion scattered around the countryside, it was decided to mark the way with white tape.

The trek across sodden fields churned up the mud but met no resistance, shelling or mines. After a night march of three miles in dreadful conditions, each battalion landed exactly on its objective and was digging in by 5 a.m. The enemy had been taken completely by surprise, a number of prisoners had been taken and by dawn a disorganised German retreat was taking place. Then, however, the Germans finally reacted and both battalions were subjected to intense shelling.

The 5th lost just two men during the course of the advance, but the 2nd fared much worse. A complete platoon was lost and taken prisoner, and heavy casualties were sustained during the shelling. As a result, the battalion was reduced from four rifle companies to three, and each company was cut from three to two platoons.

At this point, 152 Brigade's part in the battle ended. On 20 November the three battalions were withdrawn behind the front and given a chance to dry out and catch up on much-needed sleep.

Over the past three days, while the battle for the Zig Canal had been raging, 154 Brigade had been resting in Roggel and its surrounding villages. Now it was called forward to prepare for the final thrust. The 7th Black Watch, starting from Neer, followed the brigade axis, a roundabout route on very narrow roads thronged with traffic. Simply reaching the marshalling area was therefore an exhausting exercise. The roads and tracks were covered with mud that had been churned into a deep paste. The Military Police struggled to keep the traffic moving. Diversionary routes were little better and some wheeled vehicles got bogged down and had to await rescue.

After crossing the Zig, the battalion headed for Helden, which had been liberated by the 1st Black Watch. There the men changed from transport vehicles to Kangaroos in the expectation that the shelling would soon become heavy. Indeed, the shelling was intense as the advance continued, but there was little sign of enemy resistance. The tanks lagged behind the infantry as they got bogged down. Kangaroos were the only vehicles that could negotiate the sodden ground, even while towing an anti-tank gun.

On entering Onder, the Highlanders found that the Derbyshire Yeomanry, the division's reconnaissance unit, had already liberated the village. The Yeomanry played a vital role for the division. Their armoured cars would scout ahead of the infantry to locate and determine the strength of the enemy. In a crisis, they could rush to a weak spot and shore up the defences. Finally, they were tasked with gathering any information demanded by the planners.

The 7th Black Watch dug in around Onder and sent out patrols, who found no sign of the enemy in the vicinity. Casualties, however, resulted from intense and accurate German shelling and Schu-mines. Meanwhile, the 7th Argylls also came forward from reserve to advance on Panningen and protect the left flank of the attack.

The next day, 21 November, the 1st Black Watch under Lieutenant Colonel Hopwood passed through Onder in Kangaroos and advanced towards Baarlo. At every turn of the road, lethal SP guns halted their progress, but the threat of being outflanked by the Kangaroos and the battalion's excellent artillery support usually cleared the way. For forty-eight hours, the Highlanders battled against stiffening resistance under an unceasing deluge of shell and mortar fire. Advancing through some four miles of mud, further hampered by mines and the return of the rain, first the village of Soeterbeek, then Bong, and finally Baarlo were occupied. Considering the conditions, this advance was quite an achievement.

As the 1st Black Watch advanced on Baarlo, 153 Brigade was also on the move. After crossing the Zig, while 154 Brigade was heading towards Helden, the 1st Gordons and the 5th Black Watch were withdrawn to Roggel to dry out and recuperate. During their forty-eight-hour rest, the Balmoral concert party arrived to give a performance in a gigantic barn. In the meantime, the 5/7th Gordons had first moved towards the Maas to occupy Kesseleik, then had followed the retreating enemy to Kessel, three miles south-west of Baarlo. Next, the 1st Gordons and 5th Black Watch moved from Roggel to occupy both Kesseleik and Kessel and give the 5/7th a well-deserved rest. Both battalions suffered such intense shelling from across the Maas that they were pinned in their trenches.

The Highland Division's involvement in Operation Ascot ended with the liberation of Baarlo and Kessel. This left just a small enemy bridgehead west of the Maas, opposite Venlo. The task of clearing this pocket fell to the 15th Scottish and the 49th divisions.

Ascot had been a miserable experience for everyone, mainly on account of the weather. It had been plagued by continuous rain that saturated the men's uniforms and depressed their spirits. The ground was perpetually sodden, vehicles were bogged down in a sea of mud and Schu-mines slowed progress. And none of those who survived ever forgot the terror that accompanied the dreaded crossing of the canals. While the enemy showed little appetite to stand and fight, their shelling and mortaring had been relentlessly intense and deadly accurate.

The two operations to liberate southern Holland tested the men of the Highland Division to the limit. But their morale was always boosted whenever there was contact with the long-suffering local population, who unfailingly greeted their liberators with open arms. In total, the Highlanders liberated twelve Dutch towns in just three weeks, and they forged many lifelong friendships along the way.

# 7

# Back to the Front

My tortuous journey back to the 5th Black Watch meant that I missed all of the horrors of Operations Colin and Ascot. After Louvain, I travelled to yet another transit camp at Leopoldsburg, just ten miles from the Dutch–Belgian border, where I was accommodated on a straw-filled mattress in a large church hall. The weather was still changeable, so it was a relief to be billeted in a building rather than a tent for the first time since arriving in Europe. Our quarters were in the town centre and there were some facilities for the troops. The army had commandeered one of the local cinemas and it showed a fair selection of films, although many of them were in French. The town had suffered little damage, so the bars and cafés were also open. The townsfolk were overjoyed to be liberated and we received a warm welcome wherever we went. Some families even invited us into their homes, and happily shared the little food they had. It was a novelty to walk around the town, seeing shops that were open to customers and life beginning to return to normal.

However, with so many crammed into the church hall, it was difficult to form friendships. You would talk to a chap and then never see him again. We were like strangers to one another and soldiers do like to have a mate. So I spent many evenings on my own in the cinema before going on to a bar that was always busy. The bar's owner soon treated me as a regular, and his daughter would come and sit beside me while I drank my lemonade. I was much younger than all of the other customers, and I think she looked upon me as a little brother. Maybe she could also sense that I was lonely. I talked with her in my schoolboy French and she would joke and laugh, which made me feel good. I had not spoken with a girl for months, so I found her kindness and company most comforting and a reminder of life back home. When the time came to leave Leopoldsburg, I made a special trip to the bar to say goodbye to her.

Next I was sent to Roosendaal, in Holland, with a number of Highland Division comrades. We were all anxious to share any information we had and find out what was happening to the division. Most of us were very out of touch, but some knew about the attack on Le Havre and the extended rest period that followed. A few were aware of the division's drive into Holland, and one young Gordon had even been involved in the fighting. He had been wounded in Schijndel on his first day in action and was vague on the details, but he did know that the division was pushing west to link up with the Canadians. This kindled a longing in our little group to rejoin the division, although we each had our own thoughts and fears about going back into battle. We were all thoroughly sick and tired of being incarcerated for weeks in transit camps, passed from one camp to another, suffering trying conditions and loneliness, lacking comradeship. The army taught you to accept the inevitable, but accepting this stretched my forbearance to the limit.

(Some forty years later, at a 5th Black Watch reunion, I finally learned the secret of how to escape the misery of the transit camps. Bill Chisholm, who had been my platoon officer at Perth, told me that he and Major Brodie had simply walked out of their convalescence depot, found an army motorbike, filled it with petrol, and were back with the battalion in three days, rather than eight weeks. En route, they enjoyed the hospitality of any officers' mess they happened to be passing. However, their triumph over the system could have had very serious consequences, as they were branded deserters for leaving the depot without permission. Fortunately, the charges were dropped once they rejoined the battalion.)

Roosendaal had not long been liberated, and the town had suffered some damage. However, repair work was already under way on the buildings and there was not even any rubble as the locals had swept clean all of the streets. Some of the shops were back in business and housewives queued for the meagre rations, which they shared among themselves. I recalled being told at school that the Dutch were the hardest-working and cleanest people in Europe – and this town seemed to prove the point. One Sunday morning, I walked into Roosendaal in glorious autumn sunshine. I passed many families who were all beautifully dressed in clothes that I guessed had not been worn throughout the dark days of occupation. It seemed that they were going to church to give thanks for their safe deliverance from the Nazis. Most impressive of all was a young girl, aged about five, who was wearing a magnificent fur coat.

While I was enjoying the relative luxury of Roosendaal, the

fighting Highlanders were still suffering the trauma of canal crossings under heavy German fire. There was quite a contrast between the bunk beds of a dry barrack room and a slit trench half full of water. While we heard guns in the far distance, they cowered under relentless shell and mortar bombardments.

The truck that finally carried me out of Roosendaal was full of Highlanders. We were also fully kitted out for the first time, with rifles and haversack rations. This, and the increasing volume of artillery fire, told us we were heading for the front. After several hours we passed through Eindhoven, which was heavily congested with traffic. An hour later we stopped in a queue waiting to cross the Nijmegen Bridge, which was under heavy German bombardment. When our turn came, we were told to get over the bridge as fast as possible. We were on the road to Arnhem, where the 1st Airborne Division had battled gallantly to hold the bridge that allowed entry into Germany. Tragically, it had taken the ground troops three days to reach the paratroopers, turning a potentially glorious triumph into a costly disaster.

North of Nijmegen, the weather grew more gloomy as we approached the front. We passed through artillery lines where large, small and medium guns pointed at the enemy, but they were all silent. Soon we were heading west, through a partially flooded region on roads that had been built above field level. This area lay north of the Maas, south of the Neder Rhine, and stretched all the way to the coast. The 101st American Airborne Division had occupied it after the Arnhem offensive, and it was now defended by the Highland Division against German patrols infiltrating across the Rhine.

Before long, the truck stopped and the driver shouted for all those returning to the 1st Gordons to climb out. A few miles later, several 5/7th Gordons arrived at their battalion headquarters. That left just seven 5th Black Watch boys in the truck. When we arrived at our battalion HQ, we disembarked to see Adjutant Captain MacIntyre standing on the veranda of a large villa. We lined up in front of him and he gave us a brief welcome. Then he asked each of us for our company and sent us on our different ways. He didn't even bother to make a note of our names, which seemed strange. I was the only one from A Company. MacIntyre pointed and said, 'One mile up that road, past D Company farm.'

A heavy, damp mist hung over the ground, reducing visibility to a hundred yards. The road stretched ahead into a grey emptiness. Weighed down by my full kit and rifle, I walked along alone and in silence, save for the lowing of a single stranded cow on a grassy bank. There was no birdsong, which was scarcely surprising as there were practically no trees in this dismal landscape. It was most eerie, and I wondered if I was heading in the right direction or wandering straight into the German lines. So it was with great relief that I saw a farm ahead. Good, that must be D Company, I thought, but when I approached there was no sign of life. I walked past, now sure that I must have taken a wrong turn, when a voice shouted, 'Where are you going?' Two sentries then emerged cautiously from behind the barn door. I asked, 'Where's D Company?' and was told they were all inside the barn, resting. They confirmed that A Company was less than a mile up the road in Opheusden and added that everything was quiet.

I was about to press on when we heard an engine, and out of the mist appeared a jeep travelling at full speed from the front. As it passed, I caught a glimpse of Captain Fry, the intelligence officer, hanging on the side. Two stretcher cases were fixed to the jeep's frame. Later, when I was within sight of A Company's lines, another jeep carrying another two casualties came flying past.

There was no one to be seen as I entered the village, but when I passed the first house I saw Lance Corporal Campbell standing like a statue in the living room. Campbell was a hero – slightly older than me, fat, cumbersome and quiet, but steady as a rock. Having led one of 7 Platoon's sections through many battles, he was highly respected by the men and highly regarded by his superiors. He refused any promotion but certainly deserved a medal.

The first person I met when I entered A Company's house was my great friend Alex Corris. I had never seen him look so bad. He was shaking and blurted out, 'God, am I glad to see you, Tommy. It's been a hell of a day. It could have been George and me.' After a moment or two, he managed to explain what had happened during a truly disastrous day:

This morning the officers went out on a recce with the plan of moving the company some four hundred yards further forward. There had been no enemy activity, so the three of them went without any guards. Suddenly, without warning, they ran into a strong German patrol. Major Smith-Cunningham was taken prisoner. Captain Johnstone escaped with Lieutenant Scott, who was wounded. Those two raced back here and told us to withdraw, and chaos and confusion followed. Then our sergeant, Bob Fowler, took charge and ordered everyone into their defensive positions. Thankfully the Jerries didn't come because the company was still in crisis. We now had only one officer instead of five, so the sergeants were in charge of their platoons. Captain Fry arrived mainly to reassure us. He explained that the Germans were on the other side of the Rhine and that there was no danger of a strong enemy attack. He told us we should stay on the alert, but that we were merely holding the front. Perhaps his reassurance made us relax too much.

It was not only the capture of our commanding officer that had upset Alex. In the back garden of one of the platoon houses lay the body of an American 101st Airborne paratrooper. One of our lads, against strict orders, went to rifle through the body for valuables. Alex condemned this act of sacrilege, but added that the lad was a recent reinforcement and did not know the infantryman's code of conduct. Then he continued:

Next thing we knew, he went up on a Schu-mine and was writhing in agony. His pal rushed into the garden to help him and he went up on a Schu-mine as well. I rushed with my pal George Kiernan to fetch our stretcher, but the other two stretcher-bearers beat us to it. They got to the door first but had barely stepped into the garden when both of them went up on Schu-mines, too. It was bloody awful. When we arrived, the four of them were rolling around in agony with serious leg injuries. It was terrible to hear their cries for help. The sergeant major ordered George and me to go into the garden and rescue them. We told him it was obviously a minefield and refused. We would have become casualties too. Then Corporal Christison came forward and took out his bayonet. He prodded his way forward to clear a path to the wounded men. It took some guts.

Once the pathway into the garden had been cleared, Alex and George went in with their stretcher and helped recover the casualties. Alex said that rescuing them was one of his most frightening experiences of the war. He was petrified every time he took a step forward, wondering if it would be his last. He was still shaking as he said, 'Tommy, if George and I had been seconds quicker, I would have lost my leg.'

I think at least part of Alex's distress was due to a build up of pressure. On the battlefield, stretcher-bearers do vital work that requires considerable courage, strength of character and a dedication to help others. They have to save others' lives while putting themselves in great danger. Alex had volunteered for the job, and I know it gave him a huge amount of personal satisfaction.

Corporal Christison was subsequently awarded the Military Medal for his bravery. Tragically, he died during our assault across the Rhine.

Once Alex had finished relating the events of the day, he filled me in on what had happened to some of our friends and how the battalion had fared during the fighting in Holland. After a hot meal, I was sent to 7 Platoon headquarters, in a house that covered all approaches to the village crossroads. I looked around for familiar faces but saw none. Ken Bidwell and Tommy Layton had been badly injured, while Dennis Westcott and Stan Suskins were walking wounded. Company Sergeant Major Latto had been killed near Haaren, and the platoon commanders were casualties. All of our reinforcements looked young and seemed rather ill disciplined. Bob Fowler went to check on the other two sections and came back with orders for the night's watch. Everyone was given a two-hour stint on duty in the sandbagged stand-to outside. Then, in his clear, authoritative voice, he said to me, 'You've been travelling all day. You get a good night's sleep.'

Bob was a former Fife miner who had been called up in 1939 and had survived the Battle of France in 1940. I was most impressed with the way he managed a platoon of young, inexperienced boys who were probably not even fully trained. You could see that he was already moulding them into a decent fighting force. Ultimately, these youngsters would fight the crucial battles that lay ahead and finally win the war for the Allies. But the hard core of senior NCOs like Bob held the battalion together and continued to fight in the best tradition of the Highland Division. I was proud to serve under him and to be part of the fraternity of our Highland regiments.

I was glad to be back, even though I was surrounded by unfamiliar faces. The company had just suffered a disastrous day, and I knew things were sure to get worse, so why was I so keen to return to my unit? I believe this homing instinct might have had something to do with regimental tradition, the desire for comradeship or possibly just a latent sense of personal pride. Whichever it was, I curled up in a corner, wrapped myself in my greatcoat, and settled down for a good night's sleep.

One crucial victory in the autumn campaign had been achieved at Antwerp, where the harbour facilities were in good order. Huge shipments of men, tanks, ammunition and supplies were already passing through the port for the final push on Germany. However, the debacle at Arnhem had dashed any hope of an early finish to the war, so by the time I arrived in Holland, it was clear that we would have to fight into the very heart of the Reich. That winter of 1944 was freezing and the Dutch people suffered terribly. Many were still trapped under German occupation and had to endure a terrible famine.

Moreover, as we contemplated a grim invasion of Germany and enjoyed the hospitality of the Dutch families who sheltered us, Hitler decided that the best form of defence was attack. He hoped to recreate the success of 1940 by launching a new blitzkrieg through the frozen and heavily wooded Ardennes. His aim was to smash through the Americans who currently occupied the area, split the Allied armies and retake the vital port of Antwerp. Then he planned to encircle four Allied armies and negotiate a peace that would allow him to concentrate on the Eastern Front, where the Russians were storming forward. It was an audacious and desperate gamble.

Hitler assigned Field Marshal von Rundstedt to implement what he dubbed Operation Watch on the Rhine. Five hundred thousand Germans, spearheaded by the Sixth SS-Panzer Army, took the Americans by surprise on 16 December. What followed became known as the Battle of the Bulge – a bloody conflict in which the Americans lost nineteen thousand troops. The US 101st Airborne famously held out under siege in the road hub of Bastogne while the Germans wreaked havoc behind the lines by infiltrating English-speaking commandos disguised as GIs. The battle was fought in sub-zero temperatures with the utmost brutality, such as the SS's massacre of eighty-four American prisoners at Malmedy. With the Americans reeling, the Highland Division mobilised and moved south to help push back the Germans. During the bitter fighting that followed, we endured the coldest, most miserable conditions imaginable.

George Sands was struck by the freezing conditions too:

The next two days were spent carrying out familiar routines, indicating an impending battle. We were faced with Arctic conditions. Snow covered the ground, and the roads were ice bound. Tanks and carriers slithered across roads and often into ditches, and their tracks had to be fitted with special shoes to keep them mobile. Anyone who experienced these conditions will tell you that they have never felt so cold.

The Highland Division took over the front-line positions from the Welsh Division on 9 January, with 153 Brigade on the right and 154 Brigade on the left. The 1st Gordons immediately attacked across country towards Hodister, marching uphill for an hour in deep snow. They suffered heavy shelling when they reached their farm objective, and Captain Brown, their medical officer, was killed.

Meanwhile, Private Stanley Whitehouse, of the 1st Black Watch, recalled:

Moving into the line and taking over from the Welsh Division was physically exhausting. We had to walk up to Waharday, high on a bald hill, dragging our food and ammo with us. It was so slippery we could barely move. Our bodies were chilled right through and our limbs had lost all feeling. We occupied a farm building on the highest point of the hill. Only two men with the anti-tank PIAT and two with a Bren were allowed outside on guard, and it was so cold they had to be relieved every twenty minutes.

The 5/7th Gordons then passed through to take Hodister unopposed.

Meanwhile, the 5th Black Watch continued the advance westwards in calf-deep snow. We marched across undulating moorland on the right flank, the bleak landscape firmly buried under a shroud of white. The sun shone brightly in a clear blue sky and there was no wind. It was hard going, but at least the exertion kept us warm. After several miles we thought we must have lost our way, but then we suddenly arrived at our objective above the village of Warizy. By now, the sun's rays had faded and it was getting colder. We deployed in defensive positions and dug a snow trench. Almost unbelievably, a Weasel carrier then appeared with a hot meal.

During the night, when we were all frozen stiff, Bob Fowler came round and chose five of us for one of the dreaded night patrols. He said there was a farmstead less than a mile ahead, and we were to check if it was occupied. We had no difficulty finding the farm in the moonlight, and as we crept closer there was no sign of life. The wind was now bitterly cold, so we headed straight for the barn and some shelter. On entering, I heard a snort, then another. Once my eyes had adjusted to the darkness, I was just able to make out two oxen. As we approached them, we were amazed how much heat they were generating, and it was a comfort just to stand near them for a few minutes. Then we heard German voices in the farmhouse. That was our signal to leave. We slipped quietly back to our positions – mission complete.

In the morning, we moved down to billets in Warizy itself, where we bided our time for twenty-four hours. The plan was for 152 Brigade to continue the advance southwards, covering the right flank; 154 Brigade would capture La Roche and push forward; and 153 Brigade would advance on the left flank, east of the Ourthe valley. All three brigades would

attack simultaneously, as time was of the essence. The aim
was to cut the enemy's main escape route and then link up
with American troops driving north, thus preventing the
retreat of the front-line German forces.

The cold was still fearful. And sometimes lethal, as
Sergeant Jeff Hayward, who was serving with the 7th
Middlesex, discovered:

> As we travelled from Hotton towards La Roche, we
> found a shelter for our night stop. A scout car of the
> Derbyshire Yeomanry drove up beside our carrier and
> we shared a warm companionship with them. We dug
> our snow trenches and settled down with our blankets
> for some sleep. The Derbyshire crew decided to sleep in
> their car. Next morning, there was no sign of activity
> from the Derbyshires, and when we went to investigate
> we found that the crew had frozen to death. Overnight,
> our carrier tracks froze into the ground and we had to
> burn them with petrol to thaw them out. We also had to
> use anti-freeze on our water-cooled Vickers to keep the
> machine-guns in action.

The following morning, the 1st Black Watch passed through
Warizy to join the Derbyshires, who were moving unopposed
down the main road from Hotton to La Roche. The
Derbyshires entered the town first, but lost three of their
scout cars on mines. Then, as soon as the Black Watch
arrived, the Germans launched an intense and accurate
artillery barrage on the town. Nevertheless, 154 Brigade succeeded in liberating La Roche in good time, and then sent the
7th Black Watch on towards Hives and Lavaux. The road out
of La Roche twisted through a forest up the side of a hill,

with a steep slope on the right and a sheer drop on the left. Thick ice and hidden mines made the road nearly impassible for the supporting tanks, whose crews were fearful of sliding into the ravine.

Sergeant Ken Tout, of the Northamptonshire Yeomanry, was there: 'If it was difficult to control the Shermans going uphill, coming down was impossible. The machines took over, chose their own route, their own speed, their own destiny. Drivers hung on to the controls and hoped for survival.'

Felled trees and enemy machine-gun nests also slowed the advance. And when the leading company finally reached open ground, SP guns drove it back. So it was dark by the time the 7th Black Watch reached the township of Hives. After some confused fighting, they succeeded in rounding up over forty Panzer Grenadiers. The battalion transport arrived a little later, but this precipitated such heavy shelling and casualties that the attack on Lavaux was postponed for the night.

The following morning, the 7th Argylls passed through Hives and continued 154 Brigade's advance. But the Germans knocked out the leading Northamptonshire Yeomanry tank during the march to Lavaux, and then Panther tanks pinned down the leading company with deadly fire. Major Peter Samwell MC, the Argylls' much-respected company commander, died in this exchange. Private Jenkins recorded the terrible event: 'he made for the telephone link at the rear of one of the tanks. There was a blinding flash as the Sherman was hit and the major fell in a hail of metal fragments.' As daylight faded, the Argylls made a flanking movement to gain entry to Lavaux, and heavy fighting followed until the Panthers withdrew.

But the Highlanders had not finished yet. Silhouetted

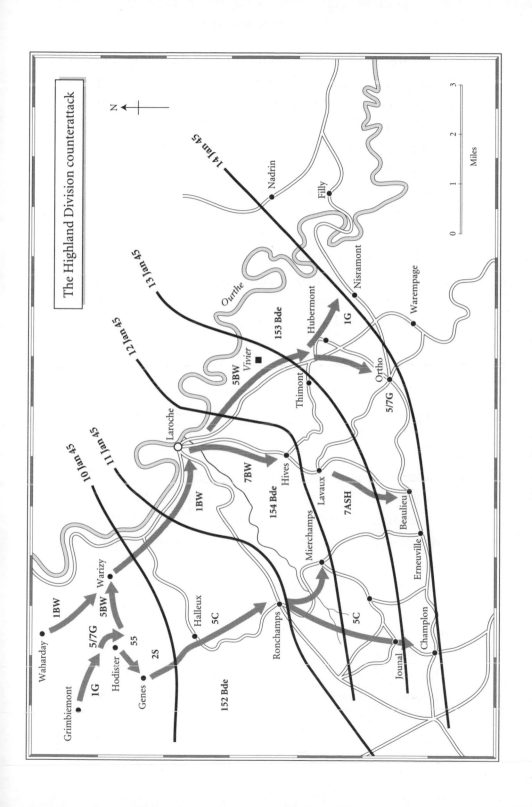

The Highland Division counterattack

Miles
0 1 2 3

N

Waharday
Grimbiemont
1BW
1G
5/7G
Hodister
55
Genes
2S
5BW
Warizy
1BW
Halleux
5C

152 Bde

10 Jan 45
11 Jan 45
12 Jan 45
13 Jan 45
14 Jan 45

Ourthe

Laroche

1BW
7BW
Hives
Mierchamps
Lavaux
7ASH

154 Bde

Ronchamps
5C
Joinal
Champlon
Erneuville
Beaulieu
5C

5BW *Vivier*
Thimont
153 Bde
Hubermont
1G
5/7G
Ortho

Nadrin
Filly
Nisramont
Warempage

against the snow-white background, they continued to advance throughout the bitterly cold night. Again German tanks and SP guns threatened their progress, but the Jocks never faltered. They had taken Beaulieu by 2 a.m., and then repulsed counter-attacks by two Panthers. The freezing cold and the fierce resistance made this an exceptionally tough advance, yet the Argylls suffered only thirty-eight casualties, due, in part, to inspired leadership from their remaining commanders.

Corporal John McCormack was one of very few men to count the weather as a blessing that night: 'The bitter cold of the Ardennes saved my life. As I approached Lavaux, I felt myself getting weaker and weaker. Only then did I realise I had been hit in the body by shrapnel. The cold congealed the bleeding and prevented serious blood loss. When I got back to the warmth of the regimental aid post, I collapsed.'

Next, it was the turn of the 5th Black Watch. On 12 January, troop carriers transported us towards La Roche, and we disembarked to march the last few miles. It was mid-morning, there was fresh snow on the ground, but once again the skies were blue and the sun was shining. We heard the sound of distant gunfire but did not suffer any shelling. Bob Fowler was still in command of the platoon because of the ambush of our officers seven weeks earlier. He ordered us to march in staggered sections – he always did things the correct way. As we neared the town, the skies began to fill with clouds and it started to snow. The snowflakes were the largest I had ever seen.

One member of my section, a wiry Lancastrian called Milligan, was carrying the bombs for our PIAT anti-tank gun. He kept falling behind and I had to tell him to keep up. We entered La Roche from the high ground, the road bounded on our right by cliffs. It was dominated by a ruined medieval castle, but now the town itself was in ruins, too. It was a miracle that only 114 civilians had died in the fighting. All the buildings had been razed to the ground, with just a few chimney stacks sticking out of the rubble. It was in a worse state than any other town I had seen, save for Caen, and could certainly no longer lay claim to being the 'Jewel of the Ardennes'.

The Royal Engineers were working in the town centre, trying to clear the rubble and open the road. The snow was now coming down hard and settling on the ground. Our morale slipped further when we saw three Derbyshire Yeomen walking towards us – the two on either side leading the one in the centre, a bloodstained bandage wrapped around his head. Thereafter, we came across more Derbyshire casualties as we marched towards our start line.

We left La Roche and continued uphill into the forest. It was now about 2 p.m., the sky was heavy with clouds, the snow was still falling, and we were really starting to feel the cold. A few shells were also heading in our direction. After a mile and a half, the leading section reached open ground and started to make its way to the Ferme du Vivier when an enemy tank opened fire. One man, Alexander Close, was killed and others were wounded, but the section managed to withdraw. The whole company was deployed in defensive positions and told to dig in. However, the ground was frozen solid, so we had to lie down in the snow among the trees, seeking whatever cover we could find.

Before long, my platoon was mortar bombed. Lacking even the rudimentary protection of slit trenches, several men were hit, including Stan Suskins – for the third time. Meanwhile, our artillery shelled the farm building. An attack was mounted but the odds were against us – A Company against enemy armour – and we failed to capture the farm. That night we launched a further attack and this time encountered no resistance. We arrived just in time to hear the enemy tanks pulling out.

Later we learned that this was one of the coldest nights during the coldest winter for forty years. We did not have our greatcoats, only oil-skin capes, which kept us dry but not warm. Furthermore, we had no rest for over twenty hours, and the exhaustion made us feel even colder. Our bodies were chilled to the bone and we began to lose all feeling in our arms and legs. Our hands were completely numb but our rifles were little use anyway, as the bolts had frozen solid. However, when the cold seemed to be at its worst and we felt as if we had reached the limits of our endurance, we were rescued by Bob Fowler. Like a big St Bernard, he appeared with a mug of rum and dished out two large spoonfuls to everyone in the section. It had some effect as I felt its warmth slipping down my throat, although I still could not feel my hands.

By now, the forward platoons had reached a crossroads where there was a row of cottages, one of them a café. After a skirmish and an exchange of fire, we drove out the Germans, who withdrew without sustaining any casualties. It was nearly dawn, we were crouching in a ditch, but I was so tired that I fell asleep in that position for twenty minutes. I was lucky someone woke me. A few more minutes immobile in that intense cold, and hypothermia might have set in.

A Company occupied the crossroads and Major Mathew, our company commander, deployed the three platoons in defensive positions. I was fortunate to be a member of the platoon that was sent into the cottages, while the others remained in the open. Day broke with clear skies and the sun shining brightly. We had come through one of the worst nights of the campaign, mainly because of the extreme cold and our utter exhaustion. Inside the cottages, we started to relax and lay down to rest.

Then, suddenly, we heard what seemed to be tanks heading towards us. We checked our rifles to find that the bolts were still frozen. Even more alarmingly, the Bren gun would not cock. Our morale was low and we started to panic. Nevertheless, when Major Mathew ordered us to get into our defensive positions we did as we were told and manned our positions by the windows. Soon we saw that the German vehicle was not a tank but a large half-track loaded with SS troops. They approached the crossroads with all guns firing but had to pass one of our platoons, which had been able to find some cover. Private Ron Grieve lay at the side of the road with the PIAT gun, ready for action. He was a hero, firing as the half-track hurtled towards him. He even managed to score a direct hit, but the vehicle continued at speed. Next it passed 8 Platoon, who were deployed on open ground, devoid of any cover. The half-track's machine-guns raked the platoon, who returned fire as best they could. Several of our comrades were hit, and one of them died on the way back to the aid post. Although one of the Germans fell off the half-track and was killed, the vehicle sped off into the distance and back to enemy lines.

The next day, we moved on towards Hubermont. As we approached the village, a recce party from the 1st Gordons, including their commanding officer and most of the company commanders, drove past. Hubermont was to be the start line of the Gordons' attack on Nisramont, a thousand yards across the valley. Once they arrived at the north of the village, they saw several German half-tracks, which they assumed had been abandoned. However, as they surveyed their objective, one of the half-tracks suddenly started up and drove past the officers' position. It was carrying ten SS troops. The two sides exchanged fire, three Germans fell to the ground, and the vehicle fled towards Nisramont. Then a second, similarly loaded half-track followed. The Gordon officers barricaded themselves in a house until they were sure that all of the Germans had gone.

A little while later, the 1st Gordons assembled in the north of the village for their attack. However, intense shelling resulted in a dozen casualties in the leading company and knocked out three support tanks. Major Napier, of 153 Brigade, witnessed the carnage: 'I went forward towards Hubermont to see how things were going. We were talking to the commander of a Sherman when it received a direct hit from a Panther at Nisramont. Unscathed, I helped to evacuate the wounded. Next thing I knew, two more Shermans were knocked out.'

The 1st Gordons' commanders postponed the attack on Nisramont until later that night, which proved a very wise decision. As the troops crept across the valley under the cover of darkness, they heard the clanking of tracks and realised that the enemy – nine tanks and two hundred men – were pulling out. They took the village without having to fire a shot.

Next, the 5/7th Gordons arrived at their start line for an attack on the village of Ortho. But a calamity had marred their journey to the front line. En route to La Roche in trucks, the convoy had halted to let some tanks pass through. German observers spotted the sitting ducks and called down a huge artillery bombardment. A Company alone suffered twenty-two casualties. Gordon Highlander John Tough was in the thick of it:

> The trucks were bumper to bumper but we did not think much about it at the time. All of a sudden, enemy shells fell out of the sky. I do not know how many trucks were hit, but a shell landed in a Bren-gun carrier full of ammunition. There were immense explosions and fire spread to several trucks. We all took refuge uphill. A tank commander pushed the carrier over the ridge into the valley.

The surviving Gordons, including Private Keith Kerr, then continued on their way as best they could:

> When our truck went on fire we had to walk into La Roche, where we spent the night. We each got a blanket, but there was nowhere to sleep. I spent the night under the canopy of a bus station. I took off my boots and next morning they were frozen solid. I was lucky to get them on, because they were size 11 and I took size 8, which allowed me to wear four pairs of socks.

Later that morning, the Highlanders stumbled upon a priest and a young girl searching for milk. The incongruous couple said that 180 civilians were sheltering from the bombardment in the cellar of a nearby hotel and were afraid to come out.

The 5/7th Gordons then advanced to take Ortho. They deployed in neighbouring woods and sent out a recce party, who took four prisoners and reported that the village was deserted. But the officers remained cautious, so the Gordons took up defensive positions around the village until they were sure that the Germans had fled.

As he gingerly entered Ortho the next morning, Private Bill Robertson came across a macabre scene:

> We could see a disabled half-track on the road just beyond the village. We spent the night in a nearby field, chilled to the bone. Next morning I went to look at the half-track and found a most incredible sight – eight Waffen-SS troopers sitting as if they were still alive. They were not wounded in any way and the vehicle was undamaged. We concluded that they had been killed from the blast of a Typhoon rocket. Each man looked a seasoned veteran, over six feet, muscular, and each carried a signed photograph of Adolf Hitler. The sight still haunts my memory.

By now, 152 Brigade was well ahead. It had taken over Hodister from the 5/7th Gordons early on 11 January. Then the 5th Seaforths, led by a troop of the Derbyshire Yeomanry, advanced towards Gênes, with tanks from the 33rd Armoured Brigade in support. However, the Derbyshires soon ran into mines buried in the snow. Trooper Denis Stanton was lucky to survive:

> I was driving the leading Humber, commanded by Sergeant Gray. After about a mile, we halted as we approached some ominous-looking farm buildings. Sergeant Gray did a foot recce and came back with a prisoner who said that Gênes was clear. We continued our advance but after about twenty yards our car went up on a mine, killing our gunner–wireless operator and injuring Sergeant Hubeny, who were standing close by.

The road ahead was heavily mined, too, which forced the infantry and tanks to advance across country. The 5th Seaforths took Gênes without opposition and found cover from the inevitable shelling, but Trooper Stanton was not so lucky: 'We took over Hubeny's Daimler and pushed on towards Halleux, but then we went up on another mine.'

The 2nd Seaforths continued the advance towards Halleux, some four miles ahead. Again, there was no sign of the enemy and the village was taken by noon, although there were some shelling casualties. By now, all the indications in this region were pointing to a well-planned enemy retreat.

That afternoon, the Cameron Highlanders set off from Halleux, but a blown bridge halted the tanks, so the infantry pushed on unsupported. At 9.30 p.m., they entered Ronchamps, which was lightly held, and captured seven 2nd Panzer Division Grenadiers. The next day, the German shelling on Ronchamps was intense, and the Camerons suffered twenty-eight casualties.

Meanwhile, the nearby settlement of Ronchampay was a possible threat to the advance and needed to be cleared. Two companies of 2nd Seaforths were sent in, captured the settlement and took several 116th Panzer Division prisoners. Again, intense shelling followed. One anonymous Seaforth Highlander remembered it well:

We captured Ronchampay at 0300 hours on 12 January without opposition, and our section was positioned in a house. When dawn came, it brought the start of shelling which lasted for two days, causing casualties and damage. One shell destroyed our Bren-gun post, one destroyed the wood shed and another whizzed past one of our lads standing in the doorway. He was near to shock when he told us and we did not believe it until we saw the hole in the wall opposite and found the unexploded shell in the pigsty. It was incredible that he was unhurt because it was a large 210mm shell. Later, he joked about it, saying it had given him a 'close shave'.

A thousand yards across the Bronce valley lay Mièrchamps, which the Germans were defending in strength, so any assault on it would be perilous. The wood five hundred yards west of the Mièrchamps road gave excellent cover right down to the river, but reaching it meant moving five hundred yards across the snow in full view of the enemy. The 5th Seaforths left their safe positions in Ronchamps at 2.30 p.m. under the umbrella of a massive artillery barrage on the enemy positions. Moving across the open ground towards the wood was a nightmare of mental anguish, with the troops fully expecting the shelling to begin at any moment and longing for the refuge of the wood. Not a single shell landed among them, and they continued to escape detection as they made their way through the wood to the river, where they discovered that the bridge had been blown. With the tanks unable to go any further, the infantry waited for nightfall, when they would press on unsupported.

Almost as soon as the assault recommenced, John Gibson had a lucky escape:

As we reached the River Bronce, we heard the whine of mortars and we all made a dash to get across at the same time. The ice broke and we found ourselves waist deep in freezing water. We managed to scramble out, by which time our trousers had frozen hard. Before we reached Mièrchamps, we were suffering agonies from the chafing of our frozen clothing. We had to carry on clearing the houses. We found a warm stove and mercifully got ourselves dried out.

The Seaforths took the Germans completely by surprise, and few of them were prepared to resist. Most were gathered around stoves, in the misguided belief that their position was secure. The battalion consolidated defensively and prayed that their tanks would arrive before the Germans could send in reinforcements. Fortunately, they did.

In the morning, a fighting patrol of platoon strength, supported by a troop of tanks, travelled three miles south to investigate Erneuville. The Germans allowed the patrol to get well into the village before opening fire. However, the British tanks then attacked the defenders with all guns blazing, which allowed all but three of the platoon to withdraw. John Gibson was one of the three who were left behind:

When the enemy opened fire, the platoon was pinned down, but my Bren-gun group managed to get into a house. The tanks charged the defenders. We went upstairs to see what was happening. Then all hell broke loose. When we came down and looked outside, we found that the platoon and the tanks had gone and we were surrounded. We kept hidden till nightfall, then the Germans all moved down to the other end of the village. We took our chance to creep out one by one and headed back to the battalion. We were able to tell the company commander details about the German positions and we were given a double rum ration to reward our initiative.

Later, the 1st Black Watch took Erneuville, which was protecting a German escape route. Meanwhile, a scout patrol of the 5th Camerons captured the village of Champlon, three miles to the west and on the same escape route. It was here that a force of the US Third Army, advancing from the south, finally met up with the Camerons. This meant that all of the German escape routes were now closed. Several isolated enemy posts remained scattered behind our lines, but most were anxious to surrender. The vast majority of these Germans were exhausted, starving and suffering from frostbite.

Sergeant Les Toogood, of the Camerons, was present at the historic meeting with the Americans:

On the 13th, I took a small patrol towards Champlon. We found no enemy in the area but did not enter the village. We heard vehicles approaching and took cover. Two German half-tracks carrying troops stopped at Champlon. Next morning, we patrolled into the village and found the enemy had departed. We then spotted a section of infantry working its way towards the village from the south and were relieved when they turned out to be American. It was the first link-up to cut the escape routes and was well reported by the media.

This marked the end of the Highland Division's involvement in the Battle of the Bulge. The 5th Black Watch had managed to thaw out a little in Hubermont, but we were still glad to leave Belgium and return to Holland, with its friendly faces and warm billets. There we would recover and regroup before facing our next challenge – the invasion of Germany itself.

One of the 'Moaning Minnie' multiple mortars that were used by the Germans to devastating effect. (IWM)

Fighting in the dense sniper-infested Bocage of Normandy cost many lives. (IWM)

Going into action in Normandy during Operation Epsom. (IWM)

The Highland Division liberated a large part of southern Holland, where crossing exposed canals was particularly dreaded. (IWM)

Snow-suited Cameron Highlanders meet up with Americans during the Battle of the Bulge, where we faced horrendous freezing conditions in the Ardennes. (IWM)

A Black Watch sniper at Gennep. (IWM)

Inseparable pals Davie Reid and Hugh 'Andy' Anderson. 'Andy' was devastated when he shot and killed one of our lads by mistake.

The Cameron Highlanders were horrified by what they found at Belsen concentration camp. (IWM)

Black Watch commander General Thomas Rennie, the inspirational leader of the Highland Division who was killed during the Rhine Crossing. (IWM)

With my great friend Alex Corris who also survived. (Renouf family)

As a young Black Watch Lieutenant visiting my grandparents in Bournemouth. (Renouf family)

Our victory parade at Bremerhaven was an amazing experience. (IWM)

Himmler's death. The feared head of the SS and Gestapo who set up the concentration camps and murdered millions was captured by the Black Watch. (IWM)

Remembering the fallen with Major Graham Pilcher MC on the right.

Meeting Prince Charles
at the rededication
of the Black Watch
memorial in Dundee.
(David Martin/Fotopress)

With fellow veteran
Dougie Roger at the
Black Watch memorial
in Dundee. (David Martin/
Fotopress)

# 8

# Into the Reich

Although still only teenagers, we were veterans now. It was February 1945 and we had come a long way since landing on the bloody beaches of Normandy just eight months before. We had very nearly buckled under the fanatical assaults of the SS divisions in Normandy but had found the resolve to push them back. We had cleared the Germans out of northern France and witnessed joyous scenes in Holland as we liberated one town after another. We had survived the murderous fighting in the Ardennes during the Battle of the Bulge. Our older comrades – many of them still only in their mid-twenties – had done all of this in addition to escaping from France in 1940, fighting their way across North Africa and liberating Sicily. But even they had never faced anything like this before.

The twelve hundred guns that roared out the greatest British barrage since El Alamein continued to blaze and ripple the earth as the morning mist slowly lifted to reveal a flat pasture field pockmarked with holes and surrounded by a spoil of rich loam kicked up by the short-falling shells. Beyond this fearfully wide-open space lay our objective: the vast Reichswald Forest, a dense natural barrier that had protected Germany's western frontier for centuries. The forest had been an exclusive hunting ground first for German aristocrats and later for top Nazis in search of wild boar. Now, it was to become a very different kind of killing ground.

The Germans had seeded the forest with bunkers, mines, snipers' lairs, machine-gun nests and tank-traps to turn it into a lethal link in their famed defensive Siegfried Line. Their gifted commander, General Alfred Schlemm, had not subscribed to the prevalent view in the German High Command that the main attack on the Siegfried Line would come in the south, so he had ordered his crack paratroopers to dig in and build effective defences in the north. His hunch was right. Operation Veritable was to have been a twin-pronged attack, but the Americans had to postpone their thrust in the south when the Germans released the waters of the Roer dams and saturated the ground, making any advance impossible.

Further north, though, two hundred thousand British and Canadian troops were poised to strike into the Reich itself, and we knew that the Germans would fight like fury to defend their fatherland. Just days earlier, the winter clouds had finally parted and the spring thaw had begun. As the snow and ice had melted away, so had our upper hand. Our tanks would no longer be able to speed across frozen ground. Instead, there was a real danger that they would be bogged down in the mud.

But the attack had already been postponed once, in order to repel von Rundstedt's Ardennes offensive, and it could not be delayed any longer. On the appointed day, 8 February, we were among five divisions launching a fierce assault.

Major Charles Napier CBE MC, Brigade Major of 153 Brigade, explained the logistics:

While an operation of this magnitude required massive forces, launching them through a narrow gap gave each of the five divisions no more than a one-brigade front. Massive stores needed to be built up in advance by the Ordnance Corps into well-camouflaged stockpiles. Every precaution was taken to show no signs of activity or movement in the area. Then five divisions would move into the concentration area hours before the attack. It was my responsibility to make sure that the battalions of 153 Brigade arrived at a given place at a given time so that the flow of thousands of men was controlled and orderly. During the first twenty-four hours, one million rounds of ammunition were fired by the artillery to protect the infantry in the assault.

On that day we were among five divisions attacking through this narrow gap between the Rhine and the Maas. We had already crossed the initial belt of organised defences, which included anti-tank ditches, Schu-mines and fortified farms and villages, but now we faced our biggest obstacle – the natural fortress that was the Reichswald.

Huddled behind the thin hedgerow that provided our sole cover, I glanced at the grimy, anxious faces around me. Some were familiar, others were rookies, but they all looked the same. Boys were men. New recruits who had been drafted mere weeks before were already grizzled soldiers, hardened in the ways of war. Killing was our daily bread, and it felt as if we had been doing it all our lives. Yet the filth of daily death had left an indelible mark on all of us. The eyes that should have been revising for exams, ogling pretty girls or aiming for goal were tarnished.

Shortly before 1000 hours, it was our turn to charge across the mine-strewn field. Just like Tommies in the trenches thirty years earlier, our mouths dried and our hearts pounded as we waited to go over the top. Then Sergeant Major Stewart started pushing us through the hedge, signalling our launch into the field. There was no time for second thoughts or prayers. 'You next!' he shouted. I started sprinting across the field, taking fire from Germans on the other side, and dashed towards the cover of the forest. A few yards out, as bullets whizzed past, I spotted one of our lads lying face down in a shell hole. I jumped in to see if he was all right and turned him over, only to find that he had a small red hole in his temple. A sniper's bull's-eye.

That macabre discovery put a spring in my step and I ran on for all I was worth. But when I finally dived into the relative safety of the forest, I found that there was not as much cover as I had hoped. There were no branches on the trees because the shelling, mortaring and shrapnel had stripped them bare. The brushwood was thigh-deep in places and presented an unexpected obstacle, making our progress very hard going and even impossible in places.

Pte. John Tough, of the 5/7th Gordons, was a forester at home:

Not only were the trees shredded of their branches, the barrage had stripped the bark off some and they were all full of shrapnel. I thought they would never recover . . .

We could hear the Germans ahead of us, but the tree trunks were so thick we could not see them.

But it could have been worse. We were in the south-west corner of the forest, on the extreme right of the attack. To the north, men of the 2nd and 3rd Canadian divisions – who were greatly admired by everyone, including us, for their fighting skills – were taking a terrific pounding in flooded terrain that rendered tanks useless.

As we moved through the mixed forest of beech and pine, we suddenly found ourselves among substantial German defences. When I glanced along the line, I saw a group of Germans completely unaware that they were about to be engulfed by British forces on all sides. I wanted to attack and take them out before they opened fire, but Sergeant Major Stewart quickly set me straight: 'Forget about them. Just keep moving. Don't forget our objectives.'

The first of those objectives was Pyramid Hill. Halfway up, Sergeant Major Stewart cried out behind me. I turned around and saw that he had been hit by shrapnel, which had torn off a large chunk of his jaw. Shrugging off medical attention, he took out a white handkerchief, held it to his bloodied face and continued to bark out orders: 'Get a bloody move on! Get up that slope!' He carried on bravely, making sure none of us lost sight of our objective. It was an inspirational and morale-boosting act of selflessness. None of us dared to let him down.

We struggled up the heavily wooded hill, wading through fallen branches and diving for cover every couple of hundred yards when waiting Germans sprayed us with Schmeisser and Spandau fire. Once we identified the sources of the fire, small units would take off and flush them out with grenades and

Bren guns. The Germans were outnumbered and were not crack troops anyway. Even so, they held us up for quite some time. But as more of our troops arrived, the enemy finally turned their thoughts to tactical retreat.

It was late afternoon by the time we reached the top of the hill, and almost dark. Our instructions were clear: establish defensive positions and dig slit trenches. As we got stuck into our task, I thought I could smell roast beef.

'Can you smell that?' I asked my nearest buddy.

'Sure can. It's definitely not Milligan's feet.'

All of the boys' noses were pointing skywards, sniffing out the mystery aroma. Shovels were dropped and tasks abandoned as we descended to the source of the mouth-watering smells.

'You're kidding me,' I said when I arrived.

The ability of the British Army to get hot meals to the front line was a constant source of envy for the Americans, who had to subsist on cold rations, but this was something special. Full marks went to our company quartermaster sergeant. I tucked into the meaty stew with true delight, unable to speak, although I did make my pleasure known through primeval grunts and fist waving. It was delicious, possibly the most welcome meal I had ever eaten. And it would serve me well over the next few hours.

Once it was dark, we were forbidden from making any sound whatsoever – even talking to our trench-mates. Tree roots enmeshed the ground, and my trench was particularly shallow, so I surrounded it with brushwood at least to give the impression of being in a defensive position. But in the blanket darkness, amid sporadic German fire, the trench still felt inadequate.

It was a terrible night. My trench-mate and I took turns to

stay awake. Scared as I was, sleep came easily, but staying alert when it was my turn for a sentry shift was a real problem. After all the exertions and terror of the day, I could not stop my eyelids drooping whenever quiet descended. But every little crackle, every snapping twig, set my nerves jangling again. I expected the Germans to come charging in at any moment. Should that happen, our instructions were not to give away our positions and to wait until an intruder was right on top of us before asking for the password. If he could not answer, then, and only then, were we to open fire.

I spotted one or two dark red glows as some of our lads went down as deep as they could into their trenches to risk a cigarette – a habit that could lead to instant death in this environment. But, to the smokers, every fag was a minor victory.

My mind raced. I thought I could see German silhouettes behind every tree and in every shadow. And it was not just my imagination. We could hear the Germans talking, and our guys would aim bursts of fire in their direction. Then there would be feigned groans from the cunning Germans, begging us to come forward and rescue them. It was a common ruse, used to try to establish our positions.

We survived the night with no losses. It had taken a heavy toll on our nerves, but we had fared far better than our mates who attacked the Siegfried Line from the north, near the reedy banks of the Rhine. Due to the unexpected thaw, the infantry divisions soon found themselves knee, if not waist, deep in mud. Much of their transport was bogged down and the tanks were unable to move forward in support. Perhaps the greatest disaster occurred at Cleve. Heavy bombing by the RAF destroyed all pathways through the town, leaving obstructions of ruined buildings and deep mud. As the 15th

Scottish Division was battling to clear the town, General Horrocks, commanding XXX Corps, gave orders for the 43rd Division to join them. But they also became heavily bogged down, which meant a complete paralysis of the advance that left them days behind schedule. Horrocks freely admitted his mistake, and it haunted him for the rest of his days.

In the morning, we received fresh orders. We were to go back down the hill and attack Gennep, a Dutch border town. This sleepy, medieval textile town had been an important staging post for German Jews fleeing Himmler's thugs in 1939 and 1940. Tragically, many of them had been swept into the Holocaust when the Germans had invaded.

In the dank and misty early light, we reached a ditch running along the southern fringe of the forest and then followed it to our new start line. As we left the forest, the Camerons prepared to take our place.

Sergeant Roy Hahn had survived El Alamein, Sicily and Normandy, but now he had a sense of grim foreboding: 'As we waited to cross the open ground, the forest was ghostly and forbidding. My spirits were not lifted when, as we crouched behind a hedge, I spotted an empty field with a sign proclaiming, "Highland Division" cemetery. I just hoped the planners had got it wrong.' (Roy survived the Reichswald, but he lost a leg later. His fate was sadly typical. Very few men who had served with the division in North Africa survived unscathed to the end of the war.)

We were glad to be out of that forest and remained in our ditch until about midday. But then came a new terror, when we took the highly unusual step of attacking in extended order, strung out across an open field instead of advancing in single file to present less of a target. Normally, we would be right behind each other, gingerly marching up a road or hugging a tree-line or a ditch. But here we were, spread out across an open field, with no cover. It was very strange and uncomfortable. We felt so exposed, like grouse on 12 August.

We put down a thick smoke barrage and stalked steadily forward in a crouch. I was saying my prayers and hoping for the best. Before we got very far, the enemy opened fire from all directions. The quaint, red-roofed farmhouses that were scattered in front of us were all bristling with German machine-guns. They must have thought it was the Führer's birthday when they saw us spread across the field.

It was petrifying. I wanted to drop to the ground and burrow down as far as I could. But Bob Fowler, revered as our 'Immortal Sergeant', was completely cool. He kept shouting: 'Six to eight yards between each man. Spread out! Keep moving! Keep moving!' He was the best soldier in the British Army, as far as I was concerned. A stern disciplinarian, he still managed to be friendly and highly respected by the platoon. He was wise and efficient, and looked after us like a grandfather. I would have followed him over a cliff.

The bullets were whizzing past us, hitting the ground and spurting up dirt in front of us as we walked towards the guns. But we kept going, battling the natural instinct to hit the deck, as Bob urged us on and steadied our nerves. At times like this, strong leadership was vital. Bob, in his unique way, ensured we did not collapse in fear because he was right there with us, shouting words of encouragement, seemingly oblivious to the imminent and savage danger.

We reached the first farmhouse and kept up withering fire with rifles and machine-guns while we crept forward and chucked grenades through the windows. Then we crashed in and took the surviving Germans prisoner. As soon as we had secured them, I collapsed against a wall with sheer relief that we had made it to safety.

But this was just the beginning. Soon, we were off again, heading across more open fields towards the next farmhouse. Even though the bullets zinged all around us, we did not suffer a single casualty. It was nothing short of miraculous.

By dusk, we had reached our fourth farmstead. We cleared out the defending Germans, held the position, regrouped and camped there overnight. Remarkably, we had still not suffered a single casualty, despite the unusual nature of the attack and the ferocity of the enemy machine-gun fire. It seemed that when the second-rate German troops saw a wide array of soldiers coming towards them, they were faced with simply too many targets. Instead of picking out one poor sod and concentrating their fire on him until he dropped, they fired willy-nilly, spraying bullets across the line without any accuracy and with absolutely no effect.

Bob billeted his sections into various parts of the farmstead. I was with him – in my new role as company runner – when three new reinforcements arrived. We were telling them of our plans to sleep there for the night when one of them collapsed to the ground and started shaking violently from head to toe. It was delayed shell-shock from the tumultuous barrage that had been raging. That terrific sound, which seemed to grow louder all the time, had the teeth rattling in our heads and affected even those who were not on the receiving end. It reduced some of our best men to sobbing wrecks. Bob had seen it all before. He looked at this wreck of a man and gruffly pronounced, 'He's no use to us. Take him back.' Sadly, as was so often the case, the other two reinforcements would not survive the next twenty-four hours.

The following morning, we encountered no serious resistance as we made our way to the River Niers, which we had to cross before launching the attack on Gennep, a couple of miles to the south-east. The Germans had blown the only bridge across the swollen and flooded river as the Gordons had rushed it, so we were ferried across in motor-driven assault boats. D Company crossed first. Then the rest of us followed in groups of ten, without meeting any fire. Once we were all across, we headed towards Gennep. The civilians had been evacuated *en masse* and the place had been heavily bombed, so we were about to risk our lives to take the skeletal ruins of a ghost town.

Frank Walker of D Company later described the night approach. When the sky was momentarily illuminated by a flash of light, they were shocked to find a German platoon right in front of them. A tremendous firefight erupted and Frank was hit by three bullets, thankfully all flesh wounds, before they drove the Germans away. His corporal was killed, though the platoon managed to take their farm objective. But as soon as they entered the farm it was hit by mortar bombs. The Germans were so expert with the mortars and had such excellent communications, that they were firing at the farm almost immediately.

We passed through their position and entered the main street of Gennep. Major Graham Pilcher's C Company went up the left-hand side, dashing from house to house, while those of us in A Company went up the right. All of the shop windows had been blown out and the roofs were close to collapsing.

We eventually reached a shop whose whole frontage was missing. I stormed inside and found three Germans. One was crying in agony with a broken femur while the other two were trying to help him. They were clearly second-line troops – older and terrified, they did not want any trouble and were relieved to be taken prisoner. I said, 'OK, get out,' and pointed down the street to where they had to go. I had no time to escort them – we needed to clear the house and get moving. They plonked the injured Jerry on a plank and picked him up, but when they reached the street his leg fell clean off and he let out a terrified scream. Poor chap. If I had remembered my Boy Scout training, I would have tied his legs together. I silently chastised myself but then shouted at them to carry him away. We had to carry on.

As we marched towards the town hall, clearing more houses as we went, checking the basements and the bombed-out attics, things were starting to heat up in Gennep. Halfway up the main street, we turned left onto a road called Picardie. Fifty yards of open ground separated each property from its neighbour, so it was a mad dash to find some cover and then regroup for the next domestic raid. The Germans, using their staggeringly good lines of communication, had already organised back-up. Unfortunately for us, these reinforcements were the big boys, crack paratroopers, who appeared from nowhere. The resistance stiffened immediately, and before we knew it they were counter-attacking. It was clear that they were steeled for battle, and we feared for our lives as they pushed us on to the back foot. These were highly skilled, well-drilled professionals, ready to kill or be killed. They evoked frightening memories of our hand-to-hand fighting with Himmler's SS troops in Normandy.

The paratroopers rushed the rear of the cottages we had just taken. We fought back and held some of the houses, but we had to abandon others as we were forced to retreat. The Germans overran 8 Platoon in number 21. Our lads threw smoke grenades and some escaped through the front door and windows, but six of them were trapped in the cellar, where they had gone for a smoke. The Germans took them prisoner.

As the paratroopers continued to rush through the back doors and windows of the cottages we had occupied, we decided our best option was to take up new positions across the street. Once we had found some cover, young Dennis Westcott, a spindly wee lad who was even more of a kid than the rest of us, was uncharacteristically boisterous and desperate to tell us something. He was a studious chap, more inclined to books than bullets, and usually liked to remain in the background. But now he stepped forward with something approaching arrogance.

'Well, spit it out, man,' one impatient wit implored.

Westcott took off his helmet and pointed down the road. 'This bloody big German paratrooper – he must've been six foot high – barged through the door. I just pulled the trigger and he dropped down dead, there and then.'

We were all aghast as his words came at us like Spandau fire. No sane soul ever enjoyed killing, especially in cold blood, but Westcott almost seemed to be proud that he had just taken a life. The details became ever more gory as he desperately tried to convince us that he had finally earned his stripes. But his eyes betrayed his boasts, and I could see that he was actually deeply troubled by what he had done. One simple act – as common as breathing in this war – would haunt his dreams for ever.

At that point, Major Eric Mathew told me to run back and tell the commanding officer that we had met some serious resistance. As I sprinted to the battalion command post on the main street, I wondered how I had drawn the short straw to become the company runner. I was probably just in the wrong place at the wrong time. To survive this dangerous job, you needed to be quick and strong, sufficiently athletic to scramble over ruins and ditches, reliable, able to think on your feet and resourceful.

I found Colonel Bill Bradford standing outside the house he had commandeered as his headquarters and conferring with other officers, who appeared to be seeking his counsel. Bradford had taken command of the 5th Black Watch after the battalion's disaster at Colombelles, and since then he had impressed everyone with his ability to weigh up situations very quickly. He also enjoyed a great relationship with the troops because of his determination to incur as few casualties as possible. His uncanny ability to identify weak spots in the enemy's defences resulted in some exceptional penetrations and achievements – and saved many lives.

I watched as the officers agreed on a way forward and then dashed back to their positions. These were all impressive leaders, but Bradford was a cut above the rest – a man at the peak of his military powers. He was dressed immaculately, with a new hackle in his tam o'shanter, freshly blancoed belt and gaiters, battle dress clean and pressed, boots highly polished. By comparison, we were a motley crew – steel-helmeted, grubby, in damp, dirty uniforms and mud-stained boots. At the time, I had no idea that Bradford had just returned from UK leave, which was why his appearance was so pristine. But I think no less of him for knowing that now.

Bradford asked, 'What can I do for you, young man?'

'Major Mathew sent me, sir. We've met stiff resistance and are in danger of being overrun. He wants you to know our position.'

The colonel immediately asked to be taken to Mathew. I could tell by his steely gaze that it was pointless telling him how dangerous the rat-run would be, so we darted from one house to the next across open gardens, fully exposed to sniper and Spandau fire. At one doorway, I cautioned the colonel to take special care on the next leg, having had a close shave there myself a few minutes earlier.

'Come on, get on with it,' he said gruffly.

When we arrived, Bradford consulted with Mathew and then gave the men some friendly encouragement. His mere presence and courageous bearing – not to mention his spick and span appearance – restored morale at a crucial moment in the battle. No amount of Sandhurst training could instil that level of stature in a man. I accompanied him back to the HQ and then returned to the front, where my comrades were already engaged in a tit-for-tat gun battle against the Germans across the street.

I found a position on the ground floor and hunkered down. Every time I popped my head around the blown-out window frame to see if I could get a shot in, Spandau fire rattled into the walls in front and behind me. I would dive down again, clutching my helmet to my head, as if that would protect me. Before long, I decided just to keep my head down. The blokes upstairs were in far better positions to pick off the enemy, so I left them to it. Private Davie Reid, of the 7th platoon, 5th Black Watch, like me, found himself in a poor position:

I was in the ground floor of a house with a very large front window. The Germans had occupied the cottages across the road, less than fifteen yards away, and we were firing point blank at one another. Corporal

Robertshaw came into the room and as I shouted to him to keep down, a Spandau burst came in through the window and killed him outright. He was an older, married man. He seemed to have had a premonition that he would be killed and had given me his wife's address, which I passed on to Lieutenant Scott. I and three others carried his body in a blanket back to battalion HQ.

The gunfight across the cobbled street of Picardie went on for hours. We expected the Paras to counterattack but Major Mathew had the company well deployed and he was determined to hold his positions. By nightfall the Paras had gone.

Meanwhile, the progress that C Company was making up the main road threatened to cut them off from their main force. As Major Graham Pilcher, watch of C Company, 5th Black Watch, described:

We were making good progress, clearing house to house up the main road, but the resistance was stiffening. Following intense small arms fire, a group of Germans from across an open space made a frontal attack on our leading platoon. Sergeant Johnston, on his own, charged the group firing full blast with his Sten gun. He killed two of them and drove off the others.

Across this open space was a house that commanded a view right back down the street, it was an obvious strong point that barred our way forward. Sergeant Johnston, on his own initiative, formed up his platoon and led a charge across the open space to the house. Grenades were tossed through the window and they cleared it room by room. It was a textbook attack, requiring inspired leadership and an injection of courage that spread throughout the platoon. It was actions like this that won battles and sergeants like Sergeant Johnston who won the war. I recommended him for an immediate DCM.

D Company passed through C and continued the advance. Major Donald Beales set up his command post in a house on the main street. In what would become a grim 5th Black Watch legend, he then sent his company runner Jocky Smith, an illiterate gypsy, back to battalion HQ with an urgent message. (Private Gerry Kingston, who always shared a slit trench with Jocky, had to read him his letters then write his replies.) As Jocky set off down the road, he shouted back to his officer, 'I'll see you in twenty minutes, sir.' In the next moment, Major Beales was killed by a mortar bomb. Twenty minutes later young Jocky suffered exactly the same fate.

But, as Lieutenant Bill Chisholm, D Company, explained, such casualties did not hinder progress:

When Donald Beales was killed we all knew our orders and continued the advance. We passed through C Company to reach the rail station and consolidated along the railway line. B Company came forward to reinforce our positions and secure the housing estate beyond. When Lieutenant McDonald, leading the attack was killed, Sergeant Hinchcliffe took command of 10 Platoon. Realising that B Company was being held up by heavy fire from a group of buildings ahead, he led his platoon in a charge across two hundred yards of bullet-swept ground and forced an entry to the main building, where his men wiped out the resistance. He then led another dash across open ground to destroy another strong point. He was awarded the DCM for his outstanding bravery and leadership.

But we managed to hold on until the main advance party of 1st Gordon Highlanders arrived the next day and cleared the final quarter of Gennep.

Meanwhile, the 5/7th Gordons liberated the smaller, adjacent village of Ottersum and then met up with the 1st Gordons. The fighting was ferocious, with dozens upon dozens of casualties. Private Keith Kerr, B Company 5/7th Gordons, recounted:

On the outskirts of Gennep, I entered a house during a halt in the advance and found German banknotes of high denomination scattered around. I was joined by Corporal Felton, a very good friend, and we both took a generous bundle as souvenirs. Next day as we pushed through 5BW and attacked Heijen, I saw some German banknotes scattered all over the road. I asked about them and was told that Corporal Felton had received a direct hit by a mortar bomb. As I passed, I saw my friend's arm with his corporal stripes lying in a garden.

The Germans could take no more and made a tactical withdrawal up the road to Goch. They would have little respite, though. Gennep was the important road centre that opened the western route into the Rhineland. It had been heavily defended by hardened paratroops and an indication of the ferocity of the battle is clear when noting that two of the six DCMs awarded to 5th Black Watch during the war were won here; and that during five days of action, forty-four comrades had been killed.

The plan was a bold one, bravely executed; highlighted by the unlikely crossing of the flooded River Niers and the building of the Bailey bridge within thirty-six hours – both achieved by the divisional engineers. Gennep was but the start of what proved to be the decisive battle in the west, which was to rage on in full fury for thirty days. And now we were heading for the hub of the battle.

While 153 Brigade was engaged in Gennep, the other two brigades were toiling eastward through the eight-thousand-yard length of the Reichswald forest. It was 154 Brigade that had won the approach to – and a foothold into – the forest, then 153 had gained the entry. When they left to attack Gennep, 152 Brigade moved into their place.

The two brigades battled through the brushwood of the southern half of the forest while the 53rd Division moved through the northern half. Both divisions had to share the only track fit for vehicles, and the congestion and the mud temporarily stopped the flow of essential supplies and equipment. The foot soldiers plodded on, mobility lost to the brushwood, visibility obscured by a wall of trees, confronted by an invisible enemy just waiting for our lads to walk into the sights of the Spandaus. Private John Gibson, B Company, 5th Seaforth, recalled:

Advancing through the Reichswald was a nightmare that is difficult to describe. The physical demands of struggling over brushwood thigh deep with a normal load were exhausting, but it was the strange mental stress, however, that took us to the brink. One minute all was clear then suddenly without any warning the enemy was there, waiting to open up at close quarters. In the dead of night when the sound of the forest tortured our imagination to distraction, the Paras would infiltrate our positions and fire at us from all quarters. The purgatory of this evil seemed to go on for ever.

152 Brigade, leading the advance to Hekkens, came under the most intense mortar and shell fire. When the brigade reached the main road running north out of Hekkens towards Cleve, it was ordered to turn south to advance on the village and the crossroads that would give our divisions contact with one another.

The 5th Seaforths attacked down the road, cloaked in darkenss and supported by a heavy barrage. But within thirty yards of Hekkens's defensive anti-tank ditch, a concentration of Spandaus along the front opened up. The battalion was pinned down – barely able to return fire – and shelled mercilessly. A three-foot-deep ditch by the roadside gave some hope that a massacre might be averted. As Sergeant Tom Smith, 13 Platoon, 5th Seaforth, explained:

The main problem was that the ditch was not deep enough to give everyone cover. If the men were laying two or three deep, then the one on top was exposed to fire, and even firing blindly in the dark the Spandaus were causing a continuous flow of casualties. Orders from Major MacKenzie were shouted along the line to wriggle and get everyone below cover. This did reduce casualties but when daylight dawned there was no way to get total protection. The Spandaus kept on firing and your fate was a mere lottery. We lay there for hours unable to return fire. The situation was crazy, the best part of the battalion was pinned down by a few machine gunners. Tanks were not immediately available and we had to suffer this nose to tail imprisonment until they arrived.

The tanks did eventually arrive, late the next morning, to allow a withdrawal. The battalion had suffered nineteen killed and sixty-five wounded. The sacrifice was not in vain for it allowed 154 Brigade following behind to attack from a different direction and take Hekkens crossroads without serious loss. It was now 18 February and we had been fighting for ten days, so we reckoned we deserved a break.

Goch was a central bastion in the Siegfried Line, but beyond it lay the German heartland. Operation Veritable was well on the way to flushing the Germans from the critical ground between the parallel Rivers Maas and Rhine, and prisoners now numbered in the hundreds. Progress had been bloody and hard fought, but we had come too far to contemplate defeat.

Our orders came with the night rain. The 5th Black Watch was to lead an attack from the north-west in the early hours, under the somewhat comforting cloak of drizzle and darkness. We were to enter the town and seize a strategic strip leading to the main square, dominated, we were told, by a church bell-tower. The 5/7th Gordons would then pass through and clear the path to the railway line. Meanwhile, the 1st Gordons would take the south end of the town and the major road leading to the south-west.

We travelled in transporters towards Goch and disembarked on the outskirts. The River Niers ran straight through
the middle of the ancient town and connected it with major
cities in Germany, Holland and Belgium. It had been a trade
lifeline for Goch, but now it was a dagger pointing straight to
the heart of this mini-Stalingrad. The Germans had turned
every cellar into a bunker, had fortified every ruined house
and shop, and had dug two anti-tank ditches. The outer one
protected Goch on its west, north and east sides, while the
inner one – a thousand yards closer to the centre – completely
enclosed the town.

Major Pilcher's C Company crept along the banks of the
Niers and penetrated far into the town before the defenders
spotted them. (We always tried to enter towns in the least
expected way, and this tactic paid off at Goch.) A Company
followed along the river, and we managed to get our platoons
right up to the edge of the main town square. Now the
Germans, realising they had been outwitted by this rather
brilliant tactical move, directed all of their available firepower
and forces against us. Their finest fighters, including paratroopers and other crack troops, soon had us totally pinned
down. They were fighting on home soil, were dedicated to
Hitler and were prepared to give their lives in the defence of
Goch.

Most of the houses lay in ruins from the persistent aerial
bombardment, but many had cellars where German troops
lay in wait, and they all had to be cleared. The task fell to
C and D companies. Initially, the favoured method was
to ease open the cellar door and toss down a grenade. But
that proved messy and ineffective, so Sergeant Maxie of D
Company adopted a new technique. Instead of a live grenade,
he told his men to hurl a rock down the cellar steps. This

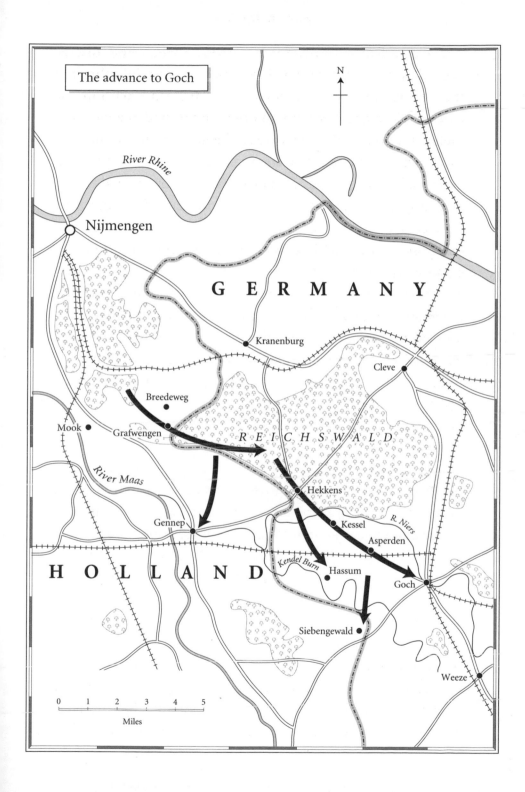

invariably resulted in a white-handkerchief-waving tide of Germans who were desperate to surrender.

Dashing to rejoin his leading platoon, Major Brodie of C Company – nicknamed the 'Mad Major' – took a wrong turn with his company runner, Private McInnes, a gritty Dundonian who had already won the Military Medal. They saw a group of shadowy figures and the Mad Major called out to them, expecting his men to greet him in return. There was a brief silence before German curses and bullets started to fly in their direction. Brodie and McInnes fled the same way they had come, found the correct side-street, and finally met up with their lead platoon.

The aristocratic Brodie was a fine leader, but he was also utterly foolhardy and entirely suited his moniker. Later, when the Battle of Goch was really raging, with bullets and shells flying from all quarters, he marched down the main street with an open umbrella, shouting, 'Jolly good fun, this war.' When someone asked what he was doing with the umbrella, he replied simply, 'It's raining, don't you know.'

From our position, the medieval church loomed large on the other side of the cobbled square. Terrible sniper fire poured down on us from the towering steeple. We ducked behind mounds of rubble and did not dare move. With no option but to settle down in the slush and mud, soaked to the bone and shivering in the extreme cold, we could only hope and pray that support would arrive soon. Thankfully, the Germans did not counter-attack, because we would have been hard pressed to hold them off if they had.

Major Mathew had set up his headquarters fifty yards from the square, in a shop. It was my job to relay messages from the shop to the platoons at the front line and back again. This task was riddled with danger. The Germans knew every inch of the town, and had spread out to cover practically every nook and cranny. So running from our makeshift HQ to the front line through ruined shops and houses was a hazardous affair. I had to dash from doorway to doorway, hedge-hopping up the street. But I met widespread scorn when I finally arrived after my first dash.

'Get down! There are snipers everywhere.'

'You'll get your lot!'

'And ours!'

I hit the deck and crawled to find the platoon commander. He gave me a report on the situation, and I ran back to HQ. I repeated this perilous return trip two or three times later that night. By then, we also had to contend with the Germans shelling at more or less point-blank range down the street with an 88mm – their lethal anti-tank gun that always frightened the daylights out of us. As I neared the HQ, I saw a shell striking its doorway. I was only feet away from the blast and felt the explosion before I heard the sound. Miraculously, I escaped injury, but I immediately started to choke when I entered the HQ. The air seemed to be filled with a pungent gas and I panicked. I hit the deck, clutched my throat and crawled to the back of the shop, where I found the sergeant major and a couple of company personnel.

'Gas! Gas!'

'What are you on about?'

'The Germans have started using gas!'

'What?'

'Come and see.' I led them through to the front of the shop.

'That's not gas, son. That's petrol fumes.'

The shell's shrapnel had struck a jerrycan full of petrol,

which had exploded. We stood and looked at the devastation. Then we heard the moans.

Through the smoke, we saw two of our drivers lying among the debris in the corner. Both had been mortally wounded. We did our best for them but they were horrifically injured and died quite quickly. They were just young lads, about my age, barely out of their teens.

Some of us had surreal experiences during the Battle of Goch. Sergeant Matthew Brown had spent most of the war manning anti-aircraft guns in the Royal Artillery. But shortly after the Normandy campaign he had been transferred from this safe job behind the lines to the 5th Black Watch, where he commanded 8 Platoon in A Company. It's fair to say that he was unable to cope with the danger and responsibilities that were part and parcel of being an infantry sergeant. But he did his best and he was good to his men, so they gave him a lot of support.

I was sent to summon Matt to a meeting at company headquarters. After the meeting, he was making his own way back to 8 Platoon when he suffered the most frightening experience of his life. Picking his way through the ruins, clutching his helmet to his head as the continuous hail of enemy shells and bullets zinged all around, he came to a closed door. Desperate for cover, he opened it and pushed inside, at which point a heinous, ghostly apparition reared to a height of twelve feet and let out an unearthly, blood-thirsty shriek. As he backed against the wall, paralysed with fear, Matt realised that it was not a ghost, nor the end of his sanity, but a tethered white stallion that had been driven mad by the noise of the barrage and the crumbling of the walls. Still in a state of shock himself, Matt could not decide what to do. In the end, he simply left the poor animal where

it was. Fifty years later, at his home in Jedburgh, he told
Davie Reid and me, 'In the inferno of Goch, you were liable
to meet the weirdest of situations but surely never a white
stallion.'

The heavy shelling continued throughout the night, inter-
spersed with mortar fire, including the dreaded Moaning
Minnies. We kept movement among the ruins to a minimum to avoid exposure to deadly sniper fire. Thankfully, by
early light, the 5/7th Gordon Highlanders had arrived
behind us. They huddled in and were given their next objective – they had to cross the square and take a hospital on the
opposite side. We all knew the perils that lay ahead of them.
I turned to a private who was firing pot-shots from behind
a pile of rubble at the unseen snipers and muttered, 'Those
poor devils.' The young Gordons, drawn from the farming
and fishing folk of Aberdeenshire, would soon have to run
the gauntlet of withering fire from the heavily defended
church.

It was simply a case of head down and charge. Watching
them crossing the square was like a horror film you could not
turn off. Despite our fierce covering fire, the bell-tower
erupted with machine-gun and sniper fire. The young
Gordons dropped like flies, one after the other. We willed
them on but our faces creased in despair whenever the next
one went down. It was heartbreaking to witness this terrible
carnage. In all, the Gordons lost 128 men and 10 officers in
the Battle of Goch.

Some of them made it across the square, though. I watched
one young Gordon dodge a hail of bullets to reach the cover
of the church, only for him to meet a flooded crater in front
of the building. A plank ran across the giant puddle like a
gangway. It seemed too good to be true, and so it transpired.

Halfway across, he detonated a Schu-mine and lost a foot. He was stranded for several minutes before two brave medics could reach him.

By now, we were all familiar with the booby-traps left in our path by the retreating Germans. They were considered fair game in war. We didn't use them much, but the Germans were masterful with them. One of their tricks was to booby-trap dead Allied soldiers, maiming comrades who came to their aid.

Eventually, D Company of the 5th Black Watch also crossed the square. Sergeant John King, D Company, was there:

> We cleared the ground floor of the hospital and it became obvious that the Germans were in the basements. A grenade failed to persuade them to give up, then after bursts of Sten gun fire, a white flag carried by a lieutenant appeared. He was followed by a major, who was followed by a colonel and a dozen men. We had captured the garrison commandant of Goch and his staff.

Several Gordons had to be physically dragged away from the high-ranking officer. Otherwise, he would have suffered the same fate as the corpses in the square.

As daylight broke, the town of Goch was revealed for the first time and I could see the dreadful destruction that had been wrought. And yet, back down the main street, I was surprised to see that some of the buildings had survived much of the onslaught. The walls were thick – constructed with the most solid stone – and shelling had only scarred them. Beyond company HQ was battalion HQ then, down at the bottom of the street, the RAP. To my horror I saw an ambulance draw up outside. I expected to see it blown apart by the 88mm gun firing down the street but the German gunner held his fire, the ambulance was loaded with casualties and drove away safely.

Shortly after that the 5/7th Gordons appeared at the bottom of the street and started moving up on the opposite side towards the square. The shelling of the street continued and the advance was slow.

Our A and D Companies were ordered to give them covering fire as they prepared to cross the square. Our full firepower was concentrated on the buildings on the far side. I thought to myself, Those poor devils are going to have a hard time of it.

The Gordons' leading company broke cover and charged in extended order across the square into heavy fire. Bullets swept the ground around them and Spandau and sniper fire erupted on our front despite our efforts to keep their heads down. The Gordons realised that their only salvation was to run like hell for the cover of the buildings on the far side. It was a most courageous feat and it was rewarded with just a few casualties.

But this was only the start of the Gordons' battle. Their objective was to clear the eastern half of Goch and that meant bitter fighting for the next few days.

Private Bill Robertson, A Company, 5/7th Gordons never forgot the horror of it:

When we arrived in Goch we took cover in the ruins at the bottom of the main street. A Company and battalion HQ were both hit by 88mm shells, which were being fired intermittently. The street was smoke-laden, littered with rubble and deserted, save for a carrier hurriedly delivering supplies and an ambulance. We advanced by dodging from one doorway to the next. We formed up for the attack across the square by sheltering behind crumbling walls and piles of rubble. I remember a bulldozer in the open filling up the bomb craters. Bullets were pinging off the engineer's machine but he ignored these and kept on working calmly. Later I was told he did not hear the bullets for the noise of the engine.

When it came to crossing the square, it was simply head down and charge. We then had to clear the houses on the far side and as we entered one of them a Panzerfaust was fired at us. The bright multi-coloured explosion blew me into limbo for what seemed an eternity. When I came round I was dazed and shaken but – incredibly – whole.

The commander of the first tank that arrived was shot right out of his turret by a Spandau burst. One of his crew bailed out and with his revolver was seeking revenge. We dragged him behind cover before he shared the same fate as his leader.

Snipers were very active and difficult to locate so I was not amused when a newsreel photographer asked me to make a dash to a doorway running into sniper fire while he filmed me. I politely refused, saying I did not want to be an extinct star.

The battle seemed to go on for ever. A two-hundred-yard advance was a major achievement. We weren't fighting garrison soldiers, our opponents were highly skilled, experienced troops, most of them paratroops but there were also Panzer units there – all of them highly co-ordinated. No sooner had we taken an objective when their mortars rained down on us.

Crossing the square at Goch might well be a story worth telling but for me it was all a bad dream, a memory I want to forget.

All who were there describe the same ferocious fighting. Like Private Neil Turner, B Company, 5/7th Gordons:

After two days and nights in Goch I came to know what was meant by 'the fanatical resistance of German soldiers fighting to defend Hitler's Reich'. They fought tirelessly; they resisted every attack and counterattacked every advance. Snipers would get you if you were not behind cover. What made Goch a living hell was the continuous shelling brought down on anything that moved. They were masters in the art of war. We fought continuously for three days before we got blankets and a chance for a little sleep and time to eat a meal.

The battle raged furiously for ten days. Each night, we had the support of massive artillery, not just from the Highland Division, but from the whole of XXX Corps, raining death and destruction down on Goch. During the night, as the flames danced to the sky and deafening explosions were followed by screams and cries, I thought to myself that hell could not be any worse than this. It was like Dante's *Inferno*.

It was only with the support of the Welsh Division, who had advanced right through the Reichswald Forest, along with the Guards' Armoured Division, coming from the left flank, that we eventually managed to gain the upper hand.

But even then, the Germans refused to surrender. They fought to the bitter end. By then, we had been withdrawn from Goch itself and moved to a small village behind the front line for a few days' rest and recuperation. It was a godsend.

We bumped into one or two German civilians, who for some incomprehensible reason had not fled the battle zone. On our last night in the village, I searched for Bob Fowler to try to get an inside word on what our plans were. I found him in a house that was still occupied by a German woman and her daughters. It was like entering a brothel, or at least a very liberal public house. I was astounded by the extent of the fraternisation. Bob had the woman, a buxom brunette, on his knee. They were canoodling, having a merry old time, and several other soldiers were also in very high spirits. It looked like plenty of drink had been consumed and the modest farmstead converted into a den of iniquity. I looked at Bob – my idol – and thought: This is not right. This shouldn't be happening.

As a regular churchgoer, coming from a sheltered upbringing, I was disappointed to see Bob in this new and less than wholesome light. The other lads were trying to latch on to the woman's daughters, who were only about fifteen or sixteen. The woman kept shouting in German, 'No, not my girls – they're only young,' but she was laughing as she said it. We all understood perfectly well what she meant, but the lads paid very little attention to her protestations. I left them to it and returned to my billet.

Our next orders were to clear the Siegfried defences south of Goch. These were mainly centred on two farmsteads, a mile or so from the town itself: Tominshof and, slightly further south, Robinshof.

Just prior to these assaults, a runner found me resting against a wall. 'Renouf, the company commander wants to see you.'

I set off immediately, nervously racking my brains for what I might have done wrong. I found the commander in a small room to the rear of a farmhouse where he had set up his HQ. He glanced up from the table, reclined in his chair, and said, 'Renouf, I want to promote you to corporal. To take charge of a section. Are you agreeable?'

I was still only nineteen, and the offer had come at me like a sniper's bullet, so I replied, 'I'd like to think about it, sir.'

'We have no time for thinking. It has to be a straight yes or no.'

I knew several people had turned down this chance, and I felt it was my duty to step up and do my best. But I was still overcome with doubts. What would the lads make of me in charge? The proposition sounded preposterous, even to me. Nevertheless, I reluctantly accepted, and rushed back to my section to inform Bob Fowler.

With a controlled smirk, he said, '*Your* section is over the road. Go and give them the good news.'

I stormed off, muttering furiously to myself, and found the section. It should have contained ten men, but casualties meant that there were now only six. In basic language, I told them of my surprise promotion and they looked at me with a mixture of disbelief, disgust and suspicion. I could see them collectively thinking: Who does he think he is?

And who could blame them? Several of them were much older than me, but here I was, a grotty teenager, suddenly handed the responsibility of keeping them alive, ensuring they see their wives, sons and daughters again. I had to convince them that I would do everything in my power to protect them, but there was little I could say to give them confidence. That would have to wait until we were under supreme duress in action. Only then would I learn how I measured up.

On the night of the 24th, we proceeded almost through the centre of Goch and headed towards our targets. Suddenly we were in the centre of a tremendous barrage – probably the biggest I heard during the war – both incoming and outgoing. I was almost deafened by the big guns, and the smell of the cordite was overwhelming. But we reached the other side and were back in almost total darkness. The only illumination came from the glow of the burning town behind us, the occasional streak from a Bofors tracer and a little of Monty's Moonlight.

The Gordons were ahead of us, already attacking Tominshof. This turned out to be a ferocious battle and they held us up. Some of our comrades were wounded by Spandau fire after a near-suicidal dash across an open field. Dave McKenzie was hit in his right side, managed to roll into a dip, and waited for the stretcher-bearers to collect him. They took him to a cellar in a nearby house for a quick patch-up and then laid him across the bonnet of a jeep for a bumpy ride to the regimental aid post. A padre held Dave in position the whole way, in spite of incessant sniper fire.

C Company of the 1st Gordons finally overcame the paratroopers defending the fortress of Tominshof, but they suffered many casualties. As we started to move on to Robinshof, I prayed we would not meet a similar reception. Before long, I was cursing under my breath, but not because of any German resistance. Just hours into my first mission as a corporal, and I had managed to lose two of my six men in the darkness. It did not bode well for my NCO career.

'Where's Milligan?' I asked nobody in particular. 'Bloody Milligan,' I mumbled when no one replied. As a result of our recent losses, he was now in charge of the section's PIAT anti-tank gun – the bazooka-like weapon that was one of our most prized assets – and he was nowhere to be seen. He still had a tendency to lag behind the rest of the section, blaming blisters or anything else he could dream up. Of course, this infuriated the rest of us. We might well need Milligan and his PIAT gun to save all our lives, but we often didn't have a clue where he was! Marching on, trying to keep what was left of my section together, I wondered whether I might have the shortest stint as a corporal in British military history.

I followed Bob Fowler through the abandoned German trenches until we arrived at the periphery of Robinshof. Bob ordered a visual recce of the place. The large farmhouse appeared to be the stronghold, and it was flanked by a large stone barn. In front of it, a sprawling munitions dump was already ablaze. It exploded occasionally, which sent us diving for cover.

After monitoring the farmhouse for a while, Bob turned to me and very casually said, 'Right, Tom. Take your section and clear the farmhouse.' He was so nonchalant, he might have been telling me to fetch him a cup of tea. It was his way of trying to instil some confidence. I gulped. My first mission, with half a section, who weren't exactly champing at the bit to follow me. I was sure we would be entering the jaws of hell. Clearing that giant farmhouse with just four men? No chance.

First, Corporal Inexperienced led his small band into the barn that adjoined the house. It was empty, so we quickly approached the door to the main house. My good friend

Davie Reid was in charge of the Bren gun, so I whispered to him, 'Give a few bursts on the door.' He looked at me twice, like a best friend who is too polite to speak up, and then rattled a short burst at the door. But his heart wasn't in it.

'Give me the Bren,' I said, taking over. Then I let rip before shouting, 'We're going in. Find cover once you're in there.'

We all expected a hail of fire to greet us, but something made us run through the shattered door. Whether it was our training or a sense duty, we always strode unquestioningly into even the most dangerous situations. And our experiences on the battlefield made us close, like a family. We were a true band of brothers, even though we barely knew many of our comrades' surnames, and we would never let one another down. Many men would rather die than do that. And death itself was so common that it almost became casual. Someone might ask, 'Did you hear old so-and-so got it today?' It was so off-hand, barely human. Grief and sorrow would only come later. During the war, our emotions were stifled by daily death – how quickly it came and went, the enormous terribleness of it all.

I charged through the door first, hoping that the rest of the section would follow, Bren gun leading. Once inside, I waved, shouted, my finger twitching on the trigger, waiting for the sound of exploding death to strike my torso. Then, to my amazement, I saw thirty or forty Germans cowering. Instead of pointing rifles, they were waving white flags, sheets and handkerchiefs, eager to surrender. What a stroke of luck, because there was no way we could have taken them on. I quickly marched the prisoners outside and led them over to Bob before they could change their minds.

One of them approached me and informed me he was an officer. In good English, he said, 'There are more of us.' There was nothing sinister about him. In fact, he seemed like a nice chap, probably glad that his fighting days were over.

'What do you mean?' I asked.

'Many more of my comrades want to surrender.'

'Where are they?' I asked, hardly able to believe my luck.

'In the cellar, below the barn,' he said, pointing.

I told the other lads to keep taking the prisoners to Bob while I went with the German officer, who showed me the entrance to the cellar. I suddenly felt very alone. All I had was the Bren gun and some grenades in my waist pouches. So I was hugely relieved when the German said, 'I will go and get them to surrender.'

'I've got a grenade here,' I warned. 'If there's any funny business, I'll drop it down there and kill the lot of you.' Strong words for a nineteen-year-old, but I had aged very quickly in this war.

'Please don't do that,' he pleaded.

He went down and emerged after a few moments, followed by one of his comrades. Then another. And another. Ten, twenty, thirty German soldiers made their way up from the cellar. I began to worry again. What chance would I have against thirty Germans? But they gave no trouble and I led them all over to Bob. In total, we took nearly sixty prisoners at Robinshof. It was unbelievable. Bob was quite casual about it though I could tell he was impressed.

There had been no need for great heroics or skilful tactics. The Germans had simply surrendered because they had wanted to surrender. I should, perhaps, have been proud and elated by such an achievement but I had no such feelings. I was simply satisfied that I had done what was expected of a corporal and hoped that I had won the confidence of my section.

Patrols were sent out south-west from Robinshof to the River Kendal across which 152 and 153 Brigades had been clearing strong points. Contact with the 1st Black Watch was made on the 27th, the day the Highland Division was withdrawn from the battle. We had fought continuously for twenty days in, arguably, the most intense battle of the campaign against resolute warriors conditioned to fight to the last in conditions that stressed the spirit beyond any normal bounds. Goch, with its incessant whisper of death, cannot be imagined. Only the survivors know the horrors of the battle inferno. And Goch, together with Normandy, were known, by those who fought there, to be among the Highland Division's finest hours.

By now, Goch was on the point of collapse. The Germans were retreating southwards, and I thought that the Battle for the Rhineland was over. How wrong I was. It would continue for another ten or more days as my comrades from other divisions fought a series of bloody battles against Germans who were masters in the dark arts of retreat. They frequently held up a whole division with just a handful of men.

Our other supporting divisions were still stranded on the wrong side of the Maas. However, thanks to our engineers, who built bridges across the wide, fast-flowing river, divisions such as the 52nd Lowlanders eventually got across and took the fight southwards. The plan was to meet up with the Americans, who had been supposed to start Operation Grenade at the same time as we started Operation Veritable, but they were fifteen days late because of the flooding on their front. The majority of the German forces were concentrated against us, so when the Americans finally did get going, their progress resembled a gentle shoulder on an open door. They sped towards us and their rapid movement captured all the newspaper headlines, as usual.

After ten days of continuous fighting, the Highland Division was told we had another battle to fight, and once again we were to be the assault division.

It was about this time, when we were back resting in Goch, that I noticed some 52nd Division trucks passing through. I asked a driver if 186 Field Regiment RA was anywhere nearby and I quoted the battery number. To my surprise he told me that the battery was just south of Goch. Tom McLean, my very good friend from Musselburgh, was in that unit.

I asked Bill Stewart, our new CSM, for permission to go and see him and got a lift in an artillery truck that took me right to his unit. Tom was, of course, surprised to see me. We began chatting but his battery guns started firing and this caused me extreme anxiety – a reaction perhaps to what I had been through.

I told Tom I couldn't stand the noise and he drove me on his motorbike – he was a dispatch corporal – back to my billet in Goch, where we had a meal. We spoke for a while and exchanged the latest news from home. When Tom left I said, 'If anything happens to me, please go and see my mother.' He didn't say much but I'm sure he saw that I had been through hell.

We had all been through hell. Captain Aldo Campbell, 2-i-c C Company, 5th Black Watch, summed it up:

Gennep and Goch were hard battles and the battalion suffered heavy casualties. I lost three of my best friends. Donald Beales and I worked closely together as seconds-in-command. Alan Foster, commanding 13 Platoon, had fought bravely in every battle since D-Day and was killed taking our last objective in Gennep. And Dick

Stuart was a Canadian Black Watch officer very popular with the men. He was killed at Robinshof and I remember his batman crying unashamedly when he came to tell me.

So we were withdrawn from the Battle for the Rhineland. Our next mission was to cross the Rhine and race into the dark heart of the Third Reich. It was not a pleasant prospect.

# 9

# Black Watch on the Rhine – Capturing Himmler

The 5th Black Watch left Goch early on 9 March and travelled in a brigade column for seven hours before arriving at Thorn, in south Limburg, at 1 p.m. The billets for our platoon were on the concrete floor of a school hall. I told Bob Fowler that my section deserved a decent bed after all they had been through and asked if I could try to find them something better. Bob agreed, so I crossed the street, knocked on the door of the nearest house and asked the woman who answered if she would take in a couple of soldiers. She did not hesitate, and gave Privates Reid and Anderson a warm welcome.

In next to no time, I found warm beds in neighbouring houses for the rest of the lads, too. All of these homes were humble, and the families were ordinary folk, but they displayed great kindness and affection. Each household had three or four children, at least one of whom had to give up their bedroom, but they did so with no complaints. We responded in kind. We knew that there was a shortage of everything, so we gave the families gifts of cigarettes (more useful than cash as a currency), chocolate and tins of bully beef, steak roll, salmon and whatever else we could scrounge.

Milligan and I stayed in the village manse. The minister was a bachelor, but he had a very house-proud housekeeper. She watched us carefully and insisted that we take off our boots and leave them at the front door before we came in. Once inside, we understood why: the manse was spotless from top to bottom.

The first three days in Thorn were set aside for weapon inspection and administration, which gave us plenty of free time and a welcome opportunity to rest. The physical exertion and emotional strain we had suffered in Goch had cut deep into our energy reserves and we needed to recuperate. I found the best therapy for the physical exhaustion was to sleep far longer than usual and to eat ravenously. We relieved the emotional strain by talking for hours with our comrades – about the war, of course, but about many other things, too. This brought some solace to our numbed minds and helped us come to terms with the grotesque life we were living.

Rumours abounded that the Highland Division was to lead the assault crossing of the mighty Rhine. As soon as these were confirmed, there was the usual outcry of being treated like cannon fodder, of always being the first to face the machine-guns of the enemy. But on this occasion, deep down, I believe our lads were very proud that they had been given the honour.

Over the next six days, discipline tightened and training intensified. The planners had been working on Operation

Plunder, the Rhine crossing, for many weeks, but only now were their ideas revealed to the divisional unit commanders. The masterplan dictated that the 51st Highland Division would attack across the river near Rees, while the 15th Scottish Division, in concert with powerful commando and airborne forces, would attack some ten miles upstream, at Wesel. Company commanders were then taken to view the crossing points. Next, battalion commanders met with their officers and sergeants to brief them on their roles in the operation and to give them information on the parts that those near by and in support would play. Finally, these details were passed down the line so that each individual rifleman learned the essentials of the barrage, the Buffaloes, the crossing, the medical support and the bridge building.

In the meantime, our own preparation for this momentous event was progressing steadily. After a couple of days of routine battle-drill training, including company attacks and loading and unloading Buffaloes, we practised a daylight river crossing of the Maas. The following night, we mounted a full-scale practice of the assault.

For the attack to succeed, the Buffaloes had to drive from the marshalling areas to the crossing points on designated routes and to a strict timetable. Moving in convoy in total darkness is not easy, and many battalions failed to accomplish the task, especially once a thick fog had descended. Consequently, the exercise ended in complete chaos. It was worrying, but we still had great faith in our friends from the 44th Armoured Division, who manned the Buffaloes. They had conducted scores of night-time operations over the last few months, and we were sure they would not be found wanting this time.

In spite of our concerns over what lay ahead, the host

families made our stay in Thorn most enjoyable. The children followed us around and treated us like heroes. On one occasion, I asked three of them their ages as I dished out sweets. Obviously, I couldn't speak Dutch and they couldn't speak English, but they soon seemed to grasp what I was asking and held up fingers. Something was wrong, though. They were telling me they were ten, eleven and twelve, but they looked more like eight, nine and ten. At first I thought they must have misunderstood the question, but then it clicked. They were so small because they were badly malnourished, and probably had been for the past four years.

The night before we left, our landladies decided to throw us a party. They invited us to the house of our favourite family and served us something similar to elderberry wine, which they called the specialty of the district. Next, they sat us at the table and presented us with two colossal tarts, one decorated with apple slices and the other with cherries. Obviously, the landladies had all clubbed together and contributed some of their meagre rations to honour us. I cut the apple tart into generous portions, which we then consumed with relish. The ladies were thrilled when we indicated to them in sign language that it was delicious. It was certainly a vast improvement on army rations.

All eyes now turned to the cherry tart, so again I gave everyone an equal share and watched the expressions of delight as they savoured this rare treat. We all leaned back in our chairs to indicate our fulfilment and satisfaction. During the conversation that followed, I asked for a cherry-stone count from each member of the section. As I went round the table, I congratulated myself on the fairness of my slicing, as they all had either eight or nine. But finally I came to Milligan, who seemed to have no cherry-stones at all. I asked him what had happened to them and he calmly replied, 'I've eaten them.'

'Do you realise that might give you appendicitis?' I said, thinking he must know no better.

I was astounded when, after a pause, he blandly said, 'Yes.'

The others called him a fool and told him in no uncertain terms that he could die. He was obviously trying to avoid the Rhine crossing. This was tantamount to a self-inflicted wound, a serious offence that carried a heavy sentence. Technically, I should have put him on a charge and placed him under close arrest immediately, which would eventually have led to a court martial. Instead, I cautioned the others not to say a word to anyone and the party continued as if nothing had happened. At the end of the evening, we thanked our landladies for their kindness and all went off to bed. But I wrestled with the dilemma of what to do with Milligan until I fell asleep.

In the morning, I decided to follow Bob Fowler's example and kept quiet. Milligan had always been a nuisance to me, and clearly he should have been charged, but we were all just trying to live from day to day, and army regulations seemed a minor consideration given what lay ahead. As we marched towards the river, true to form, he lagged further and further behind, despite continual warnings from both Bob and me. This time he claimed his feet were hurting, but we were not convinced. As far as I know, he never made it across the Rhine. The last time I saw him, he was heading for the regimental aid post. I never heard anything of him again.

The rest of us continued on to the concentration areas, located within two miles of the crossing points. The senior officers recced the route to the river and assessed the lie of the land on the far bank. Our billets were in and around

Marienbaum, with A Company occupying a farm where the livestock roamed unattended. Bob claimed a straw-filled barn, which gave 7 Platoon a cosy home for our brief stay.

The next day, 22 March, a smokescreen covered the near bank of the river for miles around the crossing points. This allowed the support units to move into their assembly positions without being observed by the enemy. It was a warm, sunny morning and our lads were able to wander around in shirtsleeves. Spring was in the air, in marked contrast to the wet, cold conditions we had left behind, and this seemed to bring a renewed sense of purpose into our lives. The lads were not as preoccupied with thoughts of tomorrow's battle as they normally would be, and they showed an increased interest in what was going on around them. Thankfully, there was no evidence of Schu-mines or booby-traps, so they poked around the farm, looking for eggs and other consumables. Later, we all gathered around a wireless to relax and listen to music that we had not heard for many weeks. A simple burst of sunshine had really boosted morale.

But it was impossible to ignore the audible backdrop. The guns of XXX Corps grumbled like a sleeping tiger throughout the day. Most of the enemy strongpoints had been targeted and these were all on the receiving end of occasional shelling. We all knew that a much bigger barrage would burst into action the next day. Other preparations were being finalised, too. These included establishing the radio link with the Typhoons that would be flying in support of the infantry, fitting swimming devices to the tanks that would follow the main assault, and laying communication cables on the river bed. Rumour had it that the Prime Minister, Winston Churchill, and the Chief of the General Staff, Field Marshal Alan Brooke, had been driving around the area, viewing the preparations for this momentous event. They were almost certainly impressed. Plunder was arguably the most extensively planned operation of the whole European campaign.

While we planned our entry into the German heartlands, some of the most evil monsters ever to blight humanity were planning their exit. Leading Nazis had already stuffed Swiss bank vaults with stolen cash and looted valuables in preparation for their escape. The Red Army was now encircling Berlin. Two months earlier, the Russians had discovered the unspeakable horrors of Auschwitz. The writing was on the wall for the Third Reich, and the world was sure to demand justice as the gruesome details of the Holocaust emerged. So escape routes known as 'ratlines' were being hastily established to smuggle war criminals to safe havens in Franco's Spain and South America. Others were acquiring false identities or planning to offer their services to the West in exchange for immunity from prosecution.

As the undisputed chief of the SS – which now boasted eight hundred thousand members – the Gestapo and, since the failure of the plot to assassinate Hitler in July 1944, the Abwehr (German Army Intelligence), Heinrich Himmler was the second-most powerful and the second-most feared man in the Third Reich. He had vowed never to betray Hitler, but he had already done so in a bid to save his own skin. Hitler had consistently refused to countenance a peace settlement in which he could not dictate the terms, but in 1944 Himmler had made secret overtures to the Western Allies. Churchill had rejected these advances without hesitation.

Himmler also sought to soften his image by producing a propaganda film that represented the Theresienstadt concentration camp as a sun-kissed holiday haven. Of course, most of the inmates who appeared in the film were eventually killed. He even opened contacts with Jewish organisations and ransomed some twelve hundred Jews from Theresienstadt in exchange for hard currency. Part of the deal was that this display of 'humanitarianism' should receive international press coverage. Hitler was furious and the episode marked the beginning of a split between the two men. From this point onwards, Himmler's main rivals – Hermann Goering, Joachim von Ribbentrop and Martin Bormann – started to exercise considerably more influence over the Führer.

Ten days before we were scheduled to cross the Rhine, Himmler had quit as head of Army Group Vistula on the Eastern Front, having failed dismally as a military commander. He claimed illness and withdrew to an SS sanatorium at Hohenlychen, but he retained all of his state and government positions.

Storm clouds may have been gathering for an increasingly anxious Himmler, but, for us, 23 March was another gloriously sunny day – the clear blue skies were vivid above the smoke curtain that hid us from the enemy's view. As we queued at the company's cook-house for breakfast, Bob Fowler ordered the platoon to be on parade in shirtsleeve order within half an hour. When we lined up, he did a head count and detailed half a dozen lads to remain behind to guard the company lines. The rest of us marched to Marienbaum and joined our comrades in a large hall that we soon filled. Colonel Bradford and his senior aides appeared, and for the first time our commanding officer addressed the whole battalion. He told us that the higher echelons had praised our role in Operation Veritable, and that he was very proud of us too. Then he briefed his men about all the preparations that had been made for the crossing and outlined the plan of attack.

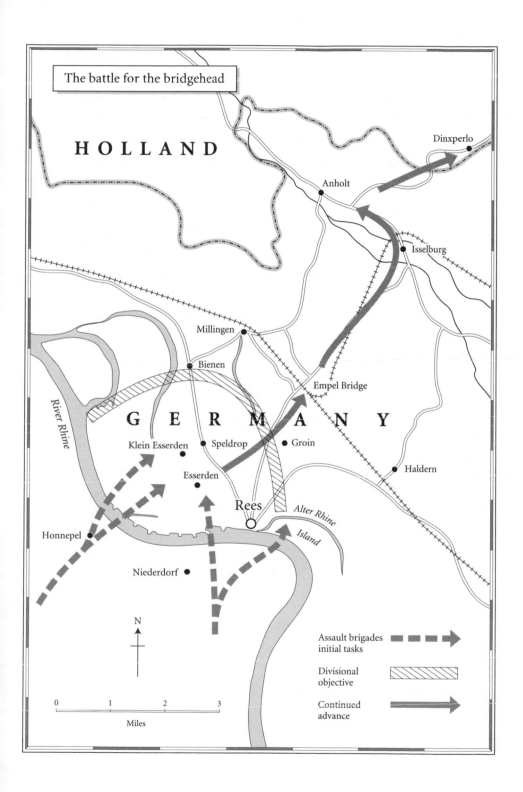

The battle for the bridgehead

HOLLAND

Dinxperlo

Anholt

Isselburg

River Rhine

Millingen

Bienen

GERMANY

Empel Bridge

Klein Esserden

Speldrop

Groin

Esserden

Haldern

Rees

Alter Rhine

Honnepel

Island

Niederdorf

N

0     1     2     3

Miles

Assault brigades
initial tasks

Divisional
objective

Continued
advance

At 9 p.m., the Highland Division would assault the Rhine on a two-brigade front: 153 Brigade, with the 2nd Seaforths, would cross the river at Rees; 154 Brigade would cross a mile downstream, near Pottdeckel. The artillery barrage would start at 5 p.m. The 1st Gordons, with the 2nd Seaforths in support, would attack Rees from the west with the 5/7th Gordons doing the same from the east. Meanwhile, the 5th Black Watch, on the left flank, would attack Esserden. It was critical to capture Rees, because this was the base for most of the German artillery. On 154 Brigade's front, the 7th Black Watch was tasked with capturing Pottdeckel and moving on to Kivett, while the 1st Battalion would attack Klein Esserden en route to its main objective of Speldrop. The 7th Argylls would capture Rathshof and Rosau before attacking Bienen. Early the next morning, the 5th Camerons and 5th Seaforths would cross and pass through the 5th Black Watch's lines to attack the strongpoints of Mittelburg and Groin.

All of these assaults demanded immediate and substantial support. It was thought that the entire success of Operation Plunder might well depend upon getting ancillary aid to the infantry in time.

The assault troops were to be ferried across the river in Buffaloes, while the back-up troops would cross in canvas boats. Amphibious vehicles and anything else that was available, including rafts, would ferry guns, ammunition, medics, transport and supplies in strict order of priority. Amphibious 'Donald Ducks' would motor across on the heels of the infantry. Casualties were to be evacuated in Buffaloes and amphibious vehicles. Heavy vehicles and equipment would have to await the building of bridges.

When we returned to company lines, I was ordered to take my section to the Hot Bath Unit – a rare opportunity that was not to be missed. We relished the chance to get clean, but when we rejoined the rest of the company we were soon cursing our luck. It transpired that Field Marshal Montgomery had just stopped by to speak to our company. Then, after a morale-boosting speech, with all of our lads gathered round his car, he had dished out packets of cigarettes. This was really something to write home about. For the rest of the day, the men relaxed in the sunshine, wrote letters, talked among themselves and casually wandered around the camp. All of this was highly unusual. Before an attack, the Jocks tended to be grim, silent and depressed. Not so on this occasion.

At precisely 5 p.m., the corps artillery opened up, concentrating initially on enemy gun positions. The noise was horrendous and quite deafening. It had been a surprisingly pleasant day, but now, after a rest period of nearly three weeks, we were returning to the dreaded battlefield to play a major part in a great event. We were given a hearty meal and issued with twenty-four-hour haversack rations and Mae West flotation jackets. Bob Fowler then called our platoon on parade, ready to move out. I checked that my section – now numbering six, after Milligan's disappearance – was all present and fully equipped. The company lined up and marched through the gathering dusk to the marshalling area, where our Buffaloes were waiting. We passed the artillery lines, where every gun – light field, medium and heavy – was now firing at an ear-splitting volume. Each platoon clambered aboard its allocated Buffalo in good time for the platoon officers to give final instructions to their men. But our platoon still had no officer, which meant that Bob Fowler had to lead us into battle while also fulfilling his sergeant's duties. Fortunately, Bob was used to this by now, and after a serious briefing everyone knew exactly what to do.

After some time, the Buffalo jerked and bumped into the clear, crisp, moonlit night. There was a series of stops and starts, and a tinge of apprehension spread through the platoon as memories of the debacle during the practice exercise came to mind. I, for one, was somewhat reassured when I noticed a red light on the Buffalo in front and saw our own co-driver standing in the stern to ensure we were still in the convoy.

Eventually, we were called forward and the Buffalo nose-dived alarmingly into the water. Then, suddenly, all was quiet and calm. It was an eerie tranquillity. The war seemed very far away as the Buffalo glided through the moonlit water. Then Davie Reid started to play his mouth organ. We all started singing as if we didn't have a care in the world. It turned into a jolly party, especially when Bob took the mouth organ to play his party piece. After that, he slipped a piece of paper into my breast pocket and said, 'If anything happens to me, write and tell my mother.' I told him he was indestructible and he laughed wistfully.

The crossing we had feared so much took less than three minutes. The Buffalo climbed the bank on the other side, took us some fifty yards inland, and we debussed in the right place at the right time. We were the front-line beneficiaries of a massive system of controllers, timekeepers, guides and beach parties, all radio linked to one another, which would succeed in moving seven battalions across this mighty river all in good order. It was an incredible achievement.

The Buffaloes of the leading companies had entered the water on time at 9 p.m. Equally crucial, however, was the mammoth task of getting the Buffaloes out of the river on schedule at the right point and debussing each battalion in formation at their designated start line. Landing parties had crossed earlier to find places that gave easy exits from the river and a clear run inland to the debussing points, where there was adequate space for the Buffaloes to turn around and make the return crossing. There was a slight mist on the river, but the bright moonlight, radio contact and light signals helped each driver to find his correct exit point. We encountered some shelling, but this was quite random because the enemy, while suffering a pounding from our own guns, did not yet know where our crossings were taking place. Consequently, nearly all of the assault battalions reached their start lines on schedule with no casualties. However, the landing party of the 7th Black Watch was attacked by gunfire, and the only one of the party to survive was the landing officer, Major Rollo. The battalion was the first to signal that they had landed on the other side, but they lost one of their Buffaloes on a Teller mine and suffered several casualties from Schu-mines, including their padre, the Reverend Bowman.

The leading companies of the 5th Black Watch, B and D, debussed in good time and made rapid progress towards Esserden. D, on the right flank, led by Major Johnston, secured the crossroads leading to Rees; B, led by Major Sandy Leslie, consolidated at Za Rees. They took thirty-five prisoners without a shot being fired. A and C companies debussed at 9.30 p.m. and formed up for the attack on Esserden. Half an hour later, with the support of an artillery barrage, our A Company, led by Major Mathew, passed through D's position and headed towards the south-east of the village. C Company, led by Captain Aldo Campbell, leapfrogged B to attack the south-west. The artillery was now firing full blast at targets further inland, and we could hear the shells, large and small, passing overhead. Bofors guns, firing their red tracer shells on fixed lines, gave us our line of attack.

Major Mathew was leading us in a long single file across flat farm fields when suddenly a machine-gun opened up on us. My platoon was at the front of the line and only a short distance from a flood embankment, so Bob Fowler yelled for all of us to run like hell and find cover. The other platoons stretched out behind us and went to ground. They were now effectively pinned down. The Spandau opened up again but there was not enough light for the gunner to see his targets. The fire was coming from a strongpoint about fifty yards along the embankment on the left. Major Mathew, knowing that any delay in the advance might prove fatal, ordered our platoon to go forward and deal with the Spandau. Bob led the way, hugging the near side of the embankment for cover, with most of the platoon following. We got within twelve yards of the Spandau nest and saw a crew of about five. Bob called me forward to tell me his plan: my section would have to rush them. The embankment was ten feet high and steep sided, so we would have to climb to the top before launching the assault. I took the Bren gun and crawled up the slope. Then, on my order of 'Charge!', we went in firing from the hip. The crew had hunkered down in their bunker so escaped injury, but they did not try to return fire. We disabled the Spandau, fired a couple more warning bursts and shouted for the Germans to come out with their hands up. One of my lads took charge of the prisoners while Bob promptly claimed the strongpoint for platoon headquarters and deployed the sections around it. My section was positioned within calling distance of a row of houses on the outskirts of Esserden. I put Reid and Anderson to the front with the Bren gun, making full use of a German dugout that was ideally positioned to

cover any enemy approach on the right, and ordered the rest
of the section to dig in and cover the left flank. Reid spotted
some movement by the cottages, so I told him to put a burst
through a window. Two Germans soon appeared, waving a
white flag. I went forward to accept their surrender and
escorted them to platoon HQ. Thereafter, several more
Germans surrendered as a result of further persuasion from
our Bren gunner.

Once we had eliminated the Spandau nest, the other two
platoons in our company had advanced further along the
embankment and on to Esserden itself. So far, there had been
no shelling, and the village appeared to be weakly held. This
was unexpected, because we had been told that several divisions of German paratroops were in the area.

Suddenly, the platoon runner came to tell me that Bob
wanted to see me. I went back to the HQ to find Bob huddled
in a corner. 'I thought you'd like a cup of tea,' he said, prof-
fering a mug. We shared the brew between us, but as I left I
sensed something was wrong. Bob usually did the rounds of
his sections, checking that everything was fine. Tonight,
though, he had remained cocooned in the bunker. There was
only one explanation: Bob had lost his nerve. It was understandable. He had shown great courage in France in 1940
and had been a tower of strength ever since. He had held A
Company together in its darkest days and had shouldered the
dual responsibilities of platoon officer and sergeant for
months. He had never previously shown any sign of fear, even
spurning a steel helmet. He could tell when his men were
troubled and knew exactly how to help them. But all of this
had placed considerable demands on his personal resources,
and now he seemed to have exhausted them. Everyone
admired and respected Bob, regarded him as a wise man of

great stature and gallantry, so I was deeply shocked by our brief meeting in the bunker.

And there was another shock when I returned to my section: Davie Reid told me that Andy Anderson had just shot a German. Davie said that he had come running towards their position from our own lines. Andy had challenged him for the password, received no reply, so shot from the hip. I went over to look at the body, which was lying face-down. When I turned him over, to my horror I found that he was one of our platoon, a young lad from Glasgow. Andy was devastated, even though I kept telling him he had done nothing wrong. It was just one more tragedy in this hellish war. Of course, I informed Bob, but he wisely told me not to breathe a word of it to anyone else. I then told the lads to do the same.

At dawn, a convoy of Scottish Horse carriers approached from the left and then turned into Esserden. I saw them as I was returning from platoon HQ and assumed the village must have been cleared. The first carrier passed safely, but when the second reached the corner there was an almighty explosion that hurled me seven or eight feet backwards. When I sat up, one of the carrier's bogey wheels was lying two feet in front of me. If it had hit me, I would have been killed. The carrier had driven over a Teller anti-tank mine and the explosion had killed two of the crew. I had walked over the same stretch of road several times during the night to collect prisoners.

A few hours later, we were told that the Gordons were having a hard time of it, so we were to go and help them. The 5/7th Gordons had crossed the river at the same time as us, landing on the right flank to launch an attack on the east side of Rees. But first they had to cross a small tributary of the

Rhine (in boats rather than Buffaloes), and they met heavy opposition. Now they were pinned down by snipers and mortars.

Meanwhile, the 1st Gordons had crossed between 11.15 p.m. and 1 a.m. without suffering a single casualty and had attacked Rees from the west. This time, the way forward was barred by a flood embankment and more stiff opposition, especially when the Jocks had to advance across three hundred yards of open ground under intense and accurate gun and mortar fire. Nevertheless, A Company fought towards Rees along the river bank, D made a steady advance on the left flank, while B and C headed straight towards the town centre. It total, the battalion suffered fifty casualties, including four officers, and fought for six hours merely to reach the outskirts of the town. Now they faced the task of clearing the ruins of Rees house by house, street by street, fighting two battalions of high-quality German paratroops who were determined to hold their ground. Every Jock would have to act like a leader, fully aware that he might meet a hail of bullets each time he kicked down a door. The operation would be exhausting, physically and mentally.

After three hours of fighting in the outskirts, C Company had forged its way towards the town centre and made contact with A, driving inwards from the river bank. By midday, D Company had joined them in the main square. It was here that all three companies would battle for the next six hours. Meanwhile, B Company fought to clear any pockets they had bypassed during the advance.

The Gordons were greatly assisted by the Royal Navy, which had supplied the battalion with four teams of 3.7-inch howitzers under the command of Captain McNair, who showed an insatiable appetite for battle. The guns kept firing

from the most unexpected positions and obliterated all suspected strongpoints.

While this battle was raging, we were ordered to attack the
north-east of the town. When Major Mathew led A Company
forward, Bob Fowler, desperately trying to conceal his fear,
assembled our platoon and followed the company trail. But
the enemy had observed the flow of reinforcements and
shelled us heavily. My section was leading 7 Platoon, so I was
marching immediately behind Bob. By now, he was in a state
of terror, scurrying for cover at regular intervals. As we
passed through a small wood, we heard the unmistakable
sound of a mortar bomb that was about to land very close.
We all hit the ground like lightning and the mortar exploded
about eight feet away. Bob let out an almighty yell: 'I've been
hit! I've been hit!' I crawled over to him and found him holding his backside. There were some bloodstains on his
trousers, but he was quite composed. When I urged him to go
back to the regimental aid post, he said with great conviction,
'No, not until we finish this attack.' The real Bob Fowler was
back. The fear and terror had left him and he had regained
his courage, his assurance and his authority. Despite his
wounds, he proudly led his cherished 7 Platoon forward into
battle.

The north-east of Rees was the industrial area of the town.
At 7.30 p.m., D Company attacked and secured a strongly
held factory, which then gave a firm base and a foothold into
the town. B, C and A companies then all attacked factories to
clear the whole industrial area. There was no serious opposition, but it took some time to clear all the hidden pockets of
resistance.

As we advanced towards our designated factory, with tanks
in support, shells started to fall all around us, but Bob yelled

at us to keep moving and not bunch. The tanks gave covering fire as 8 and 9 platoons moved into the bombed-out shell of the building. They had already cleared the ruins and rounded up the defenders by the time those of us in 7 Platoon entered.

Soon we were told that the 1st Gordons were involved in a fierce battle at the railway station. The resistance was threatening their flank, so a diversionary attack on the stronghold was essential to allow the advance to continue. A Company was chosen to lead it. Major Mathew ordered us to attack along a street that led towards the town centre, with 7 Platoon on the left and 9 Platoon on the right. Of course, we had previously experienced street-fighting in Goch and Gennep, so we were all familiar with the procedures and dangers. Those of us in 7 Platoon had another advantage, too: we trusted Bob Fowler to get us through it.

Under Bob's command, section by section, we dashed from house to house, ensuring each one was clear of the enemy. Although most of the buildings could scarcely be called houses any more as they had few walls remaining. Whenever my section attacked, we gave Davie Reid covering fire as he prepared to confront any opposition with the Bren gun. The Germans had already abandoned most of the houses, while others contained enemy troops who were more than willing to surrender, so we made good progress. But the resistance started to stiffen as we neared the centre.

Before long, we came upon an isolated house that Bob identified as an enemy strongpoint. He called a platoon meeting and told me and the other two corporals that we simply must take this house. I had never known him so positive and determined. He ordered all three sections to give covering fire as the assault was launched. On this occasion, he would lead the attack himself, accompanied by a few hand-picked men. With the full firepower of the platoon blazing, Bob led his little group forward from the flank, lobbed a grenade into the house, charged over the rubble with his Sten gun roaring and overpowered the defenders.

We took possession of the strongpoint and waited for the seemingly inevitable counter-attack. We were safe for the moment, but pinned down by three Spandaus. Bob came round the sections to check that everything was in order, then pulled me aside for a quiet word. He told me that the Spandau nests must be taken quickly. I replied that he should be making his way back to the aid post, but he insisted he was fine. Indeed, he seemed to be more committed to the fight than ever. He explained that the best way to deal with the situation was to take out a three-man patrol. I offered to go with him but he said, 'No. You must make sure that 7 Platoon holds this position at all costs.'

He was away for well over an hour. When he returned, he looked tired – as if his wound was beginning to trouble him – but his first concern was for his boys in 7 Platoon. He checked on all of us, and then casually mentioned that the Spandaus would not be bothering us again. He gave Major Mathew a report of what had happened and then finally made his way to the aid post. The major had to order him to go.

I can only imagine what Bob Fowler did on that patrol. He was a highly skilled leader who had experience of operating behind enemy lines. For instance, during the retreat to St. Valéry in 1940, when his company had been overrun by the might of the German blitzkrieg and isolated behind the enemy lines, he had shown great initiative, resourcefulness and courage to lead his men safely back to the battalion. He was just twenty at the time.

Knowing Bob nearly five years later, he would have led his patrol quietly through the ruins, taking full advantage of the darkness to creep up on his victims from the rear, closer and closer, like a stalker after a deer. Then, as soon as he was close enough, he would rush his quarry, going in alone for the kill with his Sten gun blazing. To carry out such an operation three times in one night required an immense amount of courage and a rare degree of skill and judgement. Bob Fowler had all of these qualities in abundance.

For his outstanding bravery that night, Sergeant Bob Fowler was awarded one of the five Distinguished Conduct Medals won by the 5th Black Watch during the war. It was a great honour and privilege to know him. In the heat of battle, every-one is stripped bare and the true self is revealed. Bob stood head and shoulders above the rest of us. He was an inspiration, an example to be followed. He had the rare talent of being able to relate to all of his boys, as he invariably called them, both as a friend and as a leader. I learned so much from him in those few months at the front that for years afterwards I imagined him looking over my shoulder, encouraging and watching to make sure I got things right. He was like a father to me.

(I did not see Bob again for nearly twenty years. Then, in October 1963, at a memorable Highland Division reunion, when thousands of veterans flooded the North Inch at Perth, I suddenly came face to face with him in the Black Watch marquee. We spent a wonderful day together, recalling our wartime adventures, and thereafter enjoyed a close friendship. I learned that his bravery at Rees nearly cost him his life: he was afflicted with blood poisoning and remained comatose for six days. On his recovery, he was promoted to sergeant major before being demobbed.)

The strongpoint we had captured now served as a base

through which the other companies could pass in the drive towards the station. First C Company captured the crossroads north-west of the objective, which allowed the anti-tank guns to come forward. By 5 a.m., D Company had advanced to a favourable position from which to engage the enemy. At first light, heavy fire was brought to bear on the German positions, and at 9.30 a.m. C Company, supported by Shermans, attacked and captured the station. Despite strong resistance, the two companies then cleared the whole of the surrounding area.

The Gordons were now able to continue their advance, and for the next twenty hours they slogged on to clear the town. By daylight on 26 March, they had reached the cathedral, where C Company battled courageously to overcome a strong enemy detachment. This left only the south-east corner of Rees in enemy hands. The defences here were strong, but the resistance started to weaken once the German commander of the Rees garrison was captured. By 10 p.m. that night, the 5/7th Gordons had confronted and ensnared both the original south-east defenders and their comrades fleeing from the north and west of the town.

This bloody battle entailed almost three days of continuous fighting against two battalions of highly trained paratroops. Heavy shelling throughout contributed to a total of seventy Gordon casualties, with seven officers killed. Their commanding officer was wounded, too. The 5th Black Watch suffered fifty-six casualties but took nearly four hundred prisoners.

The capture of Rees was essential in order to stop the direct bombardment of the corps engineers, who were building the bridges that were vital to the success of the whole operation. The engineers suffered 155 casualties as a result of shelling from Rees before the town was captured. Waterloo Bridge was completed at 1 a.m. on 26 March, with Lambeth finished at 8 a.m. the same day. Three days later, another three bridges had been laid across Germany's mighty western barrier.

The performance of the 1st Gordons was widely recognised as outstanding. They had pushed forward through a featureless landscape of ruins, scurrying from one flimsy refuge to the next, house to house, street to street, seeing little of the enemy but sensing him everywhere, never knowing when the barrel of a sniper's rifle might peak through the rubble. Little wonder that General Horrocks, the corps commander, visited the battalion to congratulate them on their achievement. Some observers declared that the capture of Rees was one of the greatest battles ever fought by the 1st Gordons.

But our celebrations were curtailed when we learned that the Highland Division's commander, General Tom Rennie, had been killed on 24 March. A mortar bomb had hit his jeep directly. Rennie was a legend among the whole division, but especially among the 5th Black Watch. He had taken command of the battalion in January 1942, and drove it mercilessly to the peak of battle fitness. At El Alamein, he was severe with his officers, demanding that they must do better. Thereafter, though, satisfied that his troops had performed to the high standards he had set for them, the true Tom Rennie came to the fore. While he remained a strict disciplinarian, he was a gentle man who enjoyed an affectionate relationship with his men. He held several staff appointments before being given command of the 3rd British Division for D-Day, and was wounded during the assault on Juno Beach. As we have seen, he then returned to the Highland Division in July 1944 – a critical time in the Normandy bridgehead battles.

Under his inspired leadership, the division re-established its reputation for excellence. He was admired and respected for his brilliant qualities as a soldier. His unique ability to plan a battle, his identification of priorities and his appreciation of conditions at the sharp end combined to achieve amazing results with minimum casualties. He had so much more to give, and he was sadly missed.

General Rennie was laid to rest at Appeldorn, with four Black Watch men as his pall-bearers. The regiment's pipe majors played the lament and the senior chaplain to the forces took the service. General Horrocks and the commanders of the 3rd British and 3rd Canadian divisions paid their respects at the graveside. Major Graham Pilcher delayed his UK leave to represent the 5th Black Watch. General Rennie was later reinterred at the Reichswald War Cemetery, alongside ten thousand of his comrades in arms, all killed in the vicinity of the Rhine.

Brigadier James Oliver, commanding officer of the 7th Black Watch and an original 5th Black Watch territorial, took temporary command of the Highland Division until Major General G. H. MacMillan, an Argyll currently commanding the 49th Division, could be transferred.

We left the smouldering ruins of Rees without regret on 27 March and advanced to positions beyond Empel. The 1st Gordons moved up the main road slowly in the footsteps of the engineers, who cleared mines under intense shell-fire. Meanwhile, we in the 5th Black Watch and the 5/7th Gordons made good progress leapfrogging each other on the right, and the 43rd Division pushed forward fast on the left. There was plenty of shelling but no ground resistance. It seemed as if the enemy had withdrawn to make a stand at Isselburg.

We passed through the Gordons to attack positions near the town. A Company moved forward, with 7 Platoon in reserve, but a burst of Spandau fire from a copse delayed the advance. It was our job to deal with it. Of course, Bob was now fighting for his life at the aid post, but Lieutenant MacInroy, recently returned from hospital, led us well. We moved out under good cover but the Germans spotted us and gave us several bursts of machine-gun fire. Creeping to within fifty yards of the copse, we formed up in extended order and charged, only to see the Spandau team fleeing across the fields. B and D companies then continued the advance. The latter met some opposition but dealt with it quickly and took thirty-five prisoners. Finally, C Company attacked and secured the road junction and bridge at the south end of Isselburg.

This was the last action fought by the 5th Black Watch before the whole Highland Division was rested. The next day, 28 March, I went on UK leave. I had all but forgotten that it was also my twentieth birthday.

After three days of travelling, I finally arrived at Edinburgh's Waverley Station. My mother was beautifully dressed and waiting on the platform to greet me. I wept in her arms when she hugged me tight. Thereafter, I spent most of my leave with her. My sister was now in the Wrens and had been posted to the south of England, where she had been enduring the V-1 and V-2 blitz. It must have been so hard for Mum, left all alone and knowing that either one of her children could be killed at any moment. I had always been close to her, but now the bond was even stronger.

One day, I travelled into Edinburgh and bumped into Margaret, my old girlfriend from school. We chatted in the street and she was sympathetic when I told her what I had been through. But it was obvious that she did not want to resume the relationship. I was distraught. I had carried a photograph of her ever since I'd joined up, and looking at it had always boosted my morale. I think it was her mother who advised her to move on. That was far from uncommon: many mothers did not want their daughters to be involved with someone on the front line. The risk was just too great.

My leave was over all too soon, and I travelled back down south to the embarkation camp. This was a vast, sprawling place, complete with cinema, shops and entertainment, everything laid on for us. I spent a few days there before being ferried across the Channel and into another camp. Then I boarded a transport that carried me deep into Germany – the new front line.

During the journey, we passed a camp that stood on an embankment. It was surrounded by a huge wire fence, and behind the fence stood hordes of people dressed in what seemed to be pyjamas. They were in a terrible state and had clearly been through hell. One of the chaps in the truck beside me was Jewish, and he knew exactly what we were seeing. 'It's a concentration camp,' he murmured tearfully. I was confused by the term and pressed him for more information. This, it transpired, was Belsen. The British had liberated the camp a couple of weeks earlier, on 15 April, and had already set up Europe's biggest hospital to care for over fifty thousand patients, most of them suffering from typhus. Nevertheless, the inmates were so weak that they continued to die in their thousands over the next few weeks.

The SS built Belsen to house their hostages – civilians and political prisoners whom Himmler thought might prove useful later in the war. Consequently, conditions were supposedly better than in the extermination camps of Poland and elsewhere. Himmler himself seemed to believe this fiction, and wanted to hand the camp over to the British Army because he thought it would improve his standing with the Allies. In fact, conditions inside Belsen were so appalling that they had a huge impact on British public opinion. The apocalyptic images that were broadcast around the world after the camp's liberation would haunt all those who saw them for the rest of their lives.

My view of Belsen from the back of the truck was the nearest I ever got to a death camp. The sight and smell of the camp were shocking, even from that distance. So I can only imagine what the Camerons went through as they entered Belsen with the first relief convoy. Private Richard Massey tried to put his experience into words:

> Belsen was absolutely terrible. The prisoners were in a horrific state. We had never seen anything like it. You had to see it to believe it. There were hundreds and hundreds of bodies piled up and scattered around everywhere. The stench was unbelievable and clung inside your nostrils. Skeletal figures on the point of death and dressed in rags tried to grab us and kiss and hug us. They were crying and hanging on to us. It was appalling and heartbreaking. We were all deeply affected by what we saw. I had to go and throw up. Some SS guards were still there as part of an agreement with the British. We saw this big German guard, he was like Hermann Goering – big, powerful and well fed. A friend of mine, a lad called Patterson, a very quiet lad, saw him and said, 'Hey, Fritz!' The Jerry replied '*Ja?*' and Patterson told him to come over. He had just got to within striking distance when Patterson gave him such a punch in

the face and knocked him to the ground. This mild-mannered Scot was shaking with rage and on the point of shooting the fat swine. Patterson was shouting, 'If he gets up, I'll kill him!' when our officers came and took him away. They didn't want any summary justice meted out.

We were all affected by the place. Our battalion commander, Derek Lang, who ended up as a lieutenant general, said, 'Get our bloody soldiers out of here. They're not for this.' It has stuck in my mind for sixty-five years.

The desire to punish the Nazi guards there and then was understandable. Scots Guards officer Sir Michael Gow recalled entering the camp and witnessing the soldiers' disgust at the former jailers:

We were stopped by British Military Police and sprinkled with anti-lousing powder, and I was immediately struck by the most appalling stench. We then went into a large hut full of women whose bodies had become so emaciated that it was impossible to tell that they were women. They were being scrubbed down. Outside, huge pits had been dug, into which thousands of bodies were being thrown for burial by the German camp guards. As we watched, one of them objected to having to do this, so two British officers seized him and threw him in, too.

I felt the usual trepidation about returning to the front, but was glad to see my old mates when I rejoined the battalion at Seedorf, in Schleswig-Holstein, on 1 May. Our new platoon sergeant, Tommu Nickelson, introduced himself and then put me back in charge of my section.

The next day, we came under fire as we prepared to attack the village of Horstedt. We were gingerly proceeding down a muddy track when we heard the news that Hitler was dead. It cheered us all up, and made me even more determined to survive the war now that we were so close to the end. We advanced about a thousand yards down the track and took up defensive positions. In the ensuing firefight we killed two Germans, wounded one and took six prisoners.

B and C companies passed through while we remained completely in the open. It was very cold and we were soaked from the constant drizzle. Then, just as we thought we could not be any more miserable, we were stonked by our own field guns! Fortunately, there were no injuries, and we advanced four thousand yards while the other two companies took the outskirts of the village. Nightfall was approaching and we could see the Germans moving around. Our platoons attacked with great vigour and captured more prisoners, taking the enemy by surprise. They replied with an SP gun and a 78mm anti-aircraft gun, but they were firing blindly. D Company passed through us as our artillery pulverised the village. Unfortunately, this time each company suffered a casualty when our artillery fired short. We also came under more accurate fire from the SP gun, which the Germans had pulled back.

A little later, Corporal Stevenson led a patrol to a farm on our left flank. They took twenty-four prisoners and found a signal truck with a working wireless. Stevenson ordered his men not to touch it and immediately informed his officer, who sent for an interpreter. He called the German commanders and tried to convince them to stop shelling, but they spotted the trick and opened up with more ferocity than ever. However, they eventually surrendered – thirty-two of them emerging with a white flag. We also took five private cars belonging to the Wehrmacht, including a Mercedes, a three-ton lorry, two half-tracks, a full-track and two 75mm guns, as well as a load of small-arms weapons.

The next day, 3 May, we held our positions at the farmhouse. My section was in the garden, with platoon headquarters in the bungalow. Sergeant Major Bill Stewart – a great guy who had joined us shortly after the Reichswald, where his predecessor was injured – had heard that the Germans might be surrendering the following day, so he toured our positions to tell us the good news.

But the war was not over yet. Our artillery continued to fire token shells, and the Germans responded with the occasional mortar bomb. We tried to dig trenches in the garden, but we hit water at a depth of just two feet, so we simply sat on the edges and kept an eye out. After a while, Bill asked me to accompany him to headquarters to pick up some tinned food. A shell came over just as we were setting off, and we could tell from the sound it made that it was heading straight for us. We dived behind a wood stack, heard the familiar swish and braced ourselves for the explosion. The shell landed a few yards short of the wood stack, causing shrapnel and splinters to fly over our heads. It was a lucky escape, just hours before the end of the war. Later, I was not amused to learn the shell was one of our own, fired by the 127th Field Battery.

On 4 May, we went on a recce into the Hinzel Forest and found a major German naval experimental station. The vast compound was very well camouflaged, with all the main sections located underground. It was equipped with electricity, lights, telephones, shower rooms and baths. There was even a marvellous small-gauge railway that wound for miles around the station. The place was a perfect billet, so our whole company moved into half of it and made ourselves comfortable.

The following day, our company commander, Major Mathew, announced the unconditional surrender of the German armies in North-west Europe. All along the front, Allied soldiers fired Very flares, Sten guns and revolvers into the air. We received a rum ration and later attended a magnificent dinner organised at the behest of Major Mathew, who joined us at the meal. The food was just our usual army fare, but the banquet was held in a grand dining hall, we ate off proper plates (a luxury in itself), the tables were beautifully set, we had comfortable chairs, and the quartermasters somehow managed to find a bottle of beer for every soldier. We felt like we were at the Ritz. To all intents and purposes, the war was over. Men hugged each other and clinked bottles in the air in sheer jubilation. It felt like a death sentence had been lifted from our heads.

There was a concert at the end of the meal. While we excitedly cleared the floor, pushing the tables and chairs outside the hall, I trapped my thumb painfully between one of the tables and the wall – my last injury of the war. But it did not stop me from getting behind the excellent piano. Sergeant Seeley was an entertaining master of ceremonies, and some of the other lads sang or did turns. Corporal Cheyne gave a fabulous rendition of his favourite song, 'Where or When', Davie Reid and his great pal Andy Anderson played the mouth organ, a few guys told funny stories, and others did magic tricks. But it was one of the more rough and ready corporals, a guy we called Boris because he resembled a Russian peasant, who provided the highlight of the evening. He appeared in a thick, padded suit, used by the Germans when training their vicious guard dogs, and was acting the goat when he fell over and landed on his back. As he wriggled in the massive suit, we soon realised that he was stranded, like an upturned turtle. He screamed at us to help him for a good ten minutes before we finally relented and pulled him to his feet, all of us weak with laughter.

We kicked our heels in the compound for two more days before moving on to the naval base of Bremerhaven on 8 May, VE Day. We stayed in houses on the outskirts of town and our job was to patrol the dockyard. While there, we got friendly with some Polish workers, including three bonnie young lassies. They had been forced labour workers in the camps and so must have suffered a rotten time over the last few years. After a while, I noticed that they were entertaining gentlemen callers in their rooms. One of our corporals organised these visits, and took a percentage of the profits. I was shocked when I discovered what was going on. I may now have been twenty, but I was still very innocent.

A few days later, it was announced that there would be a victory parade through Bremerhaven on 12 May. This was something the Highland Division always took very seriously, so we immediately set about cleaning our uniforms, which were caked with four or five weeks of mud and grime. The quartermasters issued us with green blanco for our webbing and we tried to make ourselves as spick and span as possible. We even polished our rifles, something we very rarely did, and tried to remember our ceremonial parade training from the distant past.

Spotter planes flew up the main route of the parade, and then the Fighting 51st marched *en masse*. The officers were all dressed in kilts and several men sported them, too. We must have been twenty abreast. Hundreds of pipers led the parade, and each battalion did its utmost to put on the best show. But there were no German civilians to impress along the route. They were all still hiding in their basements, indoctrinated by Nazi propaganda that had told them we would kill them. However, half a dozen German officers ceremonially surrendered their arms to General Horrocks, who took the salute.

We all marched with our rifles at the slope, holding them to our shoulders with our left hands. This was hard work and our arms started to ache, but we held our heads high. The Highland tunes that had haunted the Germans in the First World War and had signalled our own advances in North Africa, Sicily, Italy, Normandy, Holland and Germany now echoed off the ruined walls of Bremerhaven. We were all overcome by a deep sense of pride and a full appreciation of the significance of the occasion. The long march from El Alamein to the dark heart of Germany was over. The Highlanders had avenged St Valéry.

With the fighting finally at an end, the focus turned to catching the tens of thousands of Nazi war criminals who were on the run. Hitler and his propaganda chief Goebbels had both committed suicide. Goering had surrendered. Admiral Doenitz, who had taken over from Hitler as head of state, was under arrest. But the world's most wanted man – Heinrich Himmler, who had organised the liquidation of millions of Jews, Slavs, Gypsies, communists, socialists, Freemasons, homosexuals and the mentally ill – was still at large. He had been in hiding ever since falling out with Hitler over his proposal that Germany should negotiate a separate peace with Britain. Indeed, shortly before his death, Hitler had denounced his former right-hand man as a traitor and had stripped him of all his remaining posts. Now, the Allied intelligence agencies were desperately hunting Himmler, not only to bring him to justice, but to learn the full details of the Wehrwolf resistance organisation he had established to conduct terrorist activities in conquered Germany. We were also looking for ex-SS men and Nazi diehards in the German police who were still terrorising the civilian population.

The 5th Black Watch travelled to the village of Bremer-vörde, about twenty miles east of Bremerhaven, where we set up a checkpoint on a bridge over the River Weser. It was an important crossing point, and we had to keep an eye on the endless flow of refugees, check identity papers and detain anyone who looked suspicious. But it was an almost impossible task. The crowds flocked over that bridge as if emerging from a football stadium where they had witnessed a heavy defeat. It was a mass of human misery. There were Polish forced labourers, concentration camp survivors, badly wounded German soldiers, and poor folk pushing all their worldly belongings in prams. They were a sorry lot, and obviously desperate to escape from the advancing Russians. Most of them did not know where they were heading or what they intended to do when they arrived.

And we were past caring. Our war was over, and that was that. So we did not man the checkpoint seriously. Most of the time we just watched the mob roll past, acting more like spectators than soldiers. Twice a day, the field police would turn up, carry out a quick check of those locked in the guardroom, and then transfer any suspicious characters to an internment camp. This was a rather haphazard process. One day, I asked the field police sergeant how he determined who was a suspect. He said, 'Follow me and I'll show you.' He marched up to a young German in the guardroom and struck him sharply across the nose with a rolled-up newspaper. The young German bristled with a bitter look of defiance. 'There you are!' exclaimed the sergeant. 'You can tell by the hatred in their eyes. It's all in the eyes. Take him away.'

On 22 March, it was business as usual when we arrived on the bridge for our shift. The lads took up their positions with the usual lack of enthusiasm, so I left them to it and went to the guardroom to see if the previous section had caught anyone interesting. There were around twenty suspects, a real rabble. But in the corner sat three guys who did not seem to fit in with the rest: they were obviously well fed, which was most unusual, and reluctant to join in with the other inmates' chit-chat. Two of them were very handsome: fit, blond and burly specimens. Their companion was much smaller, and quite insignificant in comparison. His uniform resembled that of a German postman, and he had a patch over his left eye. This strange outfit had aroused suspicion, but he had been detained primarily because his papers seemed, if anything, too good. They identified him as ex-Sergeant Heinrich Hitzinger of a special armoured company attached to the secret field police. That information alone was probably enough to earn him a few hours in the guardroom; but the fate of all three men was sealed when one of his blond companions became aggressive.

While I was chatting to the guards, Nicky Henderson entered the guardroom to relieve the prisoners of their valuables. The wee guy with the eye patch was sporting an amulet around his neck and a fancy wristwatch, both of which he handed over quite meekly.

The following morning, the field police escorted him and

his two colleagues to a camp at Barnstedt for questioning. When they arrived, the small man demanded to speak to the camp commandant. Obligingly, Captain Tom Selvester made his way to the prisoner, who promptly removed his eye-patch, put on his spectacles, and said: '*Ich bin Herr Heinrich Himmler.*' Selvester, who had been a policeman in Edinburgh before the war, remembered, 'As soon as he took off the patch and put on his spectacles, I knew that I had netted a really big fish. When it sunk in that I had Himmler here in custody, a feeling of pure elation spread through me.' His two companions turned out to be a colonel and a major from the Waffen-SS.

Selvester immediately called British Army headquarters, but initially nobody believed that Himmler could escape from Hitler's bunker in Berlin, evade the Red Army, and get as far as Bremervörde. Nevertheless, Colonel Michael Murphy agreed to travel to Barnstedt, where he found Himmler and his bodyguards sitting at a table smoking cigars. Once the bodyguards had been removed, Murphy ordered a strip search of Himmler. With this done, Himmler flatly refused to wear the British uniform he was offered, so Murphy gave him a blanket instead. Himmler demanded to speak to Eisenhower and Montgomery, but instead British Intelligence officers drove him to a suburban villa in Luneburg that they were using as an interrogation centre. They asked him to sign his name, compared the signature with samples they had on file, and concluded that the prisoner was indeed who he claimed to be.

Still suspecting that Himmler had managed to conceal poison capsules about his person, Murphy now insisted on a full medical examination. But when Dr Clement Wells put his finger inside Himmler's mouth, the prisoner bit down hard, breaking a vial of cyanide. His captors immediately held him upside down and doused his head in a bucket of water in a bid to flush out the poison, but Himmler was already dead. He was buried anonymously on the bleak Luneburg Heath to stop his grave becoming a place of pilgrimage for diehard Nazis.

At least, that is the official version of events. Conspiracy theorists have long suggested that British Intelligence murdered Himmler so that he could not reveal the details of secret peace negotiations he had initiated with the British government. Unfortunately, the file on his death is subject to a hundred-year secrecy order, so we shall not know for sure until 2045.

There is a third option, though. Tom Selvester always maintained that there was nothing in Himmler's demeanour to suggest that he might take his own life. If anything, he seemed desperate to save his skin. After the war, Selvester was unable to suppress his detective's instincts and interviewed several of the men who had been involved in Himmler's arrest and interrogation. He concluded that the hundred-year order was imposed not to cover up a fiendish murder plot, but rather to conceal an embarrassing accident.

Selvester claimed that Himmler's guards at the Luneburg villa insulted and baited their prisoner mercilessly. They knew his identity and wanted to let him know exactly what they thought of him. So they jostled and slapped this pathetic figure wrapped in a blanket. He simply bit down on the poison capsule as he tried to defend himself. His death was a botch-up.

Tom Selvester was an excellent officer of great integrity, not the sort of man to say something unless he had very good reason to believe it was true. He was convinced that

Himmler's death was not suicide or murder, but an accident. I spoke with him shortly before his death in 1998 and he still maintained that Himmler had inadvertently crunched the vial of cyanide while being interviewed.

At the time, we were not particularly interested when we learned the identity of our famous prisoner. And we were even less bothered when we heard of his death. He had it coming, we reckoned. We were much more concerned about the pals we had lost since D-Day. With the benefit of hindsight, though, I can see that capturing him was one of the 5th Black Watch's more significant wartime achievements. After all, Heinrich Himmler was one of the worst mass murderers in human history – and he had almost escaped.

To this day, I possess a unique souvenir of my encounter with this vile man. Nicky Nicholson was a chain smoker – he could never get enough cigarettes. As I said earlier, cigarettes were a common currency on the continent, and I always had quite a few because I didn't smoke. I offered Nicky three hundred fags for Himmler's watch, and he readily agreed. He kept the amulet for himself, and it is now in the possession of his son.

After Himmler's death, we travelled towards Hannover and settled in Steyerberg – a beautiful place that I called the 'Enchanted Village'. Our stay there rejuvenated us all. For months, we had focused on nothing more than survival, so many of us had trouble accepting that the war was truly over. But when we finally did, in Steyerberg, the relief was enormous. I was one of the lucky ones, because the 5th Black Watch had suffered tremendous casualties right across North Africa, Sicily, Normandy, Holland and right to the very end in Germany. The more I thought about it, the more I realised that I had been very, very fortunate to survive.

As the weeks went by, I gradually stopped listening for bullets, shells and mortars coming in my direction. I no longer scanned the hedgerows for enemy strongholds that might house a Spandau nest. I was no longer engulfed by the smell of cordite from exploding shells. All of that was in the past.

In June I was surprised and very honoured to be awarded a Military Medal for my role in the Rhine crossing. Then came a commission and I became a lieutenant in the Black Watch.

Initially, non-fraternisation rules prohibited any communication with the locals, but these were soon eased. The German civilians were just relieved that we were not going to shoot them, and they were very friendly. They probably knew how lucky they were to be occupied by us, rather than the much more vindictive Russians. Soon a flourishing barter system was operating, with the soldiers swapping cigarettes and coffee for agricultural produce.

The village was so beautiful that sometimes I wondered if the war had just been a bad nightmare. I would listen to the birds singing, smell the flowers, enjoy the scenery, just absorb the beauty of the world. It was all such a contrast to the horrors we had experienced a few months earlier – one extreme to the other. I felt reborn. And I vowed that I would live a proper life from that moment onwards. I would never waste a minute. I would make full use of the time that lay ahead of me.

But when I was demobbed in 1946, times were hard in Britain. You could not just return to Civvy Street and resume your education. There was a waiting list to get into university, so I worked as a labourer on building sites in Musselburgh and then with the electricity board. It was difficult to readjust to civilian life. I frequently woke up in a cold sweat as horrific episodes from the war flooded into my mind. But slowly the night terrors began to diminish and I learned how to cope with them.

At first, I wanted to study music, but I failed to get a place. I was devastated, but it was probably a blessing in disguise. I decided I needed to pursue a more secure career, so at the age of twenty-four I entered Edinburgh University to study physics. After graduation, I joined the Royal Military College at Shrivenham, where I worked as a lecturer for the next eight years before returning to Scotland. I spent the rest of my career at Edinburgh University, where I was a research scientist and completed my Ph.D. I met my wife Kathleen, a Melrose lass, in the early 1960s and our son George was born a few years later.

In retirement, I was privileged to assist Sir Derek Lang in building up the 51st Highland Division Veterans Association. In 1990 we discovered that there was a great groundswell of demand among the veterans to get together and exchange stories – and to commemorate those who did not make it. We arranged a series of pilgrimages back to the battle sites and cemeteries on the continent, and most movingly of all to the towns we liberated in Holland. Our fundraising efforts have resulted in the erection of eight monuments in Scotland and Holland, and the weaving of a commemorative tapestry that hangs in Perth.

The veterans of the Fighting 51st are a dwindling band now, but our pride in the Highlanders has never dimmed and we have never forgotten our fallen comrades. I dedicate this book to them. We remain a band of brothers.

# About the Author

Tom Renouf was born in 1925 and, like his father before him, joined the army to see action in France against the Germans. He joined the Black Watch as a private and was promoted in the field to lieutenant. He was awarded the Military Medal in 1945 for his actions during the Rhine crossing, when the Black Watch led the British army into the heart of Germany.

On his return he graduated in physics from the University of Edinburgh and went on to become a lecturer at the Royal Military College. He subsequently returned to the University of Edinburgh where he became a research fellow and completed his Ph.D.

Tom Renouf is the secretary of the 51st Highland Division Veterans Association and has helped to ensure that monuments have been raised in Scotland, France, Belgium and Holland to the thousands of Highlanders who never came home.

# Acknowledgements

I would like to thank the following for their interest and support of our Highland Division activities over many years. Without their contributions, this book could not have been written.

The late General Sir Derek Lang KCB, DSO, MC, DL, who founded our Highland Division Association. The Highland Division Regiments and Associations for the supply of information. The Highland civic authorities for financial support. The Highland Division Trust, our parent body, for guidance and advice. Alan Heriot, our HD sculptor, for his pursuit of excellence. Maggie Savoye for perpetuating the name of the Highland Division in St Valéry-en-Caux. Adriaan de Winter of Gennep, organiser of veterans visits. Pim van Elsinger of the Haaren Welcoming Committee. Valery Parkinson, custodian of our Normandy Monument. Clan Donnachaidh, custodian of our Bruar Monument. Hugo Levels, Limburg historian.

Jack Diddon, North Brabant historian. Peter Stolte, Ardennes historian. Also Freddie de Graaf, former burgemeester of Vught, Eric Berger, former burgemeester of Gennep, and M.

Dardenne, burgermeister of La Roche, for the regard they have shown to their HD liberators.

Douglas Roger and Bill Robertson for their constant support in all our activities; and Jeff Haward, Middlesex Regiment, Ron Titterton, Derbyshire Yeomanry, and Ken Tout, Northamptonshire Yeomanry, for historical information of their regimental involvements with the division.

David Martin of Fotopress and Richard Sands. Brigadier C. S. Grant OBE, historian of the Highland Division website.

Beryl Cory was an angel at the computer and my wife Kathleen, for her support and forbearance.

Veterans of the Highland Division Association for the treasury of personal experiences contributed.

Andre Heintz, the French resistance hero who helped two Highlanders escape and who generously agreed to be interviewed for this book.

Kurt Bayer and Graham Ogilvy at Scottish News Agency and our agent Stan at Jenny Brown Associates. Also Richard Beswick and Iain Hunt at Little, Brown.

# Select Bibliography

Bavistock, K. (2002) *Breaking the Panzers*, Sutton

Borthwick, A. (1994) *Battalion: British Infantry Unit's Actions from El Alamein to the Elbe, 1942–45*, Baton Wicks

Cameron, I. C. (1946) *History of the 7th Argylls, 1939–45*, Thomas Nelson and Sons

Diddon, J. (1994) *Colin*, De Zwaardvich

Doherty, R. (2006) *None Bolder: The History of the 51st Highland Division in the Second World War*, Spellmount

Ferguson, B. (1950) *The Black Watch and the King's Enemies*, Collins

*Harder than Hammers* (1947)

Lindsay, M. (1946) *So Few Got Through*, Collins

McGregor, J. (1988) *The Spirit of Angus*, Phillimore Press

Ministry of Information (1944) *The Eighth Army*

Russell, D. F. O. (1948) *War History of 7th Battalion Black Watch*

Salmon, J. B. (1933) *History of the 51st Highland Division*, Pentland Press

Stolte, P. (1999) *The Highland Division in the Ardennes*, Arnhem

Todd, A. (1998) *The Elephant at War*, Pentland Press

# Index